EXPLORING
EATING DISORDERS
IN ADOLESCENTS

EXPLORING
EATING DISORDERS
IN ADOLESCENTS

The Generosity of Acceptance

VOLUME II

Edited by

*Gianna Williams, Paul Williams,
Jane Desmarais, & Kent Ravenscroft*

KARNAC

LONDON   NEW YORK

First published in 2004 by
H. Karnac (Books) Ltd.
6 Pembroke Buildings, London NW10 6RE

British Library Cataloguing in Publication Data

A C.I.P. for this book is available from the British Library

ISBN: 1-85575-261-1

10 9 8 7 6 5 4 3 2 1

Edited, designed, and produced by Communication Crafts

Printed in Great Britain by Biddles Ltd, *www.biddles.co.uk*

www.karnacbooks.com

CONTENTS

ACKNOWLEDGEMENTS

The editors would like to give special thanks to Lyndsay Macdonald for her invaluable work on the two volumes, and to Holly Barton, John Shaw, and Jessica Sully for their assistance with preparing the typescripts and proofs. We would also like to mention Andrea Chandler, at the Library of the Institute of Psychoanalysis, for her cheerful assistance with last-minute references.

EDITORS AND CONTRIBUTORS

Sue Brough is a Consultant Child and Adolescent Psychotherapist employed by Solihull PCT. Her interests are working with children and adolescents with eating disorders and their families, and she is presently temporarily seconded into Sure Start where she is able to observe the emerging difficulties in the infant–parent relationship which may later develop into an eating disorder.

Jane Desmarais is Lecturer in English and Art History, working in the departments of English & Comparative Literature and History at Goldsmiths College, University of London. She is the author of *The Beardsley Industry* (Ashgate, 1998) and author and editor of other books, essays, and articles on the nineteenth century. She is currently writing *A Cultural History of Decadence* for Polity Press (2004), co-writing a book on cancer and psychoanalysis with Lawrence Goldie (Routledge, 2004), and has written (in the journal *Soundings, 18,* 2001) on anorexia and passive resistance in Hermann Melville's 1853 tale, *Bartleby.* Her future projects include a book on skin, based on the work of Didier Anzieu's *Le Moi-Peau.*

Hélène Dubinsky is a Consultant Child and Adolescent Psychotherapist in the Adolescent Department of the Tavistock Clinic and is an Adult Psychoanalytic Psychotherapist. She has been a member of the Eating Disorders Workshop and she teaches in the Tavistock Model Child Psychotherapy training of the Centre d'Études Martha Harris in Larmor Plâge (Brittany). She is co-editor (with Alex Dubinsky, Maria Rhode, and Margaret Rustin) of *Psychotic States in Children* (1997), and co-author with Jonathan Bradley of one of the books on adolescents in Tavistock series, *Understanding Your 15-17 Year-Olds*.

Jeanne Magagna is Head of Psychotherapy Services for Great Ormond Street Hospital for Children. She works with young people with eating disorders in the Mildred Creak Inpatient Unit and the Eating Disorders Outpatient Team. She also works at the Ellernmede Centre for Eating Disorders in London. She trained as a Child, Adult, and Family Psychotherapist at the Tavistock Clinic and currently jointly coordinates the Centro Studi Martha Harris Tavistock Model child psychotherapy trainings in Florence and Venice, Italy.

Roberta Mondadori is a Consultant Child and Adolescent Psychotherapist. She trained at the Tavistock Clinic and teaches a number of Tavistock courses in England and abroad. She has been a tutor on the Postgraduate Diploma MA course in Working with People with Eating Disorders since its inception in 1999.

Diomira Petrelli is a Child Psychotherapist and Psychoanalyst and a member of the Italian Society of Psychoanalysts (SPI). She qualified as a Child Psychotherapist in the very first Tavistock Model course in Rome. She has been, until recently, President of the Associazione Italiana di Psicoterapia Psdicoanalitica Infantile (AIPPI), and is Associate Professor of Clinical Psychology at the University of Naples. She has a special interest and considerable experience in treating eating disorders.

Emanuela Quagliata is a Child Psychotherapist and a member of the Association of Child Psychotherapists and of the Associazione Italiana di Psicoterapia Psdicoanalitica Infantile and is also a Psychoanalyst and a member of the Italian Society of Psychoanalysts and of the International Psychoanalytical Association. She is co-author and editor of the Italian edition of *Closely Observed Infants* (Duckworth, 1989), editor of *Un Buon Incontro* (Astrolabio, 1994), co-editor with Margaret Rustin of the English edition of *Assessment in Child Psychotherapy* (Duckworth, 2000), and editor of *Un Bisogno Vitale: l'importanza del rapporto alimentare nello sviluppo del bambino* (Astrolabio, 2002). She is currently a doctoral student in Psycho-analytic Psychotherapy at the Tavistock Clinic and University of East London. She works in private practice in Rome and teaches in several courses in Child Psychotherapy in Italy and at the Univer-sity of Aquila.

Kent Ravenscroft was a Clinical Associate at the National Institute of Mental Health, where he trained in adolescent family therapy with Roger Shapiro, Helm Stierlin, and John Zinner. Trained in child and adult psychoanalysis at the Washington Psychoanalytic Institute, he is an Associate Clinical Professor at George Washing-ton and Georgetown Medical Schools, where he formerly served as Training Director in Child and Adolescent Psychiatry, as well as Director of Family Therapy. He currently supervises and teaches on the Faculty of the International Institute of Object Relations Therapy and is in full-time private practice.

Luisa Carbone Tirelli is a Psychologist and Psychotherapist. She is the President of the Associazione Italiana di Psicoterapia Psico-analitica Infantile and co-editor of the journal of psychoanalytic studies of the child and adolescents, *Richard e Piggle*. She has also promoted and directed a service for the treatment of young adults and adolescents in the public sector.

Gianna Williams has trained as a clinician for work with children and with adults. She has been on the teaching staff of the Tavistock Clinic since 1970 and subsequently became a Consultant Psycho-therapist in the Adolescent Department of the Tavistock, where she founded the Eating Disorders Workshop in 1987. She is now co-organizing tutor of the Postgraduate Diploma MA in Working with People with Eating Disorders (Tavistock Clinic and University of East London). She has been a Visiting Professor at Pisa and Bologna Universities. She has founded numerous Tavistock Model courses in Italy, France, and Latin America. She has published widely in England and abroad, and her book, *Internal Landscapes and Foreign Bodies: Eating Disorders and Other Pathologies* (3rd edition, Karnac, 2002) has been translated into a number of languages, including Chinese.

Paul Williams is a member of the British Psychoanalytical Society and of the Royal Anthropological Institute. He is Joint Editor-in-Chief of the *International Journal of Psycho-Analysis* and Visiting Professor of Psychoanalysis at Anglia Polytechnic University, U.K. He has written widely on the subject of personality disorders and psychosis.

INTRODUCTION

The receiver's capacity to be given to is a return gift to the original giver.

E. Bott-Spillius, 1993

This book consists of a collection of chapters, selected by Gianna Williams with the assistance of Paul Williams, Jane Desmarais, and Kent Ravenscroft, written by current and past members of the Eating Disorders Workshop in the Adolescent Department of the Tavistock Clinic and by clinicians in Italy who have completed Tavistock-model courses in child and adolescent psychotherapy. All the patients were treated with a psychoanalytic approach, though there are variations in the frames of reference used by the authors. The chapters in Volume I are about work with children, while those in Volume II concentrate on adolescents. In spite of the different focus of each volume, there are many recurrent issues that connect the cases of children and adolescents. For example, many cases describe the anxieties and strategies of defence used against feelings of dependence and the risk of accepting from another. This is a core theme in both volumes and is the principal idea behind the paradoxical title, *The Generosity of Accept-ance*. This title applies primarily to the struggle of some patients to accept from another, to become dependent on another, but it also refers to the need of clinicians to accept generously the sometimes violent projections of their patients. The gift of help often involves a risk of rejection, and the chapters in these two volumes vividly describe the courage and generosity it takes to persevere with patients suffering from serious eating disorders.

Psychoanalytic perspectives

Central to the psychoanalytic thinking behind the cases presented in these two volumes is a perspective principally defined by Melanie Klein's theory of object relations. This perspective may be divided, as far as these two books are concerned, into two main focuses: one relates to the reversal of the early dyadic relationship between mother and infant, the process defined by Wilfred Bion (1962a) as "container–contained"; the other relates to the failure to work through the oedipal situation. The two focuses are intimately related. In the first instance, Bion's notion of a container–contained relationship fails and is transformed, as Gianna Williams has noted, into a *receptacle–foreign-body* relationship. The infant or child is not only not contained, but is at the receiving end of parental projections. This is vividly illustrated in Chapter 6 of Volume I by the drawing entitled "An Exchange of Smoke between Houses". The smoke trails from the five houses, representing each member of the family, colliding in a vacuum. Everything, it is suggested here, is being emitted and projected, and nothing is being con-tained. For some, the introjection of projecting objects can become unbearable, and there is an imperative need to disgorge, emit, or block off these "missiles". Williams's accounts in *Internal Land-scapes and Foreign Bodies* (1997) of the cases of Sally, a 17-year-old anorexic, and Daniel, an 18-year-old bulimic, illustrate a "no-entry" system of defences. So afraid of penetration of any kind, Sally revealed in her assessment a "vast array of 'no-entry' defences", which included finding the sound of the alarm clock and the telephone unbearable. Unable to cope with parents overflowing with projections, Daniel, a more "porous" patient than Sally, binged on white bread, which, when vomited, served as metaphorical blotting paper to mop up the mess of his internal world. The displacement of the chaos within to food that then can be brought up, discharged, projected, is striking in bulimics. In Volume II, writing from a different perspective, Ravenscroft describes "projective vomiting" in the case of the bulimic patient: "the bulimic uses expulsive elimination as an emergency manoeuvre—a psychosomatic defence" [Volume II, Chapter 3].

The second focus is concerned with the failure of triangulation—that is, a denial of the space within the dyadic couple and an accompanying wish and fear of fusion of subject and object. H. Boris (1984) and Dana Birksted-Breen (1989) have described the poverty of the "transitional" space in the anorexic's relationships and her desire for or fear of fusion with her mother, in particular. Marilyn Lawrence has developed this idea in "Loving Them to Death: The Anorexic and Her Objects" (2001). She describes the anorexic's terror of separateness and differentiation, and the concomitant need to control the objects of her internal and external worlds. Unable to symbolize and accept the inequalities and differences of human existence, the anorexic seeks to protect her oedipal illusions (in which mother and child constitute the central couple) and defend herself against unbearable pain and the anxieties of the depressive position.

The chapters in these two volumes explore the implications of both these obstacles to development for understanding the conditions of anorexia and bulimia, and several key themes emerge that shed light on some of the more central aspects of eating disorders. These may be identified as (1) failure in some aspects of early relationships; (2) fusion and projective identification; (3) attacks on the "paternal function"; and (4) the presence of an ego-destructive "superego" (Bion, 1962a).

The "fit" or "lack of fit" between mother and baby, for example, is a principal concern of Volume I. The work of G. Williams (1997) and Likierman (1997) is relevant here. They both emphasize the mutually destructive link between mother and child when needs remain unmet in infancy, and, drawing on Klein (1955), they connect a dread of dependence established in the early relationship with a desire later to obliterate otherness through fusion and projective identification. We see many instances of projective identification in the chapters of both volumes, but most notably in those in Volume II by Brough, Tirelli, Mondadori, Quagliata, and Petrelli. In this state of fusion between subject and object, what we might call the third element or the "paternal function"—the space between the dyadic relationship—is obliterated too. In both volumes, we encounter patients who exhibit an overwhelming desire to denigrate the actual father and, by extension, obliterate the intermediate space the father symbolically represents in the family relationship.

These characteristics make the therapeutic process very difficult and, as the clinicians in these two volumes demonstrate, the task of treating patients with eating disorders requires extraordinary patience and courage. This task is made more difficult by the presence of a destructive superego on the side of death that speaks to the patient and through the patient and engenders persecutory feelings that are potentially fatal. This is the voice described by Magagna in her chapter, "I Don't Want to Die, But I Have To". In the following sections, further consideration will be given to the ways in which individual chapters address these key themes.

Early relationships

Several chapters suggest or imply that the rejection of a feeling of dependence might be related to a failure in some aspects of early relationships. This failure is essentially the lack of fit between mother and child, meaning the absence of an ability to give and receive reciprocally. This lack of fit is given symbolization by Petrelli's patient [II, 8], who describes a "black button"—a sign of mourning—very reminiscent of the work of Frances Tustin (1972), and Petrelli suggests that this could be the "sign of the loss of the breast, an empty hole, something related to the lack of an early fit". This view is endorsed by Tirelli [II, 2] who also makes the case that the lack of the "function of receiving" (cf. Likierman, 1997), may be due to difficulties in weaning and achieving the depressive position. An emotional "misfit" due to an extreme lack of boundaries and separateness is described in the first chapter of Volume I by Miller, in her account of a two-year infant observation of Jenny and her daughter, Anna. Here the breast could not be mourned because it became for Anna "a devalued and at times contemptible object". In Perocevic's chapter [I, 3], we learn that Miral, 6 years old, had refused food in infancy and later would only eat mashed food in front of the television, "one item at a time". Briggs [I, 4], too, suggests that his 9-year-old patient, George, might have experienced a "catastrophic weaning". George restricted the acceptable items of food to a minimum, and, like Miral, never ate more than one item at a time. In her chapter on "Aspects of the Body Image and Sense of Identity in a Boy with Autism", Rhode [I, 5] describes the re-enactment of a catastrophic birth experience when her patient, Anthony, falls off the desk and struggles to reach the safety of a chair. We shall return to this theme later when we consider the idea of triangular relationships.

In Volume I, Pinheiro [I, 2] describes two cases, one where the child did not accept food at all, and another where the child refused solids. In both these cases, there seems to be not only a lack of an early fit, but a double failure of containment—that is, a reversal of the container–contained relationship, resulting in a receptacle–foreign-body relationship. This is also the case of Perocevic [I, 3], whose patient was taken at the age of 10 days to hospital with a gastric problem and whose mother, unable to bear the anxiety, rushed out of the ambulance in a panic. This child clearly developed a no-entry system of defences (Williams, 1997) when used as a receptacle of parental projections. Pinheiro [I, 2] suggests that the infants' "capacity to signal their hunger might have been diminished in a context of parental unavailability to explore and try to understand the meaning of their crying".

In Volume II, which concentrates on adolescents and late-adolescents, there are many examples of failure in some aspects of early relationships. For instance, Mondadori's patient [II, 4], Lydia, had problems with food in primary school. We know nothing about the early relationships in the case of Yufang, the extremely regressed patient of Magagna [II, 5], but it is as if we follow an infant observation in the detailed narrative of this case. The tiny amounts of Chinese food that are eventually acceptable to this patient affected by pervasive refusal syndrome are virtually baby food. In these two volumes, it is possible to formulate a hypothesis about early failures of containment and other problems going back to the nursing couple, even when factual information about the history is not available. The generosity of acceptance, crucial to a healthy feeding relationship, may not be possible because of a severe dread of dependence, and one of the ways of avoiding receiving from another is to obliterate otherness by projective identification and fusion.

Fusion and projective identification

Petrelli [II, 8] describes the relationship that her patient, Ivana, wished to have with both her mother and also with Petrelli herself in the transference as "growing old together trapped in a kind of paralysed equilibrium". The fusion is idealized but deadly. Lack of separateness is graphically shown by Perocevic's chapter [I, 3], in which the family of four are described as sleeping in the same room as the grandparents. The family found great obstacles in leaving the grandparents' house although separate premises were available. In the patient himself, Miral, lack of separateness takes the form of massive projective identification. He is constantly inside the object, rather than with it. This mode has a clearly defensive function for him, as *being with* implies the unbearable experience of *being without* when the object is absent. Miral's intolerance of separation and separateness is also evident in the transference to his therapist.

Projective identification is a significant feature of the chapter by Quagliata [II, 6], where the patient constantly migrates from one identity to another to the extent of becoming depersonalized. Her functioning, like Mondadori's Lydia, is strikingly reminiscent of that described in Klein's paper, "On Identification" (Klein, 1955). In this paper, quoted by Mondadori, Klein refers to a novel where the main character is allowed to take over the identity of anyone he envies, as long as he keeps his own name in his pocket as a sort of return ticket into his own identity. Quagliata's patient, Deborah, often appears to lose her sense of identity in her projective identification and clearly does not keep her name in her pocket. The definition, "intrusive identification" (Meltzer, 1986), would apply to Deborah. She even intrudes in her analyst's space and time by leaving countless telephone messages on her answering machine between sessions. This case supports Lawrence's hypothesis (Lawrence, 2001) that anxieties about being intruded upon in patients with eating disorders may be due to a projection of their own intrusiveness.

Loss of identity is the high price many patients pay in order to avoid the experience of separateness and dependence, acknowledgement of which would involve a costly feeling of gratitude. An arresting example of lack of identity is given in Mondadori's chapter [II, 4], where we see the patient literally step into the "manager's shoes" at a time when she starts working in a shoe shop. When her state of projective identification lessens, Lydia very graphically gets rid of the many characters she has impersonated by donating to Oxfam thirty-six pairs of shoes.

Confusion of identity between patient and mother—"I am you and you are me"—is also described in the chapter by Rhode [I, 5], in which she refers to an anorexic patient's phantasy of starving in order to harm her mother. Brough [II, 1] describes her patient, Rebecca, as exhausting herself in cross-country running and as using her body to attack her mother, with whom she is identified. In a large number of cases of anorexia, the patient is in projective identification with the mother's body and attacks it by means of his or her starvation.

Freud provides a striking example of this type of phantasized attack on another in his famous case study of the "Rat Man":

One day while he [the patient] was away on his summer holiday the idea suddenly occurred to him that he was too fat [German *dick*] and he must *make himself slimmer*. So he began getting up from the table before the pudding came round and tearing along the road without a hat in the blazing heat of the August sun. Then he would dash up a mountain at the double, till, dripping with perspiration, he was forced to come to a stop. . . . Our patient could think of no explanation of this senseless, obsessional behaviour until it suddenly occurred to him that at that time his lady had also been stopping at the same resort; but she had been in the company of an English cousin, who was very attentive to her and of whom the patient had been very jealous. This cousin's name was Richard, and, according to the usual practice in England, he was known as *Dick*. Our patient then had wanted to kill this Dick. [1909, pp. 188–189]

It seems that Freud's patient slips into the identity of his rival Dick and he attacks the "fat one" [*dick*] by exhausting himself. This is an interesting anticipation of the use of Klein's concept of projective identification.

In the case of Aurora, described by Tirelli [II, 2], we see the patient eventually becoming more separate and we follow the difficult route that leads to this achievement. In witnessing the magnitude of the struggle to achieve separateness and accept a relationship of healthy dependence, we as clinicians can better appreciate the magnitude of the defences mobilized against psychic pain and envy. They offer protection from depressive feelings, such as gratitude (Klein, 1952), which are engendered in relationships where there is "generosity of acceptance". We are also helped to understand the extent of the control exercised by many eating disorders patients. This is described in many of the chapters, but particularly in Dubinsky's [II, 7]. Her patient, Julie, achieves spasmodic control over her food and over her objects, but also, as Dubinsky points out, primarily over her needs and her needy self. In this case, the control is chiefly exercised in order not to experience the threat of needing another or depending on another.

Attacks on the paternal function and the couple

The states of mind of fusion and projective identification obliterate the differentiation between the subject and the object. Siamese twins, it has been observed, may be aware of their sibling as "another" because there is some physical space that separates them. The equivalent of this space, the emotional space, between "you and me", is obliterated in the state of mind of fusion. An important distinction, however, needs to be made here. In a relationship of two people, a dyadic relationship, there is always a third element—that is, the space between them—and in a state of mind of fusion that space is lacking. A dyadic relationship is therefore in effect always triadic, the third element being constituted of the space between the subject and object. The term "dyadic" might imply twoness in its etymology, but in its application the term actually refers to a triadic relationship (Williams & Judd, 2002).

This third element may be referred to as the "paternal function", whether this function is performed by the mother herself or the actual father or is the provision of a boundary between mother and child. It is important to underline that this is a *function* and not necessarily a *person*. In many of the cases where fusion, lack of separateness, and projective identification are present, there is a strong attack on the paternal function. This can take a violent form, as in the case of Mondadori's Lydia [II, 4], who cut out the father from all the family photographs, and who brought this attack on the paternal function into the transference relationship. Mondadori notes: "Since I was in control of her time, I ceased to be a supportive and available mother for her. I became instead a cold and rejecting father figure whom she wanted to cut out of her life." Something similar is described by Brough [II, 1] when she observed that her patient, Rebecca, "looked at her or watched her when she was thinking" because "she didn't seem to know what was happening". This description can be linked to the one given by Britton in his 1989 paper "The Missing Link", in which the patient perceives the analyst's thinking as an internal dialogue, an intercourse within the analyst's mind. Wishing to stop it, or at least interfere with it, Britton's patient exclaims, "Stop that fucking thinking!"

The clinicians in these two volumes give many examples of the attack on the paternal function. It is present in the here-and-now of the transference relationship, but it is also present in references to the actual father whom the patient so often wishes to obliterate. In Mondadori's case [II, 4], the onset of anorexia may have been intimately connected with the separation of the patient's parents, a "mission accomplished" in Lydia's phantasy which could have evoked in her persecutory guilt.

In some cases, not only the presence, but the very existence of the father seems to be obliterated. Perocevic's patient [I, 3], Miral, uses skin colour as proof that his father does not exist. Miral, whose skin was white like that of his mother, used this perception to confirm that he was totally at one with his mother. This helped him to deny the existence of his father as a parent, as he had a different skin colour. At times the father is a rather shadowy figure. In Petrelli's chapter [II, 8], the father is described as a weak man, withdrawn into himself, suffering from epilepsy, and perceived by the patient as more of a child rival than a paternal presence. The paternal function also seems conspicuous by its absence in the case described by Ravenscroft [II, 3]. Mother is unable to set any boundaries to the patient, Paula, although she feels that "she did not have enough milk to satisfy a demanding, all-consuming, bottomless pit" which was "running her ragged". Anxious about being restricting and ungiving, like her own mother, and fearing Paula's anger and rejection, she never limits or denies Paula food or social licence.

At times we have no objective evidence of the lack of the paternal function, but we see a marked denigration of the father and the parental couple in the patients' material. This is evident in Brough's Rebecca [II, 1], who turned the parental intercourse into something that could only be damaging to mother—indeed, the cause of her depression. Rebecca develops an obsession with her father's snoring at night. This could be a denigration of "primal-scene" noises. It is not unusual in eating disorders for the patient to describe the father as making "animal" or "disgusting" noises when eating.

It is difficult to imagine a more inappropriate couple, less likely to unite and perform a creative intercourse, than the "frog and the goldfish" of Briggs's patient, George [I, 4]. It is clear that this patient's feeding difficulties are an attempt to keep the parents separate, as separate as the items of food on his plate. Like Miral [I, 3 (Perocevic)], George eats one item at a time, and never two together; so, for instance, never bread with parmesan or pasta with parmesan. His parents had to be kept separate since, when mother and father came together, they were experienced by him as terrifying, persecutory figures threatening his survival (cf. Britton, 1998).

Rhode's Anthony [I, 5] also seems to experience the parents as uniting against him to form a cruel and impervious object. When he sits between them, he smiles in a way that Rhode perceives as cruel, not joining the parents but separating them. This child has very complex phantasies connected with his difficulties with food. "Eating and growing . . . is confused with separating a parental couple. By implication, the child . . . makes himself vulnerable to be devoured by the parents when they come together." The child makes a violent oral attack on the parents that turns them into a formidable devouring object.

The ego-destructive superego

There seems to be, in the internal landscape of some of the patients described, a fierce presence that caricatures a paternal function and masquerades as a moral imperative. This has been termed, follow-ing Bion (1962a), the ego-destructive superego, and there are many instances of its presence in the "internal landscapes" of some of these patients. We meet a less extreme version of this superego in Marco's "policeman" [I, 6 (Catena)], and in Ivana's second mouth [II, 8 (Petrelli)], and the placation of a harsh superego is described in Dubinsky's chapter [II, 7]: "a bargain had been struck—if she starved herself it would stop the incessant accusations and de-mands from within". We meet a very ominous superego in Magagna's patient, Yufang [II, 5], as it is the voice of the destructive superego that speaks through her when she says: "I don't want to die, but I have to." This superego engenders persecutory feelings of guilt in the patient that make reparation impossible. A benign parental or paternal function (i.e. a benign superego) helps to sustain the hope that reparation is possible.

We might conclude where we began, with the idea that under-pins these two volumes on the generosity of acceptance. In every case described, reparation is only possible when there is a flow of giving and receiving between patient and clinician. Profound anxi-eties about the preservation of life are often split off and projected by patients into almost intolerable attacks on the analyst, who may feel bombarded and under siege. The relationship between "giver" and "receiver" in clinical work is described with a richness of modulation in E. Bott-Spillius's article, "Varieties of Envious Experience" (1993).

The *return gift*, as demonstrated by the careful work observed in these two volumes, is to receive—and to receive generously. The degree of patience, courage, and open-heartedness that this requires from clinicians is perhaps a defining characteristic of the task of treating patients with eating disorders.

Gianna Williams
Paul Williams
Jane Desmarais
Kent Ravenscroft

EXPLORING
EATING DISORDERS
IN ADOLESCENTS

CHAPTER ONE

"Who's that girl?"
An anorexic girl's search for identity and fear of contamination by the damaged (internal) parental couple

Sue Brough

The first time I saw Rebecca, she was standing outside the entrance to the clinic in tears and gasping for breath. She was wearing a vest, running shorts, and trainers and could easily have been mistaken for a boy, given her matchstick figure. Most of all, though, she looked gaunt and ill, with a face that could have been that of a 40-year-old. This face, I was soon to see, was the mirror image of her mother's. Rebecca was, in fact, just 14.

On that occasion, our first assessment session, I was told by both Rebecca and her parents that she wouldn't be able to come inside the clinic. The temperature was such, they said, that she wouldn't be able to breathe (it was a hot August day). Rebecca then said that, even if she entered the clinic, she couldn't possibly stay inside for the full fifty minutes that my letter had suggested. So I was forced, at the entrance to the clinic, to interpret her mounting panic of becoming "trapped inside" before she had even entered the psychotherapy-room.

Rebecca seemed surprised by my comment and agreed to come in with me, provided that she could leave at any time and if she could sit at an open window. In fact, she then stayed "inside" for the entire time of the two assessment meetings and for all of her

1

subsequent thrice-weekly psychotherapy sessions, although, at first, for much of the time she was in tears. It was the presence of the tears which gave me some hope.

This chapter is a description of my work in progress with Rebecca and my occasional contact with her family. I try to convey the enormous countertransference impact she had on me as I attempted to engage her in a treatment relationship. The *type* of relationship I was offering her was based on a mutual agreement to meet at prearranged times. Her misgivings about my possible cruelty, and about my motives for doing so, were to preoccupy Rebecca throughout the second half of the first year of work. This experience is consonant with Donald Meltzer's view (1992) that in certain claustrophobic states of mind "the atmosphere of sadism is pervasive and the hierarchic structure of tyranny and submission forebodes violence ... there is only one value: survival ... it is absolute loneliness in a world of bizarre objects" (p. 91).

Our work around her struggle to achieve a separate sense of self continuously left me with a feeling of "Who's that girl?", as she both physically and emotionally "ran" past me.

* * *

My own first meeting with Rebecca came three years after a previous referral to another clinic a few miles away from her home. She had been referred there by her GP when she was 11 years old. We were told that, at that time, she was described as "obstinate, obsessed with running, had strange eating habits and had lost a lot of weight". She initially attended with her parents and two elder brothers and had met a child psychiatrist who assessed the problem as "an issue of control". The family cancelled subsequent appointments, saying that they were not happy with the psychiatrist's approach to Rebecca's problems and preferred to deal with it themselves.

Rebecca was then referred to our clinic two and a half years later by her GP. At this time we were told that the eating problems "had sorted themselves out", but Rebecca was refusing to be inside the family home other than to go to bed. She was spending most of her time doing solitary, long-distance running or sitting at the end of the garden. She insisted on staying outside, regardless of weather conditions, all year long, even after dark.

They were all seen again at this second consultation—Rebecca, her brothers John and Peter (aged 20 and 17 years), and her parents, Mr and Mrs A. They were initially seen by my colleague, who took a careful history and tried to engage them in family therapy. However, Rebecca would not stay in a room with her parents. My colleague then asked me to assess Rebecca, with a view to offering her intensive individual psychotherapy with the possibility of doing some family work later. Interestingly, no one in the family had apparently recognized that Rebecca was seriously claustrophobic, despite them all seeing that she could not stay inside the building or the family home.

The first session

The first meeting with Rebecca both surprised and moved me. After I had "talked her into the room" she began by moving her chair closer to mine and saying "at last, someone is taking my situation seriously". I felt that the issues of "emotional distance" (i.e. coming closer) and "ambivalence" were instantly being put on the agenda for work between us.

I began by saying that I could see she was unhappy and was feeling "trapped" by certain feelings. I asked if she could perhaps tell me "a little" of *her* view of what these feelings were. In retrospect, I realized that in using these words, I too was identified with the feeling that emotions had to be allowed only a "teaspoon at a time". The immediacy and the distress of her response was the surprising factor—as if she had not had the experience of someone getting alongside her emotionally before. She immediately began to cry and to talk about herself as a 9-year-old. At first she talked in a disjointed way, through her tears, using phrases like "I got left behind". Then she began to speak more coherently about how she and her brothers always used to play together, or, rather, she had always "tagged along" when they were with their friends. She had thought of herself as "one of the boys", able to do anything that they did—play football or cricket, swim. She could even keep up with them when they had races in the garden. As she was telling me this, her face looked "young", like the child that she was describing. She then moved on to talk about how her father used to join in these kind of games with her middle brother and herself, and how the three of them were all good at sports.

The distress returned as she then described how this brother, Peter, had begun to change five years earlier, when he was 12 years old. He suddenly seemed to outgrow her as a playmate and turned more and more to friends of his own age, excluding her. In her own words "Suddenly there was no one but me—I was on my own." Later I understood that her father stopped taking part in the shared sporting activities once Peter withdrew, and this led, in her view, to her father putting on a lot of weight—"just giving up and collapsing", according to Rebecca. What struck me at the time was the significance of Rebecca's comment "I was on my own", given that her parents were alive and that they lived a comfortable, middle-class life. In addition, there was no mention of her mother at all in the first session. In fact, "the threesome" she described seemed to be Rebecca's phantasy, uniting her in this masculine domain which actively excluded mother. I wondered why there was so little space or significance given to "mother" in Rebecca's mind, and what connection there was between this and Rebecca's claustrophobia. The "threesome" must have defended Rebecca against some anxiety, for her world collapsed once the "threesome" disintegrated.

Given the nature of the symptoms, my colleague wondered whether Rebecca had been sexually abused, since her parents told him they thought Rebecca was now waging a "hate campaign" against her father (I was to hear more about this campaign from Rebecca later). I instinctively felt, however, that the apparent "oedipal" configuration in Rebecca's material was a defence against something more primitive and terrifying—as if Rebecca felt she were fighting for her (psychic) survival.

The running

In her third individual session with me, Rebecca returned to the theme of her loneliness once her brother and father stopped playing sport with her. She became thoughtful and said that it had just occurred to her that perhaps she had become "obsessed" with running to stop herself from feeling lonely. She then added, "I started to run every day and to go further and further. Running became like 'a friend' to me." She described how when she was running she did not feel empty and lonely, she felt "in control . . . and *strong*", not like the "panicky, quivering jelly" she felt just before a race. I thought of her description of a father who had "collapsed" after her brother left their threesome, not just physically but, for Rebecca, in his psychic function within the family. Rebecca's actual words, "panicky, quivering jelly"—the description of her psychic state just before a race—evoked in me a sense of an absent, internal mother and a passive, formless father unable to provide a backbone for her and the family. So the running was also a running away from her femininity, and a way of seeking identification with a strong phallic figure—both the potent father, and the boy she seemed to wish herself to be. It enabled her to identify with the young and virile father of her childhood (at a time when he, too, had been a competitive runner), while now putting as much physical distance between them as possible, perhaps as a counter-reaction to her overly strong and frightening oedipal feelings towards him.

The eating disorder

It was only in telling me the importance of the running that I began to hear from Rebecca about the true nature of her eating disorder. Far from having "sorted itself out", as the GP had suggested, it had become more subtle and sophisticated. At first Rebecca linked it entirely to her running, telling me how she had looked at the girls in the sports club who were running faster than she and had decided that the common denominator between them was that they were thinner than she, so she decided to lose weight. At first she just stopped eating and was amazed at how quickly she lost weight, and how easy it was—"at last . . . this was something I *could* control".

Rebecca constantly surprised and concerned me with how little she understood her own body. When she cried, it was like watching a 5-year-old who has no idea where the tears are coming from, nor how to wipe them away (further evidence of a lack of a good internal mother). She described how she "enjoyed" the feeling of

hunger, thinking that it was a sign of how "strong" she was. To my
surprise, however, she described how she came to dread the light-
headed feeling that accompanied the hunger—she felt herself to be
in a "dream-like" state, and said that it was "like a nightmare. . . .
Each morning I would wake up and hope that it was a bad dream
which was now over, but it never was." The most upsetting aspect
of this part of the therapy for me was to hear the description of
routines she had developed for helping her to do certain activities
without fainting—like holding on to certain items of furniture in
her bedroom to help her get from the door to the bed. The question
I kept wondering about in my mind was, "Where was her mother
in this?" I realized that Rebecca had little concept *in her mind* of a
mother who would be attentive to her needs and who would worry
about her. I found myself thinking of a "depressed mother"—a
mother who appears either not to notice or not to be affected by her
daughter's distress. Rebecca managed to convey to me a feeling
that her behaviour was unremarkable and should pass unnoticed. I
had to hold this in opposition to the part of me that wanted to take
hold of her and actively intervene in her neglectful and punitive
regime. The expectation that I wouldn't notice or care about her
feelings, representing a state of mind belonging to one of Rebecca's
internal objects, was, I felt, "pushed into" me, by projective identification.

Simultaneously I realized that Rebecca was studying my facial
expressions and seemed interested and surprised by my responses.
In particular, I became aware of Rebecca watching me while I was
"thinking"—not, I felt, to see what effect she had had on me, but
more because she didn't seem to know what was happening. I
found this experience, of her "watching" me thinking, immensely
moving. A simple, commonplace experience for me seemed fascinating for her—perhaps reflecting something missing in her
mother, a type of early emotional deprivation.

The face as mirror

Winnicott has written at length about the importance of the mother's face for the infant: "In individual emotional development the
precursor of the mirror is the mother's face" (1971b, p. 111).

Winnicott's metaphor of "the face as mirror" is very important in understanding the relationship between Rebecca and her mother because for both of them their faces convey a "damaged" look. Rebecca's own face is disfigured, as I will explain later, and her mother's face looks like a "death mask"—a truly frightening, unresponsive, "frozen" face. As Winnicott (1971b) emphasized, when a child meets with an unsmiling response from mother's face, the child will "scan" the mother's face to try to decipher and predict her moods. Rebecca seemed to be watching my face in order to see what I reflected about *her* (in truth, I found her very interesting) but also, I think, to find relief from aspects of her troubling world of internal objects.

The first six months of the therapy was something of a "honeymoon" period, as it gave Rebecca an opportunity to talk about the "nightmare" of the previous four years. The sense of relief this gave her at first outweighed any other factor. Only later did I experience the other side of Rebecca—the side that was most evident to her family.

I heard from her about how she felt "overshadowed" by both her brothers, who were highly successful both in academic work and in sport. Her eldest brother, John, had just been awarded a first-class honours degree in mathematics. Also, during the course of the therapy her other brother, Peter, heard that he had been offered an unconditional place at a prestigious university, and he had already been selected to represent Great Britain athletically. Despite telling me this with evident emotion, Rebecca seemed surprised by my use of the word "jealousy" in connection with her feelings, reflecting more a difficulty in conceptualization and symbol-formation than denial. When I used emotionally toned words, Rebecca did not seem able to make the link between the "feeling" and the "concept".

In our occasional meetings with her parents, my colleague and I found this same difficulty in them in a more pronounced form. Despite being professional people, both parents exhibited a type of thought disorder—or, as we came to think of it, an "emotional eating disorder"—in which "feelings" failed to develop into "concepts". Rebecca herself, despite being an A-grade student in all her subjects, did not know her way around the world of feelings at all. In fact, she did not know how to name them, though her descriptions of family experiences were usually stunning in their accuracy. I often felt that Rebecca was the most perceptive member of her family.

She described her family to me as "only able to operate in a threesome", involving, in my opinion, the fantasy of there only being one child in the family, and perceiving herself—rather than her mother—in the "couple" relationship with her father. Her competitiveness expanded to include both the girls at school and her sports club, with her main focus being the attempt to get her father's individual attention. Her father was an official at the sports club where she ran, and she bitterly resented the attention he paid to the other girls. She felt that he "flirted" with them in front of her and that they enjoyed calling him by his first name also in front of her. This was why "winning" meant everything to her—she wasn't interested in coming second or third; winning meant "having your name in the paper and becoming well-known ... having people nudge each other and say 'there's Rebecca'."

"Winning" satisfied her oedipal wish to displace her mother and have her father, as the "Club Official", announce *her* as the winner of the race; it also enabled her to "pass" her brothers in her fantasy and to be the winner of the "sibling race". I was told that they had run races in the garden as young children. Most of all, it gave her *her* moment of significance, of recognition, and of identity. Her preferred style of winning was to set off just behind the "pack" (she could never run "with" them), and then to come from behind and run past them all. When I asked her what was in her mind at that time, she said that she would be thinking of the other girls' parents who would be watching—"usually it would be their *fathers*"—and they would have their attention turned from their own daughters and would focus on *her*. Then, in her fantasy, they would all turn to each other and say, "Who's that girl?"

This would be Rebecca's moment of triumph. Not only would *her* face and *her* name be in the papers, just like her brother's had been after being selected for Great Britain, but *she* would be No. 1— the "winner". Later in the therapy, I too was to have the same experience of wondering "Who's that girl?"

The inner hunger

It was five months into the analytic work before Rebecca began to remember what she was like before the onset of the anorexia. She had started a session by telling me a long list of digestive problems she had been experiencing since the start of therapy—constipation, diarrhoea, stomach-aches, and so on—which had only recently been diagnosed as irritable bowel syndrome. I had responded by saying that it sounded like I was giving her something that was "indigestible"—that what I was offering her was either too little, too much, or simply the wrong kind of food for her emotional growth. She usually asked me to repeat comments like this and seemed to be saying them over and over to herself as if psychological relief could be gained by just knowing that these things can be thought about privately and spoken about with others. Much of the time I felt that I was not just being an "analytic mother" to her; it was as if I had to give her a map of her own body, in much the same way a mother would help a very small child make sense of aches and pains. At one point I simplified it by saying that it sounded like her stomach was letting her know how she was feeling. Her reply stunned and moved me. She said that she thinks "it's all to do with this strange feeling I get at the end of the day" (pointing to her stomach area). She added that she has a "funny feeling that there's something missing". When I queried the "something missing", she said that she couldn't really put it into words—but that it was a "feeling of emptiness". "I would feel that I had been to school, done my homework, and was about to go to bed—and it had all been done 'on my own' and I would know that tomorrow I would do the same all over again." She then paused for a while, looking strained and gaunt, before finally adding "It's the fear that I'll always be on my own."

When I asked whether the pain of the "something missing" was located from the beginning in her stomach, Rebecca told me how the eating disorder had begun. She then began to tell me how if she needed to talk to her mum when she came home from school, her mum would always be "too busy". She would begin to try to talk to her mum, and her mum would give her a cake and a drink (referred to by Rebecca as "my snack"), and tell her to watch TV in the lounge while she was cooking the evening meal. There followed a long description of how she and her brothers would then watch TV in the lounge until their mum brought their tea in on trays. Their parents ate later, also in front of the TV; the whole family then watched TV before going to bed. She added, "Mum and dad always offered food or money, but what I really wanted was more of *them*." She then described a feeling of being "trapped" into her family's lifestyle—a "lifeless lifestyle . . . they never *do* anything . . .", which she could see was making her mother unhappy.

Rebecca's attempt to change things began with her giving up the "after-school snack". Although she didn't know it at the time, it seems that the "snack" was identified by her with an attempt to fill a "gap" or a hunger in a private, concrete way. Then it evolved into Rebecca only eating *one* item from the communal meal and preparing the rest of the meal herself. Eventually Rebecca was preparing *all* of her food herself and "hiding" it around the house. We talked about this in terms of a hamster or squirrel "hoarding" its food for fear of a lack of supplies. At one point, when she was describing how she plans menus to allow herself one "treat" per day, she suddenly added that if she goes out running in the evening she deliberately plans a special supper for herself and spends most of the evening thinking about it so that she has "something to look forward to when I return . . . something there for me". She called these her special "hearty suppers". She was now doing for herself what her mother had done for her when she returned from outside activities.

The night feeds

Over the next few weeks, which preceded a holiday break, she let me in on a "secret aspect" of her eating disorder. She referred to it as "my night-time feeds". This information had followed on from her description of her special "hearty suppers". She, of course, appeared not to recognize her use of the word "hearty". Talking about these planned treats, she said that it's easier for her if she doesn't eat before bedtime, because it's only on the nights when she's eaten supper that she wants something else in the middle of the night. She also linked it with the evenings ("two or three times a week") when her father brings "take-aways" in. She would criticize him for eating them after he had already had his evening meal. She would then wait until he had gone out of the kitchen before eating his left-overs in the containers, "even if it's cold". She shuddered with disgust as she said this. I commented that she might be frightened and disgusted by her own needy/greedy feelings, and that this is why she is so appalled by her father— because he represents the greedy aspect of herself. I asked what it was that was so frightening about her greed. Again, her answer was very evocative.

She said that she was frightened that she would go on eating long after she was feeling full—and that it was her fear of *fullness* rather than fear of *fatness* which most frightened her. I felt that she associated this fear of "fullness" with her own intrusiveness and greed. She described occasions when she had eaten so much that she had been "doubled-up in pain". This had usually been subsequent to her scavenging the empty containers of her father's take-aways. Later, in her words, "In the middle of the night . . . I would creep down to the kitchen and take *huge* chunks of crusty bread and eat them in the dark." She admitted that this greedy aspect of herself would not weigh, count calories, or cut up the food, but would be specifically interested in "*huge* chunks of bread . . . something filling . . . something to really get my teeth into". She then went on to describe her fear of somebody walking into the kitchen and finding her there "with saliva running down the sides of my mouth . . . like a vampire". I queried what would "need filling", and she linked it with "trying to fill in all I've missed out on", and she gave examples of all the "normal" things of the last four years that she hadn't done, like playing with other children in the playground, or going with them into town; during all the time that she should have been doing this she was "on her own". She added, in a moment of great poignancy "If I had a best friend, I would not have become anorexic". I told her the way she had described these "night-feeds" made me think of quite a young infant who can't get through the night without the "four-hourly feed". She smiled at the irony of this and said, "It's funny . . . but the feeling *I* have at night is that I'm going to starve to death and that I won't get through the night if I don't eat . . . and also I think that I must eat *all* there is, in case when I wake up there's nothing left."

I realized that she was able to tell me about a fear of herself being a "vampire baby", because she had found a "best friend" in me, at least for the time being. This coincided with a time of great improvement for her. She began to eat more and to grow. She began to show more interest in her appearance in an age-appropriate way. She also began to realize just how "out of step" she was with her peer group, causing her considerable distress.

It was meaningful that the information about the "night feeds" and the "fear of starving to death" came up just before our holiday break, a reminder that she was not "solely in charge of the supply", that it was a time of great dependency on the therapy, and that she anticipated missing it. Despite my frequent references to the break and the impact of it, Rebecca, rather predictably, did not turn up for the last session before the holiday.

The claustrophobia

The symptom that caused Rebecca's parents the greatest sense of frustration was her determination to stay outside the house—or *any* building, for that matter—during all of her waking hours. Usually Rebecca presented this to me in a highly "rationalized" form—disparaging people (i.e. me) whom she felt to prefer "unhealthy" lifestyles by spending too much time indoors. Further exploration of this fantasy usually led her to her listing the health benefits of fresh air, exercise, and so forth, compared with its opposite—a slothful, indolent "couch-potato" lifestyle (which was one of her descriptions of her father).

She told me that the desire to stay "outside" had started a year before we had begun to meet, about three years into the eating disorder. At that time, with no real friends and no social life, she would spend most of her time in her bedroom. She would stand at the window "looking at the stars and the moon and the wind in the trees. . . . I began to feel that the house was too small. . . . I wanted to get out there to be with nature. At first it was enough to open the bedroom window and stand by it . . . but then it wasn't enough and I had to go outside." Reluctantly, Rebecca had to concede that it wasn't just that she preferred to be outside, but that she *has* to be "outside"—and that if she were forced to stay inside she would feel ill: "panicky, muddled in the head, I can't think straight, but most of all just 'ill'." She then elaborated that she feels she can't breathe and that something terrible is going to happen to her, "like a heart attack and I'm going to die". I felt that she was telling me that if she stayed in the house she would be "contaminated" or "intruded into" by some kind of "diseased" or "damaged foreign body" which would infect her and possibly kill her.

The nature of this "contaminated" or "damaged" object intrigued me. What kind of object could be so frightening? She told me, with an air of "absolute normality", that she had her own table and chair outside, and that she could move it to shelter under the awning of the shed if it rained or could place it in the beam of light coming from the kitchen window in order to do her homework. She took all her meals out there and waited until no one else was in the kitchen before coming in to "retrieve" her meals, which she had previously wrapped, labelled, and hidden in various places in the kitchen, laundry and garage. If her food was ever "found" in its hiding place, or "touched" by someone else in the fridge, she would throw it away.

This fear of "contamination" particularly applied to her father. Rebecca would refuse to enter the kitchen in order to "retrieve" her food if he was in there, and she would re-scrub any cooking utensils he may have used. I heard about this in connection with her disgust with his dietary habits. Her father was the only member of the family not health-conscious or using low-fat spreads. He also had frequent bouts of constipation. Rebecca would deliberately get up early so as to use the bathroom *before* him, refusing to go in after him. If he dared to get up in the night and use the toilet, she would immediately wake up and go and open the bathroom window, insisting that it be kept open the rest of the night.

I was often struck by the *force* of Rebecca's anger towards her father. It had an "irrational" and very "intrusive" quality to it. This emerged very clearly, in a session during the summer term, in a tirade against him when she was describing sitting outside revising for her exams. She complained bitterly to me that he had made it "impossible" for her to revise by his repeated stamping-down of his "midden" (compost heap), and she obviously felt that he had done this deliberately, in order to spoil or "rob" her of her chance to do well. She objected to the noise he was making, as if it was intended to disturb her. There was fury evident in her eyes when she described this situation, and a feeling of "paranoia" was in the room. This seemed to show very clearly the projection of her own envious, controlling, and intrusive phantasies.

Rebecca's fear of being "trapped inside", which she had shown me so vividly in our first meeting, was also linked, I think, to her fear of contamination by her father's presence in the home. His "stamping-down" of the midden, which is literally a "dung-heap", seems to have been experienced by her as a provocative noise linked with her father's sexuality concretely imbued with faecal qualities. Her vitriolic description of her father's "bulging eyes . . . and bulging stomach" reflected her concern about and contempt of his greed, which she believed to have brought about his "collapse" from the virile potent father of her childhood. I felt that Rebecca's anger and panic were also related to the "damage" that she perceived her father to have done to her mother. In her phantasy, the parental intercourse was seen as damaging, and attacking. I could therefore understand the nature of Rebecca's panic, for not only did she phantasize about herself as her father's partner (through the projection of her own oedipal wishes) but also as the product of a damaged sexual union.

Rebecca had good reason to feel "trapped" by the relationship between her parents. In less paranoid moments she did agree with my comments about her fear for her father's health because of his physical "collapse" through sudden weight increase and change in lifestyle. It was through this association of ideas that I heard about the fact that Rebecca's parents had slept in separate bedrooms for the last four to five years (the same length of time as the eating disorder), and that Rebecca also blamed this on her father's increased weight. She recounted to me on several occasions that her mother had seemed to be very unhappy during the years when she had not been working (i.e. Rebecca's childhood). She recalled her mother packing her father's case for working trips abroad, accompanied by comments such as "It's alright for men. . . . They're the ones who lead exciting lives. . . ." She also remembered that her mother had moved out of the marital bedroom on the day that she had returned to work because of the need "to get a good night's sleep", so that she could cope with work.

According to Rebecca, her father's weight increase had made his snoring so loud that "the whole house echoed with the noise". Then, when her mother moved out of the marital bedroom into the spare room at the end of the corridor, the arrangement left Rebecca sleeping in the bedroom next to her father. This proximity was too close for comfort, and Rebecca would regularly wake her mother up with her screaming at her father in the middle of the night to "stop snoring". She described in graphic detail to me why this should be so disturbing for her—for *her* bed was right next to the wall that her father's bed also touched on the other side. Rebecca was also furious with her mother for abandoning her father to her care. This made me suspect that both her obsession with running and her claustrophobia were defences against eroticized feelings towards her father that had become too dangerous, hence the total denigration of him. At first I had thought that Rebecca's "night-feeds", which happened "two or three times a week", were attempts to fill a "hole". This might have been due to her feeling of maternal deprivation, or to oedipal feelings of being excluded by a sexually *active* couple. Later I thought that the night feeds were an empathic response, in lieu of a sexual response, to father's take-aways—the mistress—which he often took upstairs to his bed-room. Rebecca agreed with my comment that she seemed to think her mother must be sexually repulsed by her father and said, with great embarrassment, "I can't *imagine* what it's like to have a man as fat as him on top of you. . . ." Which means, as I pointed out, that she *has* imagined that very thing. I felt that there was a clear link in Rebecca's mind between her father's sexual damage to mother, mother's depression, and father's greedy relationship to food.

Her fantasies were also enhanced by the perception of herself as a damaged object of the intercourse, because of a mark on her face. She had had, from birth, a large strawberry-coloured forceps scar on the rounded part of her left cheek—quite close to her mouth. It was several months before Rebecca mentioned it in her sessions with me, and she alluded to it as if "in passing". Over the course of several months Rebecca had begun to recall how she had disliked her body from a really early age. She had thought of herself as a fat, unattractive child, and she had desperately wanted to look "rough and tough" like her brothers. She even resorted to cutting and scarring her arms and legs so that she would look "tough" like a boy. She described in detail her joy, at about the age of 6 or 7, in being able to run around on holiday with no T-shirt on and just shorts so that people would mistake her for a boy. It was within this context that Rebecca pointed to the forceps scar and said that it was "the last straw", immediately followed by the comment that her mother thinks "it's the least of my problems . . .". I asked, "And what do *you* think?" She looked very strained and anguished when she replied—"I just can't believe that I've got it . . ."—and she described how, when she sees herself in the mirror, she is always shocked at the sight of it and that *is all* she can see. She described how, when she was very young, even at nursery, other children would come up and touch her face and ask, "What's that?"

With great poignancy she told me how she always felt "different" and thought that the mark on her face was a handicap and a sign that there was "something wrong" with her. She explained that she thought it was an indication that eventually something else would be found "wrong" with her—for instance, her heart—because she wasn't perfect. She remembered feeling frightened by the scar as a little girl, and angry about the origin. Each morning she would wake up and "look in the mirror and hope it had gone, but it never had". This last description was so familiar to her description of her experience of her faintness connected to her eating disorder—"like a nightmare . . . each morning I would wake up and hope it was a bad dream which was now over, but it never was . . ."—as to make me think of the eating disorder as an extension of the birth scar in her mind. The eating disorder was then the "living out" of an unconscious phantasy of being "different", "damaged", "not perfect"—her mark of Cain (*Genesis* 4: 1–16), which the birth-mark seemed to symbolize in a concrete way.

I became very interested in understanding Rebecca's feelings about this "scar"—the very word seemed to convey her feelings about herself as marked out from birth (or before) to be the carrier of the family's (mis)fortunes. I asked her what thoughts she had about how it *had* got there. She clearly hated talking about this scar—it seemed to be associated with such *shame* for her. With great difficulty she said that she thought her mother had caused it—that she had always blamed her mother for as long as she could remember. I puzzled aloud as to *how* her mother could have caused it (thinking of the forceps delivery), and she said that her mother had told her that she had suffered from high blood pressure throughout the pregnancy. She'd had a long and difficult delivery, involving the use of forceps. My comment to Rebecca was that it seemed to be unclear for her as to "who had damaged whom" in her relationship with her mother, but that it appears *something* frightened them and intruded into their feeding relationship. I said to Rebecca that the anorexia was both a symbolic and a literal *rejection* of her mother's food and her mother's care. I added that it seemed to me that Rebecca was using her body in a self-punitive way, in order to punish her mother and get vengeance for what she felt had been done to her. Rebecca was able to understand this, and she acknowledged that she *did* want to punish her mother but hadn't realized that she *had* been doing so. I was able to talk to Rebecca about the internal damage that a desire for revenge entails. I spoke about the pleasure that she seemed to be gaining from seeing her mother's distress at the damage she was doing to herself, which made it difficult for her to move on—as if she was somewhat addicted to this. Very tearfully, Rebecca did accept that she had a cruel streak inside—cruel towards her parents and, most of all, cruel towards herself. This cruel streak was also symbolized by the "scar".

As the therapy progressed Rebecca became more and more aware of the real nature of her dilemma. In external terms she described it as the need to "grow up" without "growing out". This seemed to look like a dilemma that was seriously impeding her success in running. In order to compete in the next group—that is, the "women's" rather than the "girls'"—she had to be able to compete against them on *their* terms—that is, with a physically mature body. The pressure on me in the transference also grew as this "dilemma" came more and more into the room. I had to withstand a whole variety of denigratory comments about "women's bodies"—the ugliness of "big hips and big thighs", and her view that after sexual maturity a woman's body "collapses . . . while a man's body goes on getting stronger . . .". Her intense competitiveness with things female and envy of the male body and phallic prowess made it almost impossible for her to move on developmentally, and it also made it difficult for her to accept what I could offer. I interpreted this as her fear of being "trapped" in her relationship with me. In order for her to "grow" (i.e. emotionally or "inwardly" rather than "up" or "out"), she would be having to acknowledge that *I* have something worth offering her and that therefore I was not as "collapsed" as she would like to think. However, I also spoke to her about her *fear*—that if she *did* grow, physically and psychically, this would be at my expense, leaving me depleted and defeated by her.

The question of "who had taken from whom?" was therefore a considerable problem for Rebecca in all her relationships, and it became a real issue in our work together. She acknowledged my comments that if she allowed me to help her she would experience this as at the expense of *her* independence. *Helping* her was therefore experienced by her as an intrusion into her mind, like being taken over by her parents, "robbing" her of her autonomy. Her fear was of me "pulling something out of her", just as she felt she had robbed her mother of her liveliness. I suggested that she was frightened of depleting me—of pulling my "liveliness" out of me and being left with something "dead" or "damaged". Rebecca seemed to associate the "birth scar" with her needy/greedy self, as if it were a constant reminder that her babyhood had robbed her mother of her "liveliness". I also realized that her anxiety about being so damaging contributed to her preoccupation about her "mark of Cain".

Rebecca showed me how hard it was for her to allow any "parenting" to take place—either internally or externally. Internally she seemed to be in an omnipotent place: in a state of mind that does not require nurture or protection or development. Externally she was very suspicious of my motives in wanting to work with her. The ambivalent communication about distance and closeness which I received in our first session was to be a hallmark of the therapy. She was clearly very relieved to share with someone the nature of her terror as to what the future would hold in store for her, but of course I was not to be allowed to make too much inroad into her *thinking*, or to be misled into believing that I had anything valuable to offer her.

She never missed an appointment during the first term, until it came to the last session before the Christmas break, which she did not attend. I then found that before each break and sometimes on Fridays, Rebecca had to take control of the separation by missing the session, leaving me waiting for her and wondering if she would reappear after the break. This reminded me of a situation her mother had described when the early history was taken—that Rebecca had "refused to let go of the breast" and that her mother had "forced the issue" by abruptly weaning her at the age of 18 months. I felt that this was being repeated in our relationship, as Rebecca pre-empted the break. I was also aware that the closer I got to Rebecca emotionally, the more persecuted she became. At the same time as hearing about her terror of starving to death and her "night-feeds" when she "attacked huge chunks of bread", Rebecca also began to complain to me more and more of what she felt *I* was doing to her. She accused me frequently of taking up "huge chunks of her time" (as if I were a greedy breast intruding into her) and tearfully blamed me as being the reason why she felt she was "going to fail all her exams" because I wasn't allowing her the time to revise for them (although she did, in fact, get straight A grades).

By the summer term at the end of our first year of individual work, Rebecca was bringing aspects of her more infantile self into the room, even including photo albums of herself as a young child. This was done initially because she wanted me to see just how awful she had looked when she was at her most anorexic—in the first term of her high school—at the age of 11. She did indeed look truly *awful*—like a miniature wizened version of her mother—with a look of absolute terror on her face. I imagined that she must have been very close to hospitalization at that point, yet we had been told by her parents that they were *not* the first people to be worried about her—it was Rebecca's Outward Bound leader who had first alerted them to her eating disorder after her attendance at camp. Even on giving her history, it would not have been apparent from Mr and Mrs A.'s descriptions and reaction just how ill their daughter had been—and still was. But then, being in their presence gave my colleague and myself a vivid and disturbing experience of the emotional atmosphere of denial engendered by "projective identi-fication—refusing" objects (Bion, 1962b). We had ourselves to learn how to process our own distress at their imperviousness to any-thing other than factual, concrete information.

The high-school photographs of Rebecca at the age of 11 led to her bringing in photo albums of family holidays when she was very young (between the ages of 3 and 6 years). In each photograph

I saw a little girl turning her face away from the camera or holding her hand up to cover her left cheek. Rebecca herself also seemed to see this, as if for the first time, and her explanation was that she was always aware of her "chubby cheeks" and was trying to hide them. I said that what I saw was not "chubby cheeks", but a little girl frightened by her own appearance, with a sense of *shame* or guilt about what this birth scar indicated. I described her perception of her "chubbiness" as her association to the scar, which is on the "rounded" part of her cheek and therefore a sign, for her, of her greed. This is what led me to refer to her view of her scar as her "mark of Cain". She readily agreed that she saw it as the physical evidence of "guilt" for her greediness (in *Genesis*, Cain has to carry his disfiguring mark on his face as evidence for the murder of his brother). I was very aware of how much the birth scar looked like the areola area around the nipple. Was the fantasy of a stolen nipple increasing Rebecca's feelings of guilt?

As the sessions developed a more "psychotic" feel to them, I began to understand more of how very ill and frightened Rebecca had been as a child. At times she could be quite irrational as well as being amazingly perceptive and capable of describing feeling "persecuted" by me. She accused me on many occasions of trying to "get inside her mind and influence the way she thought". I interpreted that she was feeling that I was trying to intrude into her *time* and into her *mind*, robbing her of what she felt were her very limited resources. My occasional contact with her parents helped me to understand better the nature of this fear. Their persistent unavailability for emotional communication left me feeling that I would have to "break in by force" in order to get through to them. I also interpreted Rebecca's fear that any change or growth on *her* part would be exploited by me—that I would "wallow" in this and use her infantile dependent feelings to feed my "greedy" self.

The *violence* of Rebecca's projections was striking—for there were times when I felt that I took her home with me emotionally. I had the fantasy of feeding her seated at my family dinner table, and I recalled her mother saying in our initial meeting, "there's no room left in my mind for John or Peter. . . . Rebecca whirls round and round in my head" (indicating that her head was "spinning"). Both these experiences would seem to me to indicate Rebecca's enormous capacity to use projective identification for the purposes of control, rather than just communication.

The central focus of the transference involved the question, "Who has control of the quantity and frequency of supplies?" I was often left wondering whether I had offered Rebecca too little or too much—like a mother with food waiting on the table but not knowing if it is the right kind of food. If it appeared that I offered too little, I was treated with contemptuous disdain and Rebecca would say, "There's *nobody* who really understands me . . .", but if I got in too close or gave too much, she would get angry and say, "You're trying to change the way I think"—that is, "force-feed" her. Sometimes my interpretations came as a relief to her, providing an outlet for her feelings of being "trapped", but often they seemed to be "intrusive" (and I sometimes reviewed myself as intrusive). I became aware that the "normal parenting" I was providing felt intrusive because there was no previous backdrop of emotional nourishment into which it could fit. For, if the normal process of projective identification—that is, for the purposes of communication and detoxification—of anxiety breaks down, then an abnormal or pathological use can develop. This has a different *motivation*, which gives rise to an experience of intrusion, because it is an act of "breaking and entering" into one's object in order to take possession of it. Some time into the therapeutic work Rebecca began to associate her house with her parents' "lifeless, joyless relationship".

Trapped in a tomb

Rebecca's constant complaint to me was that once a girl becomes a woman, she has "no life". Her fantasy was that a woman then has to use all her energy in looking after her husband and children and has none left for herself. This, she said, was the reason why she thought she shouldn't have children, as she didn't think she would be a very good mother. She would be too selfish and would want to live her own life. Rebecca was also convinced that women have nothing interesting to talk about—just cooking and sewing. I puzzled aloud about this and queried whether she and I just spent our time talking about cooking and sewing. She seemed unsure about this at first but then decided that the example didn't count, as "this is your job and you're doing what you're paid to do". This remark felt both hopeful and demeaning, implying that during sessions she felt that she enlivened me, and outside sessions I lay in a collapsed state, joining the ranks of her "collapsed objects". This seemed to be the outcome of attacks from her own envious "vampire" parts and a turning of "mother" (albeit, in my case, analytic mother) from something "life-giving" to something "life-threatening".

The question "who has taken what from whom?" was therefore experienced as a question between the two of us as an "analytic couple" and, in her fantasy, between herself and her mother as a "nursing couple", and between her parents as a "sexual and fighting couple". For Rebecca, this later seemed to represent some kind of deadly intercourse between an internal deadpan mother and a "collapsed" father—a heap of rubbish. It's as if, for Rebecca, her father had turned her mother's womb into a place of destruction—a compost heap (hence the fantasy about the damage she incurred while inside it). A "midden", a rotting waste-ground/womb, seemed to be for Rebecca the home of the "combined object".

Rebecca's constant injunction to her parents, but especially her mother, was to "live more". I think she wanted some external confirmation that her mother had not been totally drained of her life-blood/milk. This could also give another interpretation to the eating disorder and claustrophobia, suggesting that she might have a fantasy of being entombed in, and feeding from, a depleted, dead object.

By this stage of the individual work with Rebecca, my colleague had also been meeting with Mr and Mrs A. fortnightly. He had been told much more detail of the circumstances surrounding Rebecca's birth. He had heard that Mrs A.'s own mother, to whom Mrs A. did not feel close, had become seriously ill halfway through Mrs A.'s pregnancy with Rebecca, and that she died very soon after Rebecca's birth. Mrs A.'s mother had herself been emotionally unavailable for her daughter, and much of her time had been spent as an inner-city missionary for a small, tightly knit evangelical Christian sect. Mrs A.'s relationship with her own mother was therefore highly ambivalent, and she constantly needed to seek her mother's approval—hence all three children had been given biblical names. It soon became clear to my colleague that Mrs A. had fallen into a deep depression after her mother's death. Mrs A. had been unable to recall much detail about the feelings associated with Rebecca's first few years.

In her own way, Rebecca was also able to describe to me, indirectly, the experience of her mother's face as "unreflecting" and "cold". It was a warm and sunny day in June, and Rebecca had begun by commenting that she liked to see my white jacket hanging up in the therapy-room as it "shows that summer is here". I queried why this should feel so significant. Her reply stunned me. She described her routine upon waking—that she would immediately go to her bedroom windows and stand looking out (they would always be wide open, with curtains drawn back, even in winter). She would then instantly know how she would be feeling for the rest of the day in accordance with the weather. "If, when I look out, the sun is shining and the sky is blue, then I know that it's going to be a good day and I'm going to feel alright. But if it's overcast or if the sky is grey, then I immediately know that I'm going to be feeling bad for the rest of the day". She added that then she feels just as bad outside the house as inside.

I felt instinctively that this was an unconscious metaphor for her experience of her mother's face reflecting upon an infant's development. I also began to wonder about the significance of the "panic" or "fear of dying from a heart attack" which would be triggered off if Rebecca were to stay indoors.

Who's that girl?

Throughout the summer towards the end of the first analytic year, Rebecca felt more and more persecuted by me. As indicated earlier, this, at first, took the form of an accusation that I was robbing her of her capacity to do well by taking "huge chunks of her time" for myself. Then I had a month of disparagement during a period of particularly good weather when Rebecca raged at me for keeping her indoors. She clearly felt in danger of being "contaminated" by the "unhealthy lifestyle" she accused me of. She started to arrive five or ten minutes late for some sessions, something she had never done before. In one session she spoke about a boy who had left her school unexpectedly over a year before, and a member of staff had only recently told them that he had had "some kind of break-down". I could see that this applied to many facets of our work together.

Rebecca herself had begun to use the word "breakdown" when describing what had happened to her at the age of 11. She had also blamed me for the "breakdown" in her success as a runner which had occurred somewhat dramatically as soon as she entered psychotherapy. I had felt that the "heart" had gone out of it; maybe it was no longer needed as a reaction formation to her fear of a "collapsed" jelly-like state. She also became more aware of how "mad" she could be, and this frightened her. Rebecca surprised herself with the degree of vitriol she sometimes "spat out" at me—usually when she was accusing me of trying to turn her into someone "normal . . . ordinary and boring". Clearly, the summer holiday break was looming in her mind, and this also represented for her a "breakdown" in my capacity to keep a firm hold on her. It also coincided with the "first birthday" in our analytic relationship.

A couple of weeks before the agreed holiday break, Rebecca began to arrive late and would be carrying a paper bag of "supplies" with her which she promptly set out on a convenient table-top. She would apologize for being late and say that she had been to the nearby row of shops "to get my tea" but that the service had been particularly slow. Her "tea", which was usually quite visible on the table nearby, consisted of either low-fat yoghurt or cottage cheese and a chocolate bar. I said that it was important for her to have me see that she had a rival set of "supplies" for the holiday break and that it reminded me of her fear of "starving to death" during the night.

During the last two sessions before the holiday break, despite all the interpretations I had made about this, Rebecca did not arrive for her sessions at all. Despite the fact that her home was in the opposite direction to the clinic, I saw her running provocatively past the clinic entrance with just the top of her head and her mop of unruly hair showing as she disappeared past the therapy-room window. I was left thinking "Who's that girl? . . . is it Rebecca?" as she disappeared from view. I wondered whether she would return a few minutes later with her "supplies", as she had previously done. But she did not turn up for the sessions at all, and *I* was the one left wondering whether I should see her again after the holiday. To make matters worse, the clinic receptionist, who had got used to seeing Rebecca arrive, would ask me in a very concerned (and admonishing?) tone, "Isn't that your little girl?" (i.e. patient) as she disappeared down the road. It was as if Rebecca was experienced by us all as a parentless 6-year-old having to make her own way in the world. This gives another portrayal of Rebecca's fantasy of the parents taking their eyes off their own daughters to watch her in the race—this time the "Who's that girl?" would perhaps also carry the implied parental criticism of "*Whose* girl is that?" I certainly was momentarily overcome by the feeling of being a negligent mother who was allowing her daughter to go home on her own before she was ready.

Conclusion

I was confronted with a vast range of strong feelings during the long summer break. To begin with, the break, which was to be four weeks long, had now become six weeks. In the last session that Rebecca attended (the first session of the final week before the break) she abruptly announced that, in addition to her family holiday, she had arranged to spend two weeks with her pen-friend in France. This had not been part of our original planning for the break. As she then did not arrive at all for the last two sessions after this, we were unable to discuss it further, and I was presented with a *fait accompli*. I realized that I was being given the same treatment as her parents received when they regularly found that she had set up "house" in a tent at the end of the garden, or that she had taken her desk and chair to shelter under the awning at the side of the shed. Much of Rebecca's behaviour seemed to be a reaction-formation to her fear of feelings of dependency and helplessness. In missing her last two sessions before the holiday I felt that Rebecca was spurning the opportunity for mental "food for thought" in anticipation of the famine ahead. This made me feel very sad, as it indicated the level of her self-neglect.

My initial response to seeing Rebecca run past the clinic entrance and the therapy-room window—and running straight past it again on the way back from the shop where she had bought her "tea"—was extreme irritation. I felt provoked to explain to everyone who knew of my involvement with Rebecca that *I* had been available for her but that *she* had chosen not to come. I felt "set up" by her to look like a neglectful and uninteresting mother—a mother who had been too preoccupied with herself to notice that my "daughter" was close at hand but apparently not feeling close to me.

I knew Rebecca deeply resented and feared the feeling of being "trapped" by her relationship with me. She felt claustrophobic within the therapeutic relationship, describing how she felt "taken over" by me so that I "could control her mind". I have been helped to understand the nature of this projection of Rebecca's intrusive fantasies by Melanie Klein's work (1946). Klein describes how an infant's fantasies of attacking and sadistically entering the mother's body give rise to the fear of being imprisoned and persecuted inside her and are therefore linked with both paranoia and claustrophobia. Klein extended this idea in her paper "On Identification" (1955) to the view that claustrophobia is the consequence of being imprisoned inside the mother as a result of massive projective identification and may result in the fear that the lost part of the self will never be recovered because it is buried in the object. She describes the fear of dying inside the object (Rebecca's terror of a "heart attack") and also the fear relating to the inside of one's own body and the dangers threatening there (Rebecca's catalogue of psychosomatic symptoms). More recently, Donald Meltzer (1992, p. 4) has described the claustrophobic experience as one of the aspects of the twofold phenomenology of projective identification (i.e. projective and identificatory aspects). Claustrophobia has primarily to do with *intrusiveness*, which is motivated by a need to "control" an unreliable object from the inside. The need to "control" via intrusion seems to be a hallmark of all Rebecca's object-relationships.

I was left with the uncertainty as to whether Rebecca would return to her sessions in September, and I was aware of her need for *someone* to experience worry and distress on her behalf and to be able to sustain the appropriate level of concern. Within the analytic relationship it seemed vital that I have the experience of a mother who is *not* too depressed to notice or be able to respond to her daughter's distress.

I was puzzled by the fact that so far, despite the severity and range of her symptoms, Rebecca had been able to conduct herself in such a way that few people have really recognized the perilous state she was in. It is as if an "unempathic other"—an internal object that refuses "projective identification"—gets projected into her environment so that not even her parents or her teachers seem able to recognize the severity of her illness and distress. This gives a context to Rebecca's fear that she has got through each day "on her own", and that she will "always be on her own". An early indication of what was to come for Rebecca was given by Mrs A. in the initial consultation when she recalled that a chance remark by a teacher alerted her to the fact that Rebecca had not spoken to a single person—child or adult—for the first month of infants' school.

In many ways Rebecca developed at first in the way that was required of her within her family. She developed a premature independence and pseudo-maturity, a carapace of conformity and academic success to mask her massive failure to negotiate the vicissitudes of attachment and separation.

Rebecca's behaviour around all breaks—but this long summer break in particular—has successfully brought this issue of "attachment and separation" to the forefront of our relationship together. It looked as if the significant improvement in the quality of her life was going to deter her from wanting to explore the finer details pertaining to "relationship". The fact that she has been able to join her family on a holiday for the first time in five years is testament to this improvement. However, both my colleague and myself are aware of the need for us to have a long-term involvement. The "anorexia of the mind" does seem to affect all five family members, and progress with Mr and Mrs A., in particular, has been painfully slow. When there is such a resistance to "taking in", the therapist (rather like the mother who weans her baby onto solids by chewing the food first) has to be prepared at first to do most of the "mental digestion".

Rebecca's initial communication to me—of her fear of not being able to breathe and of getting "trapped" inside—gave me an uncannily accurate description of the quality of object-relationship that gives rise to claustrophobia and its link with her eating disorder. I also learned from her the significance for the internal world of the ordinary reciprocal to-and-fro process of projection and introjection. When it works well, it enables us to get to know, and to feel known by, others. When it works well, we do not usually notice the *process* at all but we are likely to feel the benefit of having relationships, both internal and external, that are based on respect for mutual interdependency with the freedom to act autonomously. This is the closeness yet separateness associated with healthy object-relationships. Clearly, for Rebecca things did not go well. The emotional unavailability of her mother coupled with her mother's deep depression during Rebecca's infancy seems to have intruded into all aspects of their intimate psyche-soma relationship. The intrusion affected the "to-and-fro" process of emotional exchange that gives shape and structure to the early (breast) feeding relationship and to the feeding of the mind. If the reciprocal "to and fro" process breaks down, then the omnipotent phantasy of *entering* (invading) an internal object avoids all anxiety surrounding attachment, separation, and freedom of the object. The freedom associated with healthy internal objects is replaced by the tyranny of control. However, this engenders a real confusion of identity, which leads to paranoia. For Rebecca this showed itself in a very real fear that I was trying to "get inside" her mind. Rebecca's only way of relating to another was through invasion and intrusion, leading to feelings of claustrophobia from which she tried to starve herself separate. Claustrophobia can therefore be seen to be a persecuted/persecutory state of mind associated with long-term failure of benign projective identification within object-relationships.

CHAPTER TWO

Eating disorders in adolescence: the function of receiving

Luisa Carbone Tirelli

T his chapter is concerned with disorders in eating habits, with particular reference to anorexia. Eating disorders are increasingly being diagnosed and are more frequent in girls than boys. According to epidemiological information, anorexia is most common in those countries with a high standard of living. Anorexia is typical of adolescence and is often linked to psycho-physical developments inherent in puberty. M. and M. E. Laufer (1984) have made a significant contribution in this area with their work on adolescence and their more general interpretation of eating disorders as the adolescent's failure to achieve integration of a sexual body.

I am interested to explore, particularly with reference to persistent and marked anorexic behaviour in adolescent girls, how the fear of bodily changes and the difficulties in achieving a mature female identity depend on the failure to develop what I call a *function of receiving*. By *function of receiving* I mean a psycho-physical function that was underdeveloped or badly structured during the initial relationship between the baby girl and the maternal feeding object.

The faulty development of this *function of receiving* may be the consequence of intense and persisting feelings of pain that have roots in the infant's first year of life. This situation is exacerbated by a lack of understanding and containment by the primary object and especially by projections, deriving from the mother's mind, steeped in depression and anxiety.

So the infant, in her first year of life, is prevented from integrating the feelings that come from her own body and from the body and mind of her mother. She is also unable to form a couple in her mind—first with the maternal object and later with the paternal one. Consequently, the infant is unable to conceive of the parental couple as a sexual couple, and this in turn affects the infant's later integration of the oedipal structure.

In support of this theory I wish to refer to Melanie Klein's thinking, which I shall briefly summarize. In an article written in 1952, "On Observing the Behaviour of Young Infants", Klein examines a topic she has broached before—that is, the relationship between weaning and achieving the depressive position. As this is one of Klein's last works, she is less concerned with having to defend her theories and she describes in more depth the neonate and its relationship with the breast. According to her, the breast fully assumes the meaning of a containing maternal object and one from which warmth, smell, and tenderness come, which are very important to the infant. The breast is progressively less part-object, and it comes more to represent the mother. Klein's description of a neonate endeavouring to reach the object through the activation of libidinal, sadistic, and epistemophilic drives constituted a fundamental break from Freud's theory of primary narcissism.

Klein's article and her accompanying notes are concerned throughout not only with the importance of the relationship with a fantasized mother but also with the relationship with the real mother, and with a relationship that will mark (with a move to the depressive position) the emergence of an early sense of identity. It is this sense of identity that subsequently determines affective and sexual relationships.

In light of Klein's more complex and articulated relationship with the mother, it is extremely interesting to re-read "Early Stages of the Oedipus Conflict" (1928) where she underlines that it is the frustrations linked with feeding, and in particular with weaning, that drives the neonate towards the depressive position and to-wards overcoming it for the first time. If persecutory anxieties are not too intense, the transition from the oral and anal stages into the genital stage will take place, together with a shift of love-object for the girl as she turns to the father. However, *the aim will remain the same, namely that of receiving (receptivity)*. The girl therefore disposes herself to receive from her father. If this is achieved, it is possible for the girl to face that early state of the femininity phase which allows her to discover that the vagina as well as the mouth is a receiving organ. Thus an equivalence of function is established between the mouth and the vagina. It is this equivalence with an organ so significant in the relationship with the breast-object (rep-resentative of the mother and maternal functions) that predisposes the girl to have in phantasy a receptive relationship with the father; it allows her access to the genital stage and characterizes female sexuality.

My hypothesis is that the non-development of the *function of receiving* in the relationship with the primary object determines a specific behaviour. In the latency period this behaviour can be described as diligent and peaceful adhesion to rules and instruc-tions, together with a denial of feelings and rivalry and confronta-tion. In puberty, this behaviour undergoes a transformation whereby the disorder is revealed: the rules and rhythms related to feeding are upset, consequently causing much alarm and surprise in the environment surrounding the adolescent.

This hypothesis stems from my clinical work—from consulta-tions and analytic work that have taken place with anorexic girls. The main characteristics that emerge from the therapist's experi-ence of initial sessions, and which for a long time characterize the relationship in those cases where it is possible to begin therapy, are specifically the difficulty in reaching the patient (Williams, 1997). There is also a difficulty in feeling that one's words are received, and one perceives an avoidance in the patient of establishing any sort of emotional exchange. The mouth, excessively invested in and excessively controlled, may allow verbalization, but less controlla-ble functions, such as hearing, appear to be hindered. In the pa-tient's perception of her physical self, the existence of other organs with a receptive function, such as the belly or the vagina, is often ignored. However, the image of a body that is evoked is one of a pipe suitable for the quick passage of food, without containment or digestion.

The extent of the failure in developing a receptive function and its duration is significant in terms of the degree of psychopathology. The fact that these patients are particularly good at hindering receiving in their relationships also offers an analogy to their difficulty in receiving food. It is attention to this analogy that can often engage therapeutically, although the journey is full of obstacles and setbacks. Such attention also makes it possible to identify the existence of a transference with singular characteristics where, apparently, any sort of relationship is rejected.

I shall support with case material the hypothesis that the therapeutic setting, with its rules and rhythms, functions initially as a container in which the existence of primitive anxieties linked to body-identity (Bleger, 1961) eventually are revealed. It is the setting that brings out the existence of a transference to the object. This transference is characterized by a forcefully denied and opposed search for closeness to and possession of the object, accompanied by greed. This mode of behaving is very similar to the patients' obsessive concentration on orality and food, without the consequential taking in and digesting of the food.

This chapter looks closely at some case material from an analysis with a 16-year-old girl, which lasted three years. In order to show how the setting and the relationship within the setting brought to the fore, over time, deep conflicting themes and fantasies useful to the understanding of anorexic behaviour, it seems important to describe, albeit incompletely, the way the entire therapeutic process developed with this patient.

Aurora

When I met her for the first time, Aurora was 16 years old, weighed 37 kilograms, and had not menstruated for several months. She had started losing weight about a year before, but in the last months had lost 10 kilograms. She had been persuaded to come by her mother, who was herself undergoing psychotherapeutic treatment. During the consultation with her parents, Aurora's mother appeared depressed and frightened by her daughter's behaviour. Her obsessive concern, however, did not seem to correspond with any emotional empathy nor any attempt to understand her daughter's feelings.

Although Aurora's father appeared to be a marginal figure with little knowledge of daily events, he showed a greater interest in understanding his daughter. Aurora had a sister who was one year older than she. She also had a 10-year-old brother towards whom she had shown feelings of jealousy at the time of his birth. The parents also described a long series of illnesses and surgical operations: at the age of 7 years, Aurora was taken to hospital for an emergency operation due to haemorrhaging caused by a vaginal angioma; at the age of 9 she had her appendix removed; at the age of 11 she broke her arm. They reported that all this had been borne with great patience and endurance by Aurora, who throughout had been more concerned about other people's reactions than about her own well-being.

What emerged was a picture of a good and obedient girl who did well at school. However, changes in Aurora's eating habits over several months, a tendency to isolate herself, and a silent opposition to any intervention on their part had upset her parents' image of her. She felt foreign to them. Following this session, I agreed to see Aurora and I also recommended that her parents meet a colleague of mine.

First year of therapy

Aurora was persuaded to come to therapy because she was frightened. She said that she had been told she would die if she continued not to eat, and she had recently felt unwell on a number of occasions. She gave me a detailed account of her activities. As she listed them all, she seemed relieved: she walked a lot; she went swimming nearly every day; she was good at school, but recently her mind had gone blank at times. This blankness worried her. She was also worried about losing her strength, as she had experienced this on two recent occasions when she had felt ill. She was especially concerned that she would get fat.

I proposed to offer Aurora a space where she could talk about her worries and where we would try to understand together what was happening. Furthermore, I would do nothing to pressurize her to put on weight, but she would have to make an effort not to lose more weight. She would also have to go regularly for a medical check-up, and I would keep in touch with her doctor. Aurora thought it over, and a week later contacted me to say she was uncertain but wanted to give it a try. She came for psychotherapy three times a week for three years.

Apart from her fear of physical death, what probably induced Aurora to come to therapy was the feeling that I would leave her ample room for autonomy, and that I would protect her from damaging herself physically, or protect her from dying, without imposing any changes in her habits. Aurora also felt that seeing me appeased her mother, which in turn meant that mother would leave her alone. I proposed three meetings a week, which was considered by Aurora to be excessive and elicited many protests on her part. She would have liked to come whenever she felt she needed to, as opposed to making a regular weekly commitment. I insisted, however, on maintaining the setting, and in the first months of her treatment this in fact provided an element of reassurance and regularity, perhaps even at the beginning having a soothing effect.

It became clear to me from our first sessions that, apart from being obviously irritated by words and silence, what Aurora could not tolerate was being looked at. The suggestion that she use the couch seemed to be a relief in this respect and enabled her to talk about herself. She usually did not look at me when she entered the therapy-room and it was not clear whom her words were meant for. Only occasionally did I have the feeling that my presence had been registered—and then that I was mostly perceived in an unpleasant and immediate way to be a male or female presence with whom she was determined to avoid any contact whatsoever.

Reacting to a prolonged silence in one of our first sessions, Aurora said that the evening before she was sitting in front of the television with both her parents and "they were neither talking nor fighting". Suddenly, she got up and had had several discharges of diarrhoea. She commented that: "It was strange because for her having a motion in the morning was a concession." With these

words she indicated that her need to control, which she had trans-
ferred onto her bodily functions, was mainly caused by her perception of other people's powerful effect on her. The silence in the
session, however, seemed to have put her in contact with me, and
to have given her the painful perception that, as there were two of
us in the room, we formed a couple and the couple relationship
was a dangerous one.

A few sessions later, seeing me glance at her as she entered, she
was particularly silent. Then, with difficulty, she said she was
thinking about something that had happened just before coming to
the session. She had run into a man. She would rather not have
been seen by that man as the dress she was wearing showed up her
scoliosis (slightly curved spine), and now she did not know
whether to be angry or not.

This glance that she could not accept brought to the fore her
own perception of her body as deformed and damaged inside, but
above all it created in me the feeling that my eyes had been
transformed into an intrusive object that could contaminate whatever it encountered, just as bad food would do. As a confirmation
of this, during that period Aurora would arrive so wrapped up in
layers of clothes that I was prevented from catching any glimpse of
her body.

When she felt protected from the potential contact of such
glances, she was less reluctant to verbalize thoughts and events.
Thus I came to know her interpretations of facts and events. Aurora
had dated the beginning of her refusal to eat: in her case, just as in
most of the accounts narrated by girls talking of their anorexia,
there was a significant event linked to a relationship with a boy. In
Aurora's case, her boyfriend Fabio had left her. It became progres-
sively clearer with time that this failure of her relationship with a
boy had caused her conflicting feelings. She had felt relieved but
also felt formally disqualified from "the game" compared to her
girlfriends who still had their boyfriends. Moreover, she was very
hurt by the rejection. She connected not eating and losing weight
with this event, at times justifying it as a quest for perfection and
beauty which would make up for the rejection, and at other times
experiencing it as a punishment to her body that had let her down
and therefore needed to be "put right" before she could once more
offer the sight of it to other people.

Integrating the feelings I picked up in the transference and the accounts given by Aurora, I began to intuit something that was as yet far from Aurora's own awareness. The presence of a boy in her life had put her in touch with something that felt impossible for her—that is, to receive emotionally and physically. This had produced a feeling that something was missing in her. This, in turn, caused her great anxiety because she felt there was no solution to the missing aspect. My thoughts were confirmed by several subsequent events and some dreams.

In our fifth month of therapy, the father of another anorexic girl died. Aurora was particularly interested in this girl, with whom she constantly compared herself. Aurora told me that after the father's death, her friend started menstruating again. In the same session she also told me about a few dreams that seemed very strange to her.

In one dream, *while she was with a girlfriend her scooter was stolen. This scooter, she explained, was more like a friend than an object. She would park it, and it would disappear; she would find it again, and it would disappear once more.* In another dream, *there was an old woman with a distressing face. This was the same old woman whom she had thought about with fear when she was a little girl. The woman used to steal everything from her: money, wallet, keys. She would find all her things on this old woman. She would manage to snatch back some of the things that belonged to her that she had lost and that the old woman was holding in her hands. Aurora felt anger. The old woman made her think of a witch, of death.*

In the following session, in a sequence that I linked with the dreams and events she told me about, Aurora briefly talked about the surgery she had undergone at the age of 7 on the angioma in her vagina. A catheter had been inserted, and Aurora remembered the fear she experienced when she had the urge to urinate without being able to do so. She had felt like screaming but had not done so. She said she "felt a hero". Then she corrected herself, saying she felt "a heroine, a fairy—I was the one who was reassuring everyone else!" She would draw in the hospital, and she drew portraits of the members of her family. They had praised her for her behaviour.

This traumatic event was spoken about for the first time, and it was recalled with an emotional tone, very similar to that of the dream. I tried, without success, to pick up on this and highlight it.

Aurora seemed to be unconsciously perceiving that she had been the object of some damage. Something had been taken away from her, something precious had been stolen from her. This "something" had all the characteristics of a male attribute, and once it had been taken away she had been left with a bleeding vagina that had made her vulnerable and had placed her at the mercy of anyone. Anger and despair seemed to derive from the realization that the damage was irreparable.

Further elements emerged as the summer break drew nearer, the first long break in the therapy. Aurora was far from being able consciously to register it, and although she feigned indifference, she told me at the beginning of July that when she left her session she had "looked for somebody and had cried in the street". She was angry with everyone, but above all with her sister, who did not understand her and was so very different from her. That same night she dreamt that *she was going out of the house to buy some flowers for her mother. It was night-time; it was dark. She came to a shop where there was a man. Instead of flowers, he wanted to sell her a strange object. He stuck a banana with half a boiled egg on it into her mouth. He was asking a hundred-thousand lire [£30] for that object and she did not want it.* In the days following this dream, Aurora had more dreams and fantasies about death.

In her dreams, all of her animals died. In particular, a tortoise that had been given to her when she was little died after it had broken its leg. At this time Aurora intensified her control over eating and increased her physical activities. She also spent hours lying in the sun as if to take in warmth and comfort. Twice she felt ill and was scared at the idea she had damaged herself, at the idea of dying. She would relate everything as if it were ineluctable, making me feel impotent and anxious. I felt that the meaning behind this violent resumption of control over her body was that of resisting the emotional influence that first my absence over the break and then my presence could exercise over her. But I was not to, nor could I, speak to her about this. The interruption of the continuity of the setting evoked unconscious fantasies that I assumed were linked to feelings of absence and greed. In fact, while Aurora occupied the couch in an apparently inert manner, thefts and plundering and death dominated the phantasied scene of the relationship.

It is important to understand the impossibility at that stage for me to make any transference interpretations. Sensations and emotions appeared indigestible in their concreteness, and it required time for them to be received and understood by me before being returned to Aurora as part of our relationship. For the first time, Aurora's father intervened firmly and imposed some limits on her. This seemed to curb her anorexic behaviour a little.

Second year of therapy

Aurora's return in September was characterized by a strange calmness. She used the space in the session to talk about sensations connected with heat and cold. The swimming-pool where she went daily was the centre of her thoughts. The couch on which she curled up and the blanket she used to cover herself were clearly experienced as similar to water. During this period my perception in the sessions changed. Aurora brought in a dimension in which the previous spatiotemporal parameters had lost significance. I found it difficult to be firmly aware of the end of the session and to remember to characterize the contents.

The memory of her nanny, Marta, who had died two years before, emerged. Aurora had previously mentioned her briefly conveying the feeling of anxiety she had experienced due to her sudden death. Now she was recalling other images of Marta. Marta, who had been with her since she was born, who had prepared her nice things to eat, who had a big belly on which she would lean and which gave her warmth and comfort. This warmth and comfort was very similar to the feelings of merging both in space and in time that belonged to the transference. These feelings disappeared when Aurora mentioned fantasies of Marta's death. Her nanny was too fat; the fat had killed her. She also heard people say, after her nanny had died, that Marta had had a secret relationship with a man and that she was with him when she fell ill. Orality, sexuality, and death came together and combined in the same way as they had in her dreams and fantasies linked to the surgical operation for the angioma.

The perception of me as a mother, a nanny, a womb, or a swimming-pool, alternated with the perception of my words, which proved to have an irritating impact on her when they were experienced as too intrusive. The perception of intrusiveness seemed due to the fact that I could cause emotions similar to those stirred up by the recent separation of the therapeutic break. And then I was connected with her real mother, which she perceived as obsessive and distressing in her requests and complaints.

She thus showed in the transference that she needed to keep things quite separate and reproduced this in her eating habits by increasing control over what was happening inside her with a more severe selection of food. She stopped eating solid food and began to drink milk and yoghurt—a kind of food that, she said, "passed through quickly". She compared her body to a pipe. However, the realization of the ever-increasing quantity of liquid food that she tended to take in, to the point of feeling ill at times, put her in contact with a feeling of greed, which disturbed her greatly.

For three months there seemed to me to be no third possibility: either she felt, when lying down on the couch, comfortable as if she were in Marta's belly, or she perceived every shifting from this point as something intrusive, violent, or distressing. At the beginning of winter, she stopped isolating herself and once more accepted two or three invitations from friends. She began also to talk about her desire to embrace her parents, but a new event seemed to precipitate everything into chaos.

Her maternal grandfather died, and although Aurora was not particularly close to him, she felt her mother's distress. She said she did not know how to help her. On that occasion the devastating effects of contact with her mother's depression were clearly evident. In her dreams, the swimming-pool changed into a horrible place into which she was obliged to jump, even though she was aware that it was full of mud, slime, and toads.

Although the Christmas break was short, it seemed to take her by surprise, because of her state of mind. The setting now became an unwelcoming place. Concentrating her anxieties in the analysis, she consciously directed, for the first time, her hostility towards me. She actively denied the need for therapy; she communicated that she did not want to come any more, that she was only coming because she had made a commitment and felt guilty if she did not keep to it. In the same session she related two dreams that she described as "terrible": *She was on the bed with her first boyfriend. She wanted to embrace him and felt a beautiful feeling, but Fabio was telling her that he felt like making love. While he was saying this his face changed and became very evil. She got up and ran away frightened.* She said she would have died had she remained.

In the second dream she described *a strange sea with sharks that chased her on the beach. It was getting dark. A man appeared. He put on his scuba gear and went into the sea. She was worried about that man.*

Anxieties were increasingly being concentrated on the patient–therapist relationship. It allowed me to understand how for Aurora it was through the experience of the need for another that Aurora entered a space where she could feel sensation and emotion. It was also becoming clearer how her anxiety was provoked by her fear of exploring the characteristics of this space, which was filled with ghosts that placed her own fate and that of the object at risk.

The feeling of certainty was once more shifted onto food. In that period she verbalized her satisfaction for her new diet several times. She said that taking in liquid food allowed her to evacuate easily and increased her control over what could be assimilated. She said that by not letting food stay for long in her stomach and intestines, she was sure not to get fat.

The fact that all the measures she adopted in relation to food were no longer sufficient to avoid anxiety, and that the anxiety was more and more clearly linked with the changes in the relationship between us, was confirmed when she came back after the Christmas holidays. She returned to lay ruin and death before me. With her hair completely shaved off, she verbalized her wish to stop eating. She said that she did not even want milk any more. She talked of purges, laxatives, and vomiting, of continuous diarrhoea. I understood that she was indulging in solitary binges, about which she would not talk to me, in order to fill the feeling of emptiness. Then after these binges, she would resort to drastic remedies. It was the only period in which Aurora alternated bouts of bulimic behaviour with anorexic behaviour. She was thin and saw herself as being *bloated*. She told me directly that she once saw herself in a mirror and took fright at her emaciated appearance. She used the expression "mental squint" to define her astonishment.

During this period I felt terribly guilty about having let her do this to herself, and I was seriously concerned for her health. She was also facing her last year at high school. She had her final examinations to prepare for, and this opened the way to upset all schedules and rhythms. She had thus been able to reduce to a minimum the moments in which she encountered the other members of her family and also their control. It was the most difficult period of the therapy. It was, however, possible to associate it with separation and her related need to punish and frighten me.

She gave scant information on what took place outside therapy, but a clear differentiation was beginning to develop between her being somewhat regressed in the session and more together in her external life. At the beginning of spring, she began to feel and talk about an intense interest in a boy, Pino. The desire to be with Pino induced her to keep company with a group of peers. From this point on there were no longer periods of total isolation. The group with Pino became, apart from family and therapy, the third place whereby she could explore her emotional world.

Other feelings appeared among which the feeling of shame dominated. She talked to me about it by telling me a dream: *Her parents, both together, were making fun of her and were preventing her from talking to Pino and telling him that she cared for him. The scene changed. She was on a school outing, in a camp site. She needed to do a wee and she went into a café. One bathroom was locked, the other was all wet, flooded. She fell and wet her shirt. She had to give up having a wee. Then she ran to the bus, and the deputy headmistress told her she had arrived too late and she could no longer leave.*

After relating the dream, she was silent and, in reply to a question I put to her, said she thought that other people did not think her capable of loving. At this point she began to cry and once more remembered the surgical operation for the angioma in her vagina. She recalled it in detail, which aroused much pain in me. The physical pain, the fear at the sight of blood, the anger at feeling deceived, the shame of being exposed for all to see, all emerged in connection with the events concerning the angioma.

It seemed that for the first time she was entrusting her intense feelings connected with a fragile and defenceless part of her, and which until now I had perceived only in its physical aspect. Equally intense was her distrust and fear of the maternal prohibition to attain genitality, represented in the dream by the deputy headmistress-therapist who vetoed her departure.

She associated the fear of the surgical operation with the fear felt at the onset of her menstruation. She communicated the terror she felt at the idea of a gynaecological visit and remembered with disgust the physical contact with Fabio. Mouth and vagina began to be differentiated in the perception of the different functions that they carried out.

The following nights a series of dreams enabled her to be in contact with a feeling that she had violently opposed in reality: her anger. *Once more the predominant scene was her parents fighting while Aurora was crying in the dark. To this scene was added the image of a fierce Alsatian locked up in a cage. She had to pass by unnoticed, hoping that the wire net of the cage would hold, but invariably the wire net would give way and she would be torn to pieces.*

The rage that was devouring her appeared connected with the presence of a couple interacting while she was small, alone, and in the dark. In the transference, anxiety proved prevalently linked with a feeling of emptiness expressed through the phrase "I am not able to love" and through the conflict caused by the wish to be one of a couple with the mother-therapist.

Third year of therapy

At the beginning of the third year, Aurora had an accident on her scooter which damaged her nose, and she lost her sense of smell for a long period. This fact caused her intense fears, which she expressed with these words: "Everything happens inside. I wish I had broken my leg!"

For the first time she seemed to perceive my attention as helpful, and she asked me for help to sort out the confusion and anxiety that the feeling of being damaged caused in her. She began on this occasion to fantasize about her body and about what the accident had done to her inside.

One evening, she arrived at her session saying she had just come from the swimming-pool. She had tired herself out too much, she had overdone it, and on her way to therapy she had felt like running and shouting "I'm hungry!" I received her request, saying that she was turning to me to ask for food. She was silent for a while. Then she told me she was thinking of her cat. Her cat sucked and chewed wool because it had not been without its mother for very long. She associated this thought with something she had never mentioned before: she said, "I was not breast-fed much. My mother had a lot of milk, but I did not suck a lot and my mother gave her milk to my cousin!" After a pause she added, in an apparently incongruous manner, "It annoys me when I see my cat purring, sucking, and lying on its back with its paws in the air. Perhaps it annoys me because I can't do it."

I was afraid she might have slammed the door in my face once again. Instead, something else happened. The theme of receiving manifested itself in a dream that same night and was related with a great deal of emotion: *She was letting Umberto [the boy she was interested in at that time] into her house. She was putting a duck into his hands—a white duck with a yellow beak, which she had been given as a present.*

Aurora was beginning to be able to imagine possessing and exchanging. I was struck by the words *"letting in"*, *"she had been given"*, *"putting into his hands"*. The dream had a complex scene at the centre of which was a soft, fragile object—the duck—born from a womb/swimming-pool/therapy. The conception of an inside made the union fertile.

There followed a long period of working through those themes during which she progressively drew nearer to me, bringing, for example, dreams in which her mother was able to watch and be present while a boy was kissing her. Talking at great length about Hermann Hesse's book *Narcissus and Goldmund*, she said that for the first time she seemed to be caring for someone who at the same time cared for her too. This feeling increased in the following months, together with the perception of slowly acquiring, in her eyes, feminine features.

Significantly, it was during this period that Aurora suggested the end of her therapy. Although she was aware that she was not yet fully equipped on her own, she heralded her wish to move away and go her own way by telling me about a part of a Bergman film which had made her think: "The mother said to her daughter: 'Your pain is my joy'. The daughter's pain is the mother's joy, but at the same time it is pain because they are one." She said she had thought about this, about the fact that in the beginning you are one. She was silent a while, and then she said: "Some people are able to separate immediately and some are scared. . . . Some are still scared like me, but I must go my own way."

By this point in the therapy her interests had widened and she no longer spoke about food, which she had now begun to take regularly. Just before summer, her menstruations had returned. Aurora took advantage of our third summer interval, which she prolonged, to have sexual intercourse for the first time with Umberto. She returned in September with long hair, looking very beautiful, and in the last three months that brought her therapy to an end she barely mentioned her sexual relationship. Instead, she dwelled on the atmosphere of her days. She was radiant, just like the atmosphere she was describing. This image has remained with me, and for this reason, having to select a name for her in order to write about this work, I chose "Aurora".

In a sad and concerned way, Aurora again requested we end therapy. I accepted her decision, but I asked her to reflect, in the time that remained, on the road that we had travelled and on her present state of mind.

A few sessions before her last one, Aurora told me of a dream that seemed significant: *I am leaving with my father in a car, but a policeman stops us. Fuck off! my father says to him. The policeman arrests us and says: I am obliged by the law! He takes us to a house full of children; they too were in prison. Two jailers arrive, a man and a woman. They take us to a room where there is a sort of banquet. They bring in a man and a woman, roasted. We faint from the fear that we might have the same fate. What scared us was seeing those two. . . . They did not cook the children, though. In the dream I thought: "That's why I don't want to grow up!"* She added that the policeman reminded her of her sister and that "She has such a bad relationship with my father! I, instead, want a relationship with him!"

Aurora wanted to be able to form a couple, but somehow she sensed that there was an obstacle: what could stop her was her difficulty of fully attaining genitality by integrating the oedipal structure. The oedipal dimension still appeared very concrete and difficult to symbolize and therefore remained *not digestible*. Faced with the possibility of having a cannibalistic meal, she stops and *"loses consciousness"*. Interpreting her dream, I shared her concern and her hope. The hope derived from the course she had undergone in therapy and, for Aurora, was constituted by the perception of the "We go" mental category (G. Klein, 1976). "We" was a pronoun she repeatedly used when relating her dream. Hope linked with "We go" increases space and the possibility of there being life; it allows children to exist, even if still prisoners and limited in their growth. It was the dawning of this prospect of life that made Aurora stop her attacks on her physical self, on her body.

Discussion

At the beginning of psychoanalysis, Aurora presented the three fundamental characteristics, indicated in related literature, that identify the anorexic syndrome in adolescence: *voluntary limitation of food; significant loss of weight; amenorrhoea*. Kestemberg, Kestemberg, and Decobert (1972) add to this features indicative of the psychic structure of these patients: *copious fantasies*, even if at times not shared with others; *difficulty in making contact*, a difficulty linked with the rejection of dependency, which persists a long time in psychotherapeutic treatment; *absence of any links with personal history*—memories that go back to infancy and latency are rare.

Aurora was able to present her fantasies from the initial phase of treatment and during the whole course of her therapy. Her dreams maintained for a long time those characteristics that are prevalently peculiar to pre-latency children's dreams (Carbone Tirelli, 1994)—that is, they provided a direct access to the unconscious. This work was absent or rudimentary. The dream work, which derives from a maturity of the intrapsychic structure and which, through the secondary elaboration, moves from the concrete representation to a process of symbolization, differentiates the primary object from the symbols created by the ego (Klein, 1930; Segal, 1957).

They are therefore dreams that can easily be interpreted. Although they are stimulated by the relationship with the therapist, it is difficult to connect them to this relationship, as these dreams seemed to be produced more to hinder access to the transference situation rather than to offer access to it. Paradoxically, representation was not used so much in order to maintain and give meaning to sensations that derive from the body and from the object, but rather with a function that opposes introjection. In fact, the contents of Aurora's first dreams—for example, the ones about the scooter being stolen and the old woman stealing from her—point to a poverty of libidinal investment. Her narcissistic restoration of the body self is pathologically regressive.

In the dreams with the *scooter* and the *banana*, Aurora's preoccupation seemed in fact to be connected with the loss of a phallic part of the self. The arrival of adolescence had already exposed her to this risk; it gave her an urge to enter a dyadic relationship with Fabio, through the statement of her female identity. The risk was further reactivated in the transference in her encounter with me. The arrival of puberty and the developmental needs to form a dyadic relationship required Aurora to relinquish a bisexual image of herself (McDougall, 1973). Aurora compared the loss of this completeness, with the theft in the dream by the old woman. The opening created by recognizing her need of the other person exposed her in the transference to castration anxiety and annihilation anxiety. These anxieties were represented in the *banana–boiled-egg* dream.

There was an important evolution in the therapeutic process, of the meaning aspect of the three objects that appeared in the dreams: scooter, banana–boiled-egg, duck with the yellow beak. The form in which these objects are represented is also significant as they postulate a possible fantasized reference to an early oedipal scene in which we do not see the concrete breast which contains the child, nor the concrete penis which represents the father. Instead, the male and female *characteristics* are juxtaposed and produce a combined object with the parts precariously stuck together. This precariousness immediately triggers off fantasies related to theft and something being taken away, just as when the father of the anorexic girl with whom she compared herself died.

After having examined the development of the concept of projective identification introduced by Melanie Klein (1946) and further developed by W. R. Bion (1959), R. H. Etchegoyen (1986) writes that:

> The best device in the face of separation anxiety seems to be projective identification, because if one can get into the object there is no experience of separation anxiety. However, in the first stages of development, when tridimensional space has not

yet been configured, the only device in the face of separation anxiety consists in making *contact* through adhesive identification. [§43.1][1]

Aurora represented in fantasy a juxtaposed configuration of male and female characteristics on which she fell back in a resigned manner at the beginning of the second year of therapy. This configuration was caused by the failure to report to projective identification as a tool towards knowledge and emotional exchange with the object and was aimed at hindering access to insight. In fact Aurora had retreated when faced with the desire to bring flowers to the mother-therapist.

The *difficulty in associating*, which the Kestembergs indicate as the index of the quality of the anorexic structure (Kestemberg et al., 1972), derives from the failure to achieve insight. Contact via adhesive identification is reassuring but not gratifying, because it undermines the vitality of the object as well as the feeling of having an identity. This often characterizes the behaviour of anorexic girls who frequently progress only from a diligently superficial learning modality to that of relating by mirroring, which necessarily implies an effort in order not to lose contact with the object. Aurora manifested such a need not only in the transference but also in her constant search for girls similar to herself with whom she could establish equivalencies.

Aurora was able to communicate the reasons why all this happened in the transference and through the fantasies produced in therapy. While she was able to visualize a container, she was unable to explore this space more fully because of the anxiety it created in her. The swimming-pool full of toads and terrifying images can be associated with a maternal mind that does not receive and contain and is not capable of working-through, inasmuch as it is overwhelmed by its own anxiety-provoking representations. Meltzer (1992) puts it in another way by using descriptions

---

[1] It is not possible in the space of this chapter to give due weight to the brilliant work of the authors mentioned. However, for this discussion on mental anorexia in adolescence, I use as principal theoretical references the evolution of the concept of projective identification, together with Esther Bick's (1968) concept of the *function of the skin* and Bion's (1970) concept of *container-contained*.

of a *claustrum* rather than a *container*. To enter in this space spells danger and death, as Aurora showed on the occasion of her mother's depression following the death of her grandfather.

The same characteristics of the container are attributed in an equivalent manner to one's own personal inner space, with the risk of death for the object if it ventures into this space. Aurora manifested this fear in the dream of the father-scuba diver. The alternative to conceiving an internal space capable of receiving and containing, represented both psychologically and physically by the vagina, is that of a pipe-body.

There was, however, a constant doubt that crossed Aurora's mind and at times made her condition painfully lucid, like that of many anorexic girls. Aurora visualized the existence of a space, and she knew how relationships and meetings occurred, including sexual ones. Such a notion derived from having observed, but also from having unsuccessfully tried to enter into, this dimension. Perceiving this triggered off her greed and anger. But it was probably this notion that made her structure different from a clearly psychotic patient.

The traumatic event of the separation from Fabio—and, to an even greater extent, the recollection of the operation for the angioma in her vagina—were resorted to and used as explanations for her terror of relationships and constituted an attempt to make sense of the difference she perceived. The trauma became the organizer of the experience of not being able to receive. However, it also leads one to suppose that the early feelings of deadly intrusions (into the space that love, desire, and availability towards the object had created at a very early stage) must have had traumatic characteristics for Aurora as an infant. We do not have any history regarding Aurora's earliest relationship with her mother, but the elements related to death in her fantasies, together with the characteristics of the objects that filled her dreams, lead one to think of a maternal mind occupied by an intense depression, as André Green clearly described in his work on "La mère morte" (1983).

Aurora spoke of her own pain when she proposed separation and the end of therapy. She experienced the pain of separation and was consequently able to recognize and indicate the sacrifice involved in being united to the object: Aurora says, *"The mother said to her daughter: 'Your pain is my joy'. The daughter's pain is the mother's joy, but at the same time it is pain because they are one."*

To conclude, and to underline that the origin of the disorder lies in an early stage of development, I would like to point out that in psychotherapy with anorexic patients, evolution and change occur via the surfacing of emotions that are recognizable and recognized. These emotions are often heralded by the registering of sensations and by the act of communicating them, as Aurora did by saying: "I'm hungry!" These sensations are an indication of having overcome the massive resistance to transference and the parallel perception of a body and a mind capable of receiving and therefore, potentially, able to contain and generate.

CHAPTER THREE

Paula's secret:
an adolescent with bulimia

Kent Ravenscroft

Since 1980 there has been a virtual epidemic of bulimia and other eating disorders among teenage females. Psychoanalysts have focused on the individual intrapsychic aspects of anorexia and bulimia, with emphasis on the dyadic transference. At the same time, object-relations theory offers a lens for examining the contribution of the marital-parental couple and the family to anorexia and bulimia. Using a combined individual, couples, and family object-relations approach, this chapter discusses the developmental background and onset of bulimia in a teenage girl and illustrates a typical interplay of intrapsychic and interpersonal forces operating in eating disorders.

Why does bulimic behaviour become a primary symptom for only certain individuals and their families and not others? Why does the syndrome usually develop in mid- to late adolescence? What is the core intrapsychic and interpersonal pathology? Are there structural precursors of this impulse disorder? And what are its developmental roots?

Paula:
an adolescent bulimic

When Paula's mother heard her vomiting at age 17 and realized what was going on, she was frightened and feared that her husband would accost Paula. His reaction was one of disgust and anger at Paula for not controlling herself. I saw mother and daughter together, then apart during the first session, and I indicated that I would continue seeing her but would want to see them all together, as well as the parents separately, in order to experience all levels of interaction in the family.

Paula is a tall, large-boned young woman of normal weight with an attractive figure. She was scared and anxious when I saw her, fearing her father's wrath and worrying about her mother's over-concern. She talked about fights between her mother and father, conflicts between her and her parents, and her frenetic, tension-filled life at school. Her secret bingeing and vomiting had been going on for over two years, ranging from once to several times a day. She thought it began when she got involved with a boy and then lost him. Only later did we reconstruct that she also lost her very close, love–hate relationship with her 15-year-old brother who left for boarding-school at that time.

Like her mother, father, and most of her friends, she was preoccupied with being thin, but she had strong cravings to fill herself up to relieve feelings of emptiness and anxiety. She thought that a quarter of the girls in her class induced vomiting for weight control: when her own bingeing and vomiting got out of control, she became embarrassed and secretive about it. I found myself filled with feelings of being flooded by her, wanting to control and criticize her, yet wanting to hold and calm her down, too. For her part, she gave early indirect indications of fearing that I, too, would be critical like her father or worried and overprotective like her mother.

As I sat in the initial parent sessions, I was struck by how large her parents were. Her mother was neatly coifed, fadingly attractive, and horsy; her father, imposing, rumpled, and squat. The room was filled with tension. Mother, tears streaming down her face, felt guilty about failing her daughter. She said, "My daughter needs more from me than I have to give—I can't fill her void, never could." Father exuded impatience and contempt, blaming both mother and daughter for the problem. Mother interjected that she had been trying for years to keep them together as a family, not to get a divorce despite their grave differences. In exasperation, she said that her husband would "step on the fingers of drowning non-swimmers". I felt a knot in my stomach as I sensed their anguish and anger, and I dreaded the idea of wading in between them. I finally dared to suggest that things seemed a little too dangerous between them for a psychiatrist to help them navigate, and yet I sensed they both wanted help for their child and themselves given this painful, embarrassing impasse. To my surprise, they smiled, relaxed a little, and became more reflective.

Nevertheless, the marital tension persisted for months until I recognized my over-concern about the father's vulnerability and my inhibited anger at him. My countertransference kept me from interpreting his fragile, stifling competitiveness with me and his wife. When I mentioned this, the father, a lawyer, recalled the time when his firm was splitting up. He developed panic attacks and saw a psychiatrist, and, though painful and humiliating at first, it had helped. Mother also saw someone during that period. In the family sessions, father was impatient and critical, blaming and exhorting Paula around her disgusting loss of control. Mother was alternately deferential and critical of father, protecting her. Tears would stream down the mother's face, which appeared to torment Paula. There seemed to be no space for Paula to show her true feelings. I asked why she was grimacing at her mother, and she said she couldn't stand her mother's tears; it made her feel so guilty. When I noted that she didn't say anything about her father, she looked apprehensive and then, with her own tearfulness, said she felt crushed and helpless. As the family sessions progressed, it became clear how father dominated the women with his bluster while they disarmed him with "helpless tears". They all shared a basic, ambivalently held assumption of deep dependent loyalty to the family and hostility towards outsiders. Later, we widened discussion of Paula's fearfulness about separating to the whole family's sensitivity about loss of independence, and the riskiness of being out there with others on one's own. This led to discussion of the father's firm splitting up and to associations about fears that the family and extending family might split up.

Treatment arrangements

We had a year and a half for treatment before Paula would leave home for college. I met with her weekly and alternated the family and couple's sessions biweekly. Whenever the son was home from boarding-school, he attended the family sessions and, on occasion, at his request saw me alone, as did both parents.

Description of a bulimic episode: a composite narrative

Here is a picture of one of Paula's characteristic bulimic episodes, using her own words:

"I was at school, sleepless, homework unfinished. So many people had called me the night before to gossip or get help. I had wanted to do a terrific job on my homework for once and please the teacher, but I couldn't say no to friends, they needed me so much. But then I didn't have any time for myself or my homework. At school things were buzzing socially and I couldn't stand to be left out of anything. It was exciting and overwhelming. I was flying around talking to everybody. I was a regular social butterfly trying to please everyone just like my mother felt I should and my father hated. I was into so many activities that I was way over-extended. Yet there were so many more things I wanted to do, be part of.

"Once I sat down in class I had to slow down. I began to feel empty and lonely, left out, cut off, distant. I found myself fretting about all the things I hadn't done for people, worried I had told secrets or said mean things, about people not liking me, not approving of me. I tormented myself over what I was missing out on. At the same time I couldn't help but worry I would be called on, not having my homework done, not know my stuff. I became anxious and lonely, began to have a knot, a gnawing in the pit of my stomach, thinking the teacher wouldn't like me, approve of me. I even began to think of my father, how contemptuous he'd be of my embarrassing performance. I felt so ashamed and small, misunderstood and abandoned. I felt angry at them, wanting to break away and be free from them. I was filled with feeling, anxious, empty and hungry.

"There was only one way to relieve the way I felt. I was disgusted with myself for giving in to the impulse—though as I slipped into that delicious frame of mind I could almost taste the relief. I began getting excited. Sometimes it almost feels sexual. At class break I slipped into a private bathroom and gorged on my secret supply of cupcakes and chocolates. I'm embarrassed to tell you how many. As I filled up I began to feel relief at first, relishing swallowing the forbidden rich, fattening stuff despite my own and my family's dislike of fatness. I felt so relieved and satisfied, free and together—a real high. I felt in my own special private world. You know—separate and in complete control just for a passing moment, doing my thing. Once I even masturbated a little. I never told you that before.

"Anyway, I couldn't stop myself. I kept going, and as I did so my mood and my feeling about what I was doing, about myself and the food, began to change fast, just like it always does. I began to feel the food turn rotten, bad, disgusting, as if it were turning in my stomach, attacking me. It no longer gave me absolute relief and pleasure. It always spoils the perfection. I began to think about the outside world again. I began to hate myself because I couldn't stop, because I had given in, because I was pigging out, and the food would make me fat. I had to get it out of me, get away from it, control it and control my urges. Giving in had gotten out of control. What was so good turned so completely bad that I had to get away from it or everything would be ruined. I'd be caught or collapse. Somehow I felt I had to punish it and myself. So I stuck my fingers down my throat repeatedly and vomited it all up—got rid of it—to protect myself from becoming fat, disgusting, embarrassing. I began worrying about someone having heard me, catching me at it. I wanted to avoid the other kids, my Mom and Dad, knowing, criticizing, making fun of me, though I hated myself. Actually, though, there is such relief, almost a rush, from vomiting. It's such a physical feeling, the relief to get rid of the bad stuff.

After I come out of it, the tension is gone, though I'm left with a hangover in my body and feelings. I know it won't build up again, at least for a while. I almost feel like someone else took me over, someone else did it. Yet it's so special, it's all mine, it's private and I haven't wanted anyone to know about it—or take it away. It's my baby. I know its wrong and dangerous. Maybe that's why I got myself caught by my mother. Anyway, when I leave the bathroom, it takes a while for me to feel myself again. I feel people know somehow I've been doing it, like they can see through me, smell it or something. I feel fuzzy, like they can read my mind. I have to be extra careful and good. I'm so tired from it, feel so ashamed, that I like to keep my physical distance, get away and rest. That's impossible at school, so I bury myself in a book or stay out of social things. After a while I feel normal again."

What Paula made repeatedly clear to me was that at school and at home she went through repetitive cycles every day, with the prodromal build-up of specific psychodynamic tensions with familiar content, followed by the impulse to binge and then purge. The triggers were both inner conflicts and outer events. Always involved were object-related, object-directed fantasies about herself and others, with familiar but varied psychodynamic content. As the impulse to binge gathered strength, she would first fight it, then feel compelled, and finally even eager to binge. As the urge to binge reached an obligatory phase in some safe secret place, she underwent a regression to a different psychological state—a special private world—with altered personality, reality-testing, and ego-functioning.

Summary of treatment

As my work progressed with the couple and the family, shared family basic assumptions emerged around compulsive loyalty and dependency, and shame and envy regarding outsiders. As anxiety mounted around exposure and intimacy, especially in father, the family coalesced against me as a condescending outsider and critical intruder. I felt hurt, angry, misunderstood, and inclined to counter-attack—until I identified their shared projections, expressed mainly by father, which were kindling my countertransference. I shared my sense that they were filling me with enviable things and a harsh conscience. Later, I wondered if their seeing me as critical had something to do with their own fear that being separate and different from each other, being angry or disappointed with each other, felt disloyal and aggressive, so they united against me as the divisive threatening outsider. As these shared basic assumptions became less rigid and intense, the family holding environment allowed the parents to work on their sado-masochistic relationship. They explored how they handled their tensions around intimacy, sexuality, and competition by putting feared aspects of themselves into each other, or into others, their daughter receiving most of them. They came to recognize that what they projected onto the outsiders, onto me, and onto Paula represented aspects of themselves. They began dealing for the first time with their own mid-life crises, while addressing the problem of letting their daughter grow and leave home.

In individual work, Paula feared that I would be critical like father or smothering like mother, and she kept her distance. As we worked through these transference positions, she developed a dependent, idealizing, and eventually sexualized transference. Our focus was not on the bulimia—at least not at first—but on her empty drivenness to pursue what she envied in everyone else. As we worked through each micro-projection around her peers and her parents, we began to analyse her self-denigrating experience with me based on her idealization of me. As she became more assertive, expressing her differences and accomplishments and no longer fearing my parent-like envy and competition so much, she came to trust me and herself enough to feel romantically inclined. This began to have more of an adolescent feel, indicating sufficient progression and integration that she was more developmentally on track. She was dating again by now, but not too seriously. For the father's part, he was less contemptuous of her, opening his arms and heart to a degree. Mother was less jealous as their relationship had improved. Periodically Paula would refocus on her bulimia, and more of its meaning would emerge. Slowly, we forged the linkages between her bulimic episodes, her daily life, and her inner object world. It would then drop out of sight. Finally, for long periods, the bingeing and vomiting abated as she felt more whole, full, and together. Couple and family work stopped because her parents had reached sufficient accord and were no longer interfering with her development. With the approach of termination and leaving home, the bulimia returned. At first I found myself alarmed and acting like an over-concerned parent, until I realized that this represented a termination regression. There was a couple and family regression going on too, with familiar old assumptions and projections being reactivated. We agreed to add some family and couple sessions to address these issues and re-work them again in the face of the family's intolerance for loss, anxiety, and mourning. By the time of summer vacation and our parting, Paula was more self-contained, sad but ready to go—with some remaining urges to binge and purge, and an occasional slippage. These imperfections did not panic her, as we reflected on the fact that our "termination" was really a forced "interruption" of her incomplete personal growth. I recommended that when she got to college, after taking a break for a while and settling in, she should consider further work, which she eventually did. We met by chance many years later when her baby was about to be baptized, and she said all was going well.

Narrative family and developmental history

The inner and outer worlds of the family members shed light on the development and onset of bulimia in this teenage girl. As was mentioned in the description of the family session, confidence had been shaken around father's crisis around his firm splitting up, which was not long before Paula turned 12. As a child and preadolescent, she had been chubby, on the social sidelines, and receiving school criticism about her self-centredness and temper. As she turned 12, they took a summer safari to Africa where she became deathly ill with severe vomiting, not eating for two weeks, and losing a great deal of weight. She returned to school in seventh grade and, to everyone's amusement, was trim and temperate, a popular social butterfly. From that time on, she seemed both selfless and absorbed in her world of peers. As we reviewed other family experiences during this period, they realized that the father's father had died about the same time, further precipitating the father's mid-life crisis. Each of these reminiscences led the parents on different but important tracks in subsequent sessions. Mother became tearful again, remembering her sense of loss and rejection when Paula became successful with peers. Mother was hurt and jealous. It reminded her of aspects of Paula's early years and other losses. When she was born, she reportedly cried twenty-two out of twenty-four hours and rarely slept. Mother's milk could not satisfy or soothe her, because she didn't have enough and the milk was "bad" ("black milk"). Mother followed a paediatrician-prescribed "two-hour demand schedule". Initially, there was no weight gain, and after four weeks there was a loss. Her husband had to be away for several weeks. During this period mother felt overwhelmed and alone. She felt she "had no real help", despite the fact that her own mother came before her husband left. She always felt criticized and deprived by her mother, who only supported achievement, leaving a reservoir of hidden craving and resentment. Consequently, she sought her approval and acceptance, giving her mother complete outward respect. Mother's own father, though subtly seductive, was distant and quite critical, noticing her only for her ideas and academic achievement. Her parents had a formal intellectualized, seemingly asexual, relationship covering many disappointments and hostilities that occasionally erupted towards each other or her. At such times, her mother would withdraw tearfully and father would become verbally abusive of her. Secretly she (Paula's mother) welcomed the intensity of his feeling and attention. Eventually, with a change in paediatrician and an unrestricted formula schedule, the baby began to thrive. Even so, she remained high-strung, irritable, with mother feeling she was a demanding, all-consuming "bottomless pit", running mother ragged. A sense of a misfit prevailed, with Paula being pictured as insatiable and unsatisfied. Father apparently got some sadistic enjoyment out of clapping and setting off her Mauro startle reflex. Worried that she was basically at fault for not giving her enough, mother never limited Paula, spoiling her for years yet underneath hating herself and Paula for it. From the beginning she felt that something was wrong with the baby. When Paula was a year old, mother saw early signs of her being "very social, going off with anyone"—she had no sense of family, I felt so rejected, abandoned". For fear of not being a good mother and of being restricting and ungiving like her own mother, she never limited or denied Paula food or social licence, fearing anger and rejection. Yet she found herself hurt, and secretly angered, by Paula's independence and separateness. She had to suppress the negative side of her ambivalence about her daughter. Later, she recognized that she envied what her daughter was getting from her that she had never had from her mother.

Early in the process of childrearing, the father's mother became involved when she visited, and she had a "tremendous effect on Paula, enveloping her like an octopus, and I let her do whatever she wanted". Around age 2 years her brother was born, and at age 4 years the paternal grandparents moved to the same city. Mother allowed the paternal grandmother's pervasive influence because "there were such profound differences between my husband's family and mine, between him and me, that I gave in to her so as not to risk further divisiveness and loss". Father's mother was an extremely phobic, dependent, smothering woman, who shaped her empty days around her granddaughter, catering to her, and protecting her from imagined inner and outer fears. Mother wanted to deal with nightmares and night fears and turn off the night-lights, but the mother-in-law urgently said no and prevailed. Redoubling her effort in the face of this competition, mother devoted herself even more to her daughter, wearing herself out and resenting her own mother and mother-in-law even more. The context for the focus on Paula was a bitter family disagreement suffered by the paternal grandparents in their previous city, resulting in the paternal grandfather never talking to his own brother again, followed by the move. They were a dependent, devoted couple, and mother "could not be so unkind and impolite as to assert myself, differ with them, and push her out. . . I despised her all-encompassing need to have a relationship with my daughter, but I tolerated it." Sadly, this disruptive fraternal pattern was re-enacted between the father and his brother thereafter, with his brother becoming so envious of the father's career that they stopped talking and both families quit seeing each other. The paternal grandparents were caught in the middle. A year later, mother suffered a placenta previa and lost her uterus with the child, further precipitating her mid-life crisis. She confessed that she has "never gotten over it, and my daughter must have suffered terribly because I needed that child so much—our marriage was so rocky and father wanted ten children". Paula, 5 years old at the time, could not come in and see her mother, so she cut off a lock of her hair in desperation and sent it in to mother. Perhaps as a reaction to these family impasses, father refused to let his daughter or younger brother go to camp, insisting that the family be together on vacations. Mother observed: "We were dominated by his wishes in all things and were never separated as a family. He also drank too much, but then so did I. We both had an alcohol problem. My family gave me my head, while my husband sat on my head." So mother, fearing her husband's anger, sharp tongue, and aggressive outbursts, swallowed her opinions and differences to keep the peace.

For years, until age 12, Paula was supported by her mother in thinking only of herself, expressing her negative opinions and asserting herself. Mother observed:

"I guess I allowed her to be negative and opinionated due to my completely positive attitude and suppression of myself. I never said 'no' and was the opposite of my negative, cynical husband; I felt so used and exploited, so I encouraged my daughter not to be used and exploited. It was my fault that she was so self-centred, so opinionated and hot-tempered. That's why she alienated peers, had no friends, got into trouble in junior school. As a result we were closest friends, though we actually fought a lot. . . .

"I also found it much easier to criticize her, compared to my son. He could make me laugh, but with my daughter, some of her anger and aggressiveness reminds me of my husband. I was ambivalent about her rebelliousness. She dared to do things I never did. When she began to skip classes and lie about her activities and homework in the last few years, I wondered if I was at fault. She has always had an impulsive, defiant side, though most of the fire went underground when she was 12. With my son, it wasn't so perfect either—he is dyslexic, had self-image problems, was hyperactive, and was failing courses despite his motivation and determination. He was getting into a

negative, self-defeating cycle with school and friends. My husband couldn't stand that, and I found our ideal relationship was
going sour. We felt he needed a fresh start, with more structure
away from us. So when he was 13 and my daughter 15, we
decided to send him to boarding-school. We had not anticipated how different it would feel around here without him. He
was the "love-beacon buffer" and the "shock-absorber" for us
all. We all missed him and felt sad, but his sister seemed to miss
him the most. She used to tell him everything, and vice versa.
She, incidentally, was enuretic until age 12."

In the context of the brother leaving for school, mother surprised
and upset father and daughter by arranging to go back to school
herself "to become an Interior Decorator so I can have something
meaningful of my own to do and become more financially independent".

Family developmental formulation

The marital couple

Paula's mother characterized her relationship with her parents
as one in which she felt superficially valued for good products and
performance while personally criticized and deprived. As a result,
she developed a "false self" (Winnicott, 1956), suppressing her
negative thoughts and feelings in favour of pleasing and appeas-
ing, while harbouring deep, dependent cravings and bitter resentment. Hoping to escape her parents and satisfy her longings, she
married a man with seeming strength, brilliance, and independence, only to discover that he was critical and distant—like her
father. He resented her dependency and uncertainty because of his
own counter-dependent and counter-phobic tendencies. Because
his own parents, especially his mother, were so dependent, phobic
and smothering, he sought a woman who would not challenge his
dominance and independence. Prior to their daughter's birth, they
felt trapped in a sadomasochistic struggle fuelled by mutual patterns of projections based on original familial conflicts. Mother
hoped that having a baby would save the marriage.

The "psychosomatic partnership"

When Paula was born, her strong appetite and irritability collided with mother's anxiety and inadequate milk supply, resulting in a sleepless, insatiable, inconsolable infant. Already deeply ambivalent about nurturing because of her own maternal experience, Paula's mother found herself in exactly the position she most dreaded—failing to satisfy her child and instead becoming the seeming object of her ravenous child's tormented fury. In addition, her husband was abandoning her rather than giving her more love and support, and her mother was witness to her failure to perform well as a mother. She felt overwhelmed by loss and rejection from everyone, especially by her daughter. Characteristically, she attempted to suppress her disappointment and rage and began to deplete herself by limitless giving. The resultant failure in fit and bonding (Steiner, 1985; Stern, 1977) between mother and child—the mother's failure to provide an adequate holding environment for her infant—began a very bad, even catastrophic, experience for both of them. In terms of mother's internal-object world, through role-reversal and projective identification the baby became mother's "bad demanding libidinal self" and she became her "bad rejecting anti-libidinal" mother (Fairbairn, 1954). As a result, she found herself attacked from without by her persecutory little baby and sabotaged from within by her harsh critical superego. Attempting to ward off these pernicious perceptions, she enacted with her baby her wish to become her fantasied self-sacrificing, all-loving, all-giving ideal mother. This combination of repression and splitting, suppression, and projective identification, exacerbated by the baby's temperament, caused serious distortion in the formation of their "psychosomatic partnership" (Scharff & Scharff, 1987) from this point on. Because of mother's inner conflicts and projective identifications, she found it virtually impossible to know where she stopped and her child began. Due to the distortions in her centred holding and relating, she did not create a growth-sustaining holding environment nor function as a nurturing, regulating self-object. She failed to provide, nor did she assist her child in the development of self-regulation (Box, 1981). And at first the infant exhibited a "failure to thrive" pattern. Recovering somewhat from her rage and regression—with time, defensive reconstitution, and a change to a more flexible paediatrician—mother and baby moved from a more rigid demand schedule to *ad lib* feeding. Baby became a "butterball", with mother unable or fearing to limit her in any way. Early in this process, father began his characteristic sadomasochistic overstimulating intrusions with Paula. Basically, however, mother felt that she was at fault, spoiling Paula yet failing to give her enough, experiencing her as a demanding "bottomless pit who ran her ragged" (Balint, 1968).

Centred and contextual holding

Father proved unable to protect and nurture mother, contributing significantly to her difficulties. Uncomfortable with passivity and dependency coming from his maternal experience, he remained aloof and critical of mother's efforts, contemptuous of her spoiling Paula and of her inability to control the girl. This psychological failure on father's part was continuous, though sometimes subtle. At the heart of his difficulty were his internalized yet still continuing conflicts with his mother and his father. As a result of his upbringing by his phobic, overprotective mother, he now defended against similar conflicts by his dominating abusing style, sadistically criticizing everyone else for their fearful helplessness. A striking example of his, and their, shared difficulty in creating an appropriate centred and contextual holding for Paula involved the paternal grandmother. Despite their shared awareness that his mother wanted to "swallow Paula up", overprotect, and smother her "like an octopus", they allowed the grandmother, for differing reasons, to become overly involved, overriding mother and monopolizing Paula. Father seemed relieved to have his overwhelming mother focus on mothering his daughter instead of him. Paula's mother, because of her internal doubts and ambivalence about mothering, surrendered her to her mother-in-law in order to save the marriage and preserve extended-family harmony. She sensed her mother-in-law's narcissistic sensitivity to criticism and loss, her voracious need to control everyone and everything. This was heightened by their family losses in their old home town and move to this city, making them more dependent on Paula's parents. The focus on Paula became more intense because of the competition between her father and his brother for the affection of the newly arrived grandparents (a repetition of what grandfather had just been through). Mother sensed that her husband did not want to lose his parents to his brother, despite all his counter-dependent claims, and Paula became the vehicle for capturing them. Father's brother became jealously enraged and cut him off, with the grandparents and Paula the only go-betweens. She became the sacrificial object as mother and father colluded in avoiding personal, marital, and extended family conflict. As the extended family worked out its conflicts around dependency, greed, envy, and paranoia, and enacted its tendency towards persecution and splitting off, they revealed a shared incapacity for mourning, ambivalence, and compromise. As a result, Paula's parents were not able to provide sufficiently firm generational boundaries, as mother and father reenacted their pathology and allowed his mother a primary caretaking role. Paula's mother's stifled rage at her own mother, her daughter, and her mother-in-law, fuelled by her deep sense of inadequacy and guilt, led to her surrender to all her daughter's urges and to everyone else's wishes for her. This lack of limitsetting, this failure in modulation and regulation (Box, 1981), this surrender of appropriate boundaries, all created an amorphous illdefined centred and contextual holding environment for Paula. At the same time, this holding environment was suffused with often intense, conflicted, confused feelings and interactions between Paula and her caretakers because of their individual and collective unexpressed and unresolved conflicts. These early repetitive experiences in central relationships had a profound effect on her process of internalization of her primary objects and the development of identity formation, self-regulation, and self-control around affects and impulses. This distorted family structure and functioning, with its boundary violations and intolerable affects, provided the extended family context for all that Paula was internalizing.

Triadic relationships and oedipal issues

For her parents and the extended family, the birth of her brother, when she was 2 years old, proved a contrasting relief for everyone—for a while. Early on, Paula was fascinated by him. They

became close and played endlessly. For mother's part, she mar-
velled at the fact that she never felt inadequate or enraged with
him. He seemed easy and easily satisfied. Later, instead of characteristic escalating angry interactions with her daughter, she found
her son somehow got her to smile and relax, breaking the tension.
As a result, she felt good about herself and him. They developed an
intense, positive "mutual admiration society" with each other.
Even though he proved to have learning disabilities, she felt that he
was somehow always more self-contained and self-sufficient, leaving her fulfilled, not enslaved and drained. This obvious splitting
between her daughter and son set the stage for mother's intense
oedipal involvement with him and interference with her, as well as
her later envy of her daughter's relationship as a teenager with her
brother, given the marital impasse. Two years later, the marriage
was still in precarious shape and mother hoped, with her next
pregnancy when Paula was 5 years old, that she could please father
and satisfy his "deep need for ten children". The loss of not only
this pregnancy (a male child) but also her childbearing capacity
plunged mother into deep despair about herself and her marriage,
just as her daughter was dealing with triadic phallic oedipal issues.
And death and disappointment plunged both parents further into
their own mid-life crises. Mother's post-partum and reactive depression (incorporated into her reservoir of unresolved losses) and
father's disappointed, angry withdrawal back into business left his
daughter relatively abandoned and deeply unsatisfied. To the degree her own unresolved earlier issues allowed her to make an
oedipal bid for father during this period, family recollection reveals that it was fickle and frenetic. Father would alternately displace his marital desires and frustrations onto his "hot-tempered
little darling", igniting a love–hate sequence, only to withdraw
entirely for periods. This established him further as a tantalizing
and tormenting inner object for her.

Latency

Paula, from age 6 to 12 years, emerged as a self-centred, opinionated, hot-tempered girl. Because of her impulsiveness and splitting, peers and teachers tended either to like her a great deal or not

much at all. With a style so different from mother's self-sacrificing masochism, she was much more identified with father (identification with the aggressor), though also expressing mother's suppressed rebellious side. When she and father were not keeping their distance, she engaged in heated struggles with him, unlike her more acquiescing mother. This same sadomasochistic pattern was also evident in her battles with her brother. Her libidinal interests, displaced in part from her father, were much more overt with him. She relished beating and being beaten and then making up, with her parents too much the distant but fascinated spectators. Everyone enjoyed the drama.

Despite parental looseness about boundaries within the extended family, father's absolute insistence that they spend all vacations and summers together cut Paula and the family off from peer and camp experience in later years. In fact, both mother and father held a deep shared assumption that to go off too far with others outside the family was disloyal, dangerous, and threatening—almost a phobic paranoid stance. Both parents projected bad aspects of themselves onto outsiders. As a result, the age-appropriate process of separation and object removal was partially blocked for Paula. Forced family vacations stemming from this overly rigid aspect of the family holding environment also contributed to a relatively unmetabolizable affective "hot-house effect" in this family. Because they imbued outsiders with so much harshness and danger and inadvertently set them up as external family social-control agents, family members found themselves much more painfully regulated by shame than by guilt. Internal regulation through identification with parental values and prohibitions— through the formation of conscience and ego ideals—was deficient. The agency and actions of self-control (Steiner, 1985) were defensively projected onto outsiders because parental experiences and internalizations were too painful. For the most part, the locus of control for this family was outside, and shame was the motive. Parental problems around impulse control and self-regulation were evident in other ways also. Excessive drinking and overeating were a preoccupation in the family, with the parents swinging back and forth between periods of self-indulgence and self-denial. Both bordered on obesity and alcoholism at times. During latency and early preadolescence, Paula was impulsive or incontinent in several ways. She was podgy and enuretic, as well as opinionated and mercurial.

Entering adolescence

As Paula approached pre-pubescence and preadolescence, several things conspired to alter her outer and inner worlds. Shortly before this time, as we have heard, her father's firm experienced a hostile take-over attempt from within, and he decided to split off from it. He found himself so narcissistically injured and so threatened that he regressed. Losing his confidence, he became physically shaky and shifted into a phobic and dependent state, something he suppressed at the office but showed at home. Injured, beaten temporarily, and depressed, he recovered over six months with psychotherapy and medication. Getting help for her reaction to his collapse, mother had to assume more independence and leadership at home temporarily. Acting the hero at work, father set up his own firm, suppressing his shameful rage and humiliation. At home, he was threatened by his wife's friendly "take-over from within", becoming more anxious, rigid, and critical of his "defiant impulsive wife and uppity daughter". Not too long after this, father's father also died, adding to father's depressed, hostile state. Somewhat tomboyish, Paula's identification with her father had a significant defensive aspect to it, based on identification with the aggressor and mother's suppressed resentment.

This dramatic turn of events and the relative shifts in mother's and father's positions were not lost on her. She found herself with a seemingly new and then harshly reaffirmed family reality at the same time that she was experiencing an upsurge of sexual and aggressive urges. In addition, she was becoming interested in boys and worried about her looks and chubbiness. Just as her father seemed to be softening up, only to come down on her harder, her paediatrician—usually warm and permissive—made some seemingly critical remarks about her weight problem. Mother had put him up to this to control her daughter. Unfortunately, this echoed not only mother's new weight campaign, but also stray teasing by body-conscious pre-teen classmates. Underneath, mother was feel-

ing challenged by her daughter's budding seductiveness with father and upsurge in critical defiance of mother. In effect, mother
joined father in coming down on their daughter to protect herself
and displace her own feelings. That summer, in the context of the
"fun family safari to Africa", which proved to be more of a forced
march by father, she experienced her "vomiting sickness" and lost
a great deal of weight. She had become frightened of rejection by
her mother and father for her new adolescent independence and
experimentation within the family. Because she felt so excruciatingly sensitive, threatened, and shamed by her parents, paediatrician, and peers, she internalized a harsh, rigid reinforcement of her
anti-libidinal internal objects. She experienced a consolidation of
her false self, repressing further the upsurge of her sexual and
assertive yearnings for her parents and peers.

To everyone's surprise, she came out of Africa a changed young
woman, her primitive threatening, internal objects repressed and
her central self overly civilized and constricted. No longer as self-
centred, defiant, and impulsive, she swallowed her real desires and
became a selfless appeaser, representing an identification with her
subjugated mother. Both mother and father felt, in retrospect, that
she seemed to lose her fiery directness, becoming, in father's terms,
an "air-brained social butterfly, with no depth or direction—just
like her mother". In fact, Paula became consumed not only by her
pursuit of thinness but by "being in on everything, never on the
outside with anybody". She became self-conscious about her
weight, her appearance, and her style, wanting to be pleasing to
everyone. Losing her centre, she became an "as if" personality
(Deutsch, 1942). She projected everything good outside herself into
peers and teachers, while sensing in them the potential for harsh
criticism, making every new social interaction tantalizingly precarious should she make a false move and not do the imagined
"right thing in their eyes". She repressed, or felt compelled to
suppress, any feelings or actions she suspected might trigger such
catastrophic reactions. Because her defences were fragile, she was
prone to micro-projection and misperception. As a result, she was
excruciatingly sensitive to even subtle differences or separateness,
which she experienced as criticism or rejection. Usually she drove
herself crazy trying to keep her whole social world positive and
ideal. But occasionally, when she experienced such inevitable "re-

jection" she could no longer contain her anger. The person would become suddenly entirely bad, revealing her propensity for splitting (Kernberg, 1975, 1977). The relationship would turn sour and spoil. She would experience herself as rotten, becoming frightened and disgusted with herself as she hid in shame from the other person. No longer identified with the aggressor, she suffered masochistically.

Onset of bulimia

The frequent onset of bulimia during mid-adolescence is related to both personal psychological and family developmental tasks (Ravenscroft, 1974; Stierlin & Ravenscroft, 1972). The implications of the impending second-order structural change for the family when the adolescent is preparing to leave home, as well as the special challenges for the adolescent female and marital couple at this juncture, are often cited as the reasons for the onset of bulimia in mid-adolescent females. The unusual number of losses found in bulimic families is also often cited. More probably their unusual shared sensitivity to, and incapacity for dealing with, losses is involved.

Mid-adolescence

For Paula and her family, the loss of her brother to boarding-school as she and her family were beginning to anticipate college created the over-determined circumstances for onset of her bulimia. Within the "hot-house" of the family, adolescent issues were germinating. Unfortunately, her parents did not provide an appropriate holding environment and were not available for the developmental tasks of adolescence within the family. Mother and father were so anxious about separation–individuation and oedipal-heterosexual issues that their anxiety and defensiveness interfered with their daughter's reworking of these issues. Yet they also interfered with her moving into the peer group. As a result, both Paula and her younger teenage brother entered into a highly charged sexual and aggressive relationship, tinged with and re-enacting the same regressive anal sadomasochist struggles seen with their parents. Because of their marital and, in particular, their sexual impasses, the parents alternately fuelled and criticized this hot brother–sister relationship. In this context, Paula was noted to oscillate back and forth between her peer group and her brother as she experimented abortively with separation and heterosexuality. Her parents regularly managed—although nominally for her growth—to criticize and limit her peer-group forays, citing poor judgement and shameful behaviour but implying family disloyalty and their own marital anxiety.

During this period, as Paula's brother began to have increasing scholastic difficulty, mother nevertheless idealized and adored him while father became disappointed over the embarrassing struggles of his son. He felt that his wife babied him but also secretly resented their erotic intimacy, as well as his son's intimacy with his daughter. This oedipal challenge was too threatening. For this mix of reasons, he partially rejected his son. By sending him out of the family, father broke the unwritten family rule of loyal enmeshment. Unresolved oedipal issues for the parents had been displaced onto son and daughter, leading to their splitting them up as a sibling couple and sending the son away. Father's problems around competition, envy, and shame in male relationships—inside and outside his family—were now being re-enacted with his son (Levi, Stierlin, & Savard, 1971). When the parents sent their son to boarding-school, they lost their tension-relieving oedipal displacement, and Paula lost her in-house romance. His departure, besides facing everyone with partial loss and their incapacity to grieve, also brought home the possibility of Paula leaving, too, and the parents' prospect of an empty nest and barren marriage. The result was powerful intensification of conflict, regression, and personal and family defensive manoeuvres.

Fuelling these were their separate mid-life crises (Jacques, 1965). Because of marital anxiety, father became more distant and critical. At first, mother became more dependent and tearful. Father engaged his daughter in more hot but critical encounters. Mother attempted to envelop and control her. Soon, however, mother herself broke covert family rules and assumptions as she reacted to her son's somewhat forced departure . Her assertive and defiant decision to go back to school was threatening to her daughter and

husband, implying rejection and loss. Paula had just moved tenta-
tively into her first romance, possibly in anticipation of her brother
leaving, but then, under the inner and outer onslaught of his actual
departure and mother's major independent move, she retreated
from this outside relationship, collapsing loyally back into the
family, while becoming secretly but defiantly bulimic. She could
not escape yet could not stomach what was going on in the family.

Clinical theories about bulimia

I have found most psychodynamic explanations of bulimia unsatis-
fying because they usually do not make a sufficient clinical and
conceptual distinction between structure and content. As a result, I
find myself expecting to find *the* psychodynamic explanation of
bulimia and come away with the impression that *any* psychody-
namics might be involved, including a smorgasbord of psychosexual levels. In addition, there is a tendency to get lost in
confounding secondary psychophysiologic effects of both the
binge-vomiting physiology and the guilt-, hunger-, and endorphin-
induced anorexia and starvation after a binge–purge cycle. Also,
there are the confounding psychological secondary, subsequent,
and stratified causes within the bulimic individual and the family.
Many clinicians, understandably, have been lead to the conclusion
that bulimia can arise from any developmental level and that
almost any type of personality and dynamic pathology can under-
lie the condition. This unsatisfactory conclusion overlooks certain
important clinical observations and leads us to seek an answer at a
different level. Sophisticated clinicians point to the obvious impulse disorder involved in bulimia and conclude rightly that a
structural defect in the ego must be present. Since the predominant
difficulty seems to be at the oral level and involves defensive
manoeuvres of "taking in" (bingeing) and "eliminating" (purging),
the defences of incorporation and projection must be involved.
Discussions elsewhere in this book cover these areas thoroughly.
Pathological as well as healthy defences can give form to varied
dynamic and psychosexual content, accounting in part for the
discrepancies and confusion reviewed above. Much of psychoana-

lytic thinking is predominantly drive-oriented, dealing with the vicissitudes of libidinal and aggressive drives in terms of internal structural relationships. Object-relations theorists, and especially object relations family theory, on the other hand, make the important theoretical and clinical distinction that libidinal and aggressive drives are all directed at objects, resulting not in the incorporation or projection of disembodied drives in relation to reified "mental structures", but, rather, the incorporation or projection of personified drives involving the personal self in relationship to other real significant people, as part or whole objects, mediated through internalized object relations.

Premorbid personality characteristics

With these theoretical and clinical considerations in mind, I worked with Paula's family individually, as a couple, and as a family group. The resulting detailed clinical observations give additional insights into the intrapsychic and interpersonal aspects of the bulimic in her family, and into the bulimic episode itself. Paula felt ashamed or fearful about much of her private internal world, obsessing about her feelings and thoughts about people. Like many teenagers, she spent much of her day rehearsing and sorting out her ideas and feelings, imagining everyone's reactions, and modifying her responses. For her this was more dangerous and draining because of her deep cravings, impulsiveness, and sense of impending disaster. Because she experienced so much of what she was as unacceptable, she felt she needed to hide most of her self. Not only did she have a "false self" and repressed "true self", but a sizeable conscious-to-preconscious "hidden self" in relation to "hidden others". This constituted a cauldron of doubted or feared parts of herself leading to her sense of shame and need for secrecy. As a result, Paula often felt quite isolated. In Kleinian terms, she had a tendency, when anxious, to operate from a predominantly paranoid–schizoid position (Klein, 1946), trying to relieve her sense of isolation and separateness, yet fearing "internal sabotage".

From a personal and family developmental point of view, impasses around both dyadic separation–individuation and triadic oedipal issues made it difficult for Paula to move beyond mid-adolescence. Her anaclytic dependency, intrapsychic and interpersonal boundary problems, severe identity confusion, and immobilizing projections left her psychologically unable to move out of the family into her peer group. Her failure in identity formation and mid-adolescent identity consolidation has been traced from her maternal dyadic "psychosomatic partnership", through each stage of development, to mid-adolescence. In effect, she suffers from severe difficulties in identity formation stemming from early dyadic and triadic experiences, unresolved and further distorted by later developmental experiences. Paula has serious structural and functional deficits in her ego, her available defensive operations, and her identity. Her regression into this defensive position underlying her development of bulimic symptoms represents movement into a psychic retreat (Steiner, 1993). What she could not take in entirely because of her pathological centred holding and relating with her mother she now sequesters in preconscious limbo within herself, an encapsulated part of herself—an internal saboteur—threatening to destroy inner and outer boundaries. This leaves her with a fluid and fragile identity and brittle defences, and a proneness towards projective identification and splitting. On the other hand, as another result of this process of splitting, a conscious sense of the "ideal object" develops and a failure of normal identity-formation occurs, resulting in a brittle distorted "false self" leading to Paula's unstable "as if" personality. In addition, there is a hypertrophy of the conscious and preconscious "ideal object" due to Paula's urgent projections of the good parts of herself onto her mother and others for safe keeping, split off from the bad. This is amplified by mother's unrealistic enactment of herself as all-gratifying and unfrustrating. The conscious and unconscious fit of mother's and Paula's projective systems left Paula with an internal idealized infantile cornucopia fantasy, Paula retaining the sense of badness lurking within her preconscious and unconscious, while imbuing many of her objects with exaggerated goodness, the recipients of projections of tantalizing tormenting riches now embodied in those around her.

For the mid-adolescent and her family, the developmental challenge is to promote the final formation of a coherent, integrated identity through provision of a healthy facilitating "shell" (Scharff & Scharff, 1987), so the adolescent can be "hatched" out of the family—a whole separate self capable of self-regulation, ready for emancipation and launching. Paula, like most female adolescent bulimics, found the disparate aspects of her family, now in her internal object world, and her fractured identity impossible to swallow (incorporate), metabolize, and integrate. To become a person like her parents, to become a female like her mother, to enter into a heterosexual and aggressive relationship like her parents, to leave a family such as hers, into a world such as they project—all this was too much for her to incorporate or "package". In addition, she feared that if she left them alone together, there would be both a real-life catastrophe (a parental divorce) and an internal catastrophe.

Object relations and the bulimic episode

From Paula's composite narrative of her bulimic episode, we can sense the build-up of intense craving, frustration, and anger as she seeks to satisfy her omnivorous appetites with the people in her life. Prior to the binge she uses a combination of repression and splitting, suppression, and projective identification to distribute in a characteristic pattern the intolerably good and bad aspects of her self and others, fueled by the interplay between her internal objects and her peers and teachers. She represses and splits off her devouring libidinal and aggressive self and her tantalizing, tormenting exciting other; she represses and splits off her angry, critical anti-libidinal self and rejecting other. These intolerable aspects of her self and her objects, repressed as her internal bad self and bad objects, erupt into consciousness as either tantalizing goodness or threatening criticism contained in others—and in her secret supply of food. As a result, she experiences her central self as depleted and empty. Devoid of sufficient self-organizing appetites and assertive directedness, she becomes selflessly outer-directed. At the same time, she projects onto others around her the idealized aspects of herself, experiencing herself surrounded by people filled with everything good and exciting she so hungrily craves. She then feels compelled to seek and incorporate these libidinal supplies on all psychosexual levels, giving the various oral, anal, and oedipal tinges to her interactions with her objects. In addition, because she suffered from preconscious suppressed introjects of her mother, father, paternal grandmother, and others, she constantly experiences a sense of paranoid foreboding as her cravings raise these critical ghosts towards consciousness. Because they so frequently frustrated her, stirring intolerable rage, current needful interactions with them and others occasion considerable anxiety. She is threatened in her strivings by the return of the repressed and the resurrection of introjects—hence, her particular structural fragility and affective/impulsive lability—characteristic of bulimics. This internal and projected distribution of good and bad aspects of herself and others is maintained to protect herself and others as well as to protect these good and bad aspects of herself and others from coming into internal contact with each other—thus avoiding the catastrophic risk of spoiling and destroying each other. Such catastrophic risks and failures, we will recall, were part of Paula's damaging early "psychosomatic partnership". Because of her ego defects and faulty identity formation, she maintains this fragile and precarious distribution with difficulty.

Regression and binge phase

As she approaches a bulimic episode, her mounting voracious hunger, sense of deprivation, and rage over projected criticism and rejection become intolerable. She reports not just thinking about her peers, teachers being like her parents at such times, but sensing and hearing people acting and sounding like them. As internal tension mounts, she can no longer tolerate tyranny over her appetites by her rejecting bad objects and anti-libidinal self. A loosening of boundaries, de-repression, and activation of introjects occurs, due to increasing desire, anxiety, and shifting defences. Eventually, she feels compelled to give in to her impulses and defy this tyranny. Regression to another state of consciousness occurs when she finds a safe setting for her impulsive binge. In a sense, the bulimic episode is a manic, even orgiastic, triumph and feast on all the denied and projected good parts of the self and others—past and present, internal and external. It is also a manic triumph over the tyranny of harsh forbidding and foreboding part and whole objects, whether parents, peers, or authorities. In an orgy of libidinal and aggressive incorporation, she devours omnivorously everything she desires—the forbidden ideal mother, her breast, her milk, the food, the soft, relinquished good faeces, her father's elusive but potent penis—everything about them and her peers that she envies. All the derivatives and sublimations of her appetitive goals and objects undergo regression and homogenation, and they condense into the archaic dream substance of the forbidden rich food that she craves and engulfs.

She regresses to a mental state in which food has become a densely packed symbolic equation (Klein, 1957; Segal, 1964) for all that she has been denied and forbidden. She destroys with biting, oral rage those tyrannical aspects of herself and others that have been oppressing and tormenting her—internal saboteurs and external assassins alike—swallowing them whole or barely chewing them up as she engulfs them with characteristic bulimic gulps. Often the food is selected precisely because it is highly calorific, soft and copious, sweet and fattening, and fast and easy to gorge on quickly. Bulimics like Paula will scoop up great gooey gobs of chocolate cake, or cram cupcakes into their already bulging mouths—seeking an immediate, quick explosive "fix"—revealing themselves as closet food-addicts seeking an immediate high, a powerful antidote for extremely anxious, needful, empty, low feelings. The food is also particularly designed for minimal mastication, rapid homogenization, and quick swallowing. The manic wish for undifferentiated reunion with everything ideal and good, including all later developmental derivatives, is acted out as a symbolic equation through the literal oral incorporation of her part and whole objects. Her fragile false self, her faulty identity, her defective personality structure, her ego and defences—all have collapsed under the onslaught of libidinal and aggressive impulses. Instead of suffering masochistically as the victim, she has become the gluttonous saboteur and assassin herself, joining "the Gang" lurking in her psychic retreat (Steiner, 1993). Massive self-indulgence in every sphere of deprivation leads to gluttony, biting, smearing and messing, fleeting fantasies of matricide and patricide, and masturbation and orgasm.

Transition and purge phase

Typically, this impulsive yielding to urges, this collapse and shift of defences, this manic implosion of usually separated aspects of self, results in a transient and unstable personality configuration and mental state. For the same internal reasons that these intolerable aspects of self and other were kept apart and out of consciousness, they now begin to collide and create an intolerable chaotic destructive internal state. As the reality of actual fullness and satiation sets in and the manic phase reaches its climax, she rapidly begins to experience a sense of the good food spoiling and turning rotten—the bad ruining the good, the hate destroying the love. She senses her destruction of her parents and their rules coming back to haunt her. She fears discovery, criticism, and catastrophe. She feels as if she is losing herself, being taken over by what she has consumed, being attacked by what she attacked. On a literal level, her eyes were bigger than her stomach and she is in pain. She must do something to relieve her physical discomfort and relieve a new intolerable internal tension.

In another sense, she has been omnivorously gluttonous, violating every internal and external rule, and must pay. As a developmental experience while growing up, it was intolerable to incorporate, hold, metabolize, and integrate her object-directed impulses and relationships. She never was held by her parents in a way that allowed her to take them in comfortable and fully as self-holding prototypes that would allow her to become internally tolerant, coherent, and whole. Now that she has given way to her impulses and cannibalistically swallowed them whole into her conscious self, a microcosm of the same internal and interpersonal catastrophe is occurring that she has avoided by a fragile combination of repression and splitting, suppression, and projection. Purging becomes an urgent and deeply desired escape route from this physical and psychological state. In fact, since she has regressed to the level of the "psychosomatic partnership", mind–body and self–other boundaries have dissolved. Because of this unity, the infant is essentially a body-ego. One's collapsed self now includes the other—body and soul—as a self-object. One is, in effect, a concrete embodiment of a "symbolic equation"—concretely corporeal and incorporated—for the moment. Unfortunately, the reunion with the perfectly satisfying mother rapidly dissolves. With no compartmentalization psychically or physically, the overwhelming signal anxiety of this impending implosive catastrophe—a collision of internal objects—is experienced as body-tension and action-impulse. The earliest and worst aspects of her faulty "psychosomatic partnership" experience are re-emerging. In essence, urgent purging is an emergency manoeuvre—mentally and physically—to explosively expel, redistribute, and recompartmentalize these incompatible internal aspects of self and other. First, the regressed bulimic automatically uses expulsive elimination as an emergency manoeuvre—a psychosomatic defence. I am tempted to call this "projective" vomiting, since vomiting is one of the earliest psychosomatic *Anlagen*, or prototypes, for projection. Other forms of elimination, such as cathartics and diuretics, might represent a variant on these structural and dynamic considerations since they use different body parts and functions to express, in part, the same mode and motive but probably have different meaning and involve a lesser urgency with a different time frame.

Post-purge transition and reconstitution

During the purging, the bulimic rapidly emerges from her regressed state. Impelled by near annihilation anxiety, she uses ejection, repression, splitting, and projection to re-establish her central self (false self) in relation to her unconscious, and in relation to her real objects. During this transition back to her normal self, she suffers from loose boundaries, having trouble knowing where she stops and her body—her unconscious—and others begin. She also suffers from activated but receding introjects and proneness to reality distortion. Derealization and depersonalization can occur. For these reasons, as well as cathartic/orgiastic exhaustion, the bulimic likes to go off and be alone, feeling the need to protect and nurture her fluid, re-emerging self-structure. She feels fragile, transparent, and vulnerable. After a while she gets back to feeling her old self, only to discover in time that she is in precisely the same internal and interpersonal predicament she was in in the first place. And thus the cycle begins again. It is of importance to note that the dynamics of the binge–purge cycle are a microcosm of the dynamics of Paula's underlying personality structure, as is the case with all bulimics. While bulimics can seem, on the surface, to have a range of personality styles, at their core this deep structure and dynamics are present, similar to structures described by Deutsch (1942), Kohut (1971, 1977), and Kernberg (1975, 1977).

Conclusion

It is important to differentiate epidemic peer-group fad bingeing–purging on the one hand, and post-anorectic bingeing–purging on the other, from the syndrome of true normal-weight bulimia. With the former group, most individuals do not go on to develop true bulimia, despite the exposure to vomiting as a weight-control technique. Only certain anorectics proceed to bulimia, perhaps as a result of treatment or growth in some instances. Why certain mid-adolescent females with similar peer exposure to the technique of vomiting eventually develop the full syndrome is a function of their family and personal development, their structure and function, and especially their object relations, both internal and external. Clear antecedents and a particular vulnerability are present prior to their peer-group exposure, accounting for the onset of true bulimia. Normal-weight bulimia, with its onset predominantly in mid-adolescent females, is an eating disorder caused by specific interrelated personality and family pathology. Characteristically, the mother is in a hostile, dependent masochistic relationship with her husband, while deeply ambivalent, guilty, and overindulgent with her daughter. Typically, the father is counter-dependent, counter-phobic, and sadistic with his wife, while overstimulating and rejecting with his daughter. Because of interlocking pathological familial and parent–child patterns of projective identification, there is a characteristic failure of the "psychosomatic partnership" during early childhood. As a result, the pre-bulimic child develops a "false self", a fragile identity, and a vulnerability towards regression to the paranoid–schizoid position. She also comes to suffer from sequestered or encapsulated part-object introjects (Hopper, 1991), reflecting the faulty and incomplete process of internalization and identity formation due to her pernicious object relation-

ships. Both child and parents share, to a varying degree, an underlying assumption of deep familial dependency and paranoid distrust of outsiders. They also share an intolerance of loss, mourning,
and ambivalence, based on structural ego defects, leading to excessive defensive operations of repression, splitting, suppression, and
pathological projective identification. Because of the mutual fit of
the projective systems of mother and daughter, the pre-bulimic
child retains an excessive, unmodified infantile cornucopia fantasy
about the ideal mother. She comes to feel that all the ideal oral
supplies she craves reside outside her, while her experience of her
central self is one of deprivation, depletion, and emptiness. Each
subsequent individual, marital, and familial developmental phase
is distorted in reciprocal fashion by the family's disordered central
and contextual holding capacity, as well as by their distorted direct
relationships.

Because of difficulties around boundary regulation on all levels
within the family, the pre-bulimic child comes to share the familial
difficulty around self-holding and self-regulation. The vicissitudes
of the related ego defects, identity formation, and impulse regulation can be traced developmentally, revealing that the bulimic's
ultimate addiction to an impulsive eating disorder has clear developmental precursors and parallels in the family. Given the
bulimic's pathological process of internalization, structural defects,
and particular internal-object relations, she and her family are
vulnerable to difficulty specifically around the developmental
tasks of mid-adolescence. Facing the necessity of "hatching" and
"launching" their adolescent female, the parents—themselves in
their mid-life crisis—must face the prospect of an empty nest and
their marital impasse. At some point in this process a crisis occurs
in such families, especially around their mid-adolescent daughter
as she moves towards separation and heterosexual peer relations.
This precipitates a regressive realignment in the family and the
adolescent. She collapses loyally back into the family while secretly
and defiantly developing bulimia. Her bulimic episodes, in particular, represent a biphasic regression in which she first gives way
to an impulsive oral incorporation of her infantile ideal part and
whole objects, followed immediately by an internal implosive catastrophe necessitating emergency projective elimination and re-
distribution of those objects to protect self and others. The bulimic

episode represents a microcosm of personal and family life. While there are many primary and secondary physiologic concomitants to the binge–purge cycle in bulimics, as well as secondary gain and subsequent causation as the illness progresses, the predisposition for this syndrome is based, fundamentally, on the interplay between inner and outer personal and family dynamics.

CHAPTER FOUR

The uncovering of a lack of identity

Roberta Mondadori

I have divided this chapter into two parts corresponding to two phases of psychotherapy with Lydia, a 17-year-old anorexic girl. As I shall describe, Lydia ended her therapy abruptly after one year but asked to resume eighteen months later. Fortunately I was able to accept.

This second phase continued for two years. In her first phased-type therapy Lydia mainly communicated through primitive early mechanisms such as splitting, projections, and particularly through the "no-entry system" of defences (Williams, 1997). I greatly relied on the transference–countertransference relationship with Lydia, as she seemed at the beginning to have very little space for thinking. In the first phase, Lydia used me mainly as a container of her anxieties, and it was essential for me to perform a holding function. In her second phase, Lydia began to develop sufficient trust in our relationship, and some exploratory analytic work gradually took place. The feeling of trust was furthered by the experience of reliability and the stability of our relationship, which had withstood Lydia's mental rejection and deep anxieties about her own survival.

Background and referral

Lydia was 17 years old when she initially referred to our adolescent service, after her admission to hospital because of anorexia.
Her eating problems started when she was about 13 years old.
Around that time Lydia's mother was ill herself and had a hyster-
ectomy. Lydia's parents had, however, reported that even at primary school she was preoccupied with her weight. In the past
Lydia had been seen by two female psychiatrists, both of whom left
London after a year of treating her. At the time that the second
psychiatrist left, Lydia was not considered high risk; her weight
was stable, and she was attending the last year of her A-level
studies. Soon afterwards, her parents' marriage broke up and her
parents separated. It was around this time that Lydia's weight
went down to seven stone, and she needed hospitalization.

Lydia comes from a middle-class background. When I started
seeing her, her brother was attending a prestigious university
outside London. After her admission to hospital, Lydia asked to see
a therapist since she felt she needed to talk about her problems
again.

Meeting Lydia

When I first met her on the hospital paediatric ward, Lydia struck
me as being extremely graceful and slim, but not emaciated. She
looked at ease in the hospital environment and welcomed me with
a big smile. Her first words were how pleased she was to have
somebody to talk to. She had not seen anybody since her last
therapist left London eight months before. She said she had been
considered to be able to manage on her own, but clearly her
therapist had been wrong because she had ended up in hospital.

I tried to explore the link between Lydia's parents' recent separation and her admission to hospital. Lydia denied any possibility
of a link. She said that she was glad that her parents had finally
split up; her father had always been very cold towards her, and she
was not prepared to forgive him. Her parents had always been
unhappy together, and she had encouraged her mother to let her
husband go. She felt very close to her mother but said that her

insistence that she eat irritated her deeply. She felt that her mother should be there for her but should leave the worries about her eating to the doctors. Another problem was her studies: she had dropped one of her A-level courses, even though her teacher had been against it because he thought that her work was sufficiently good. Lydia wanted it to be perfect—any imperfection was, to her, a failure.

Already in this first meeting Lydia's extreme fragility and rigidity of thinking were evident: the mental representation of her parents as figures seemed to contain cold, distant, unreliable, and uncommitted objects, like her father and her two previous therapists, and a demanding, intrusive object, like her mother.

I was very struck by Lydia's denial of any connection between her parents' separation and the sudden worsening of her anorexia, thus clearly showing that she was not prepared to make a link between her physical state and her emotional state. I had the impression that if she allowed herself to think about her own contribution to the collapse of the parental couple, she would have broken down.

Lydia's refusal to think and link manifested themselves also as a total lack of curiosity about the possible reasons for her eating problems, and the contradictory image she had of herself when she thought she was too fat but at the same time knew she wasn't. She had no views and no wish for exploration.

I wondered what sort of relationship she would have with me—if any. Lydia did not seem to see me as a person in my own right, but as "another therapist" who had finally been allocated to her because of somebody's sense of guilt. I was part of a picture, of a system where the adults were failing. In this first meeting, she conveyed considerable satisfaction and even triumph in proving the professionals wrong in their insistence that she could manage on her own. I felt from the outset that she was warning me that I should always be there for her without burdening her with my demands and concerns. There was apparently no concept of the possibility of being helped and of using my analytic "food".

Lydia and I agreed to meet twice weekly on the ward. It soon became clear that she understood the seriousness of her predicament; she was frightened of putting on weight and, therefore, of having to leave the hospital. She was scared of her own suicidal impulses, a fear that she had had since she was 13, and she told me that she often thought of throwing herself out of a window or of running in front of a car, without knowing why. Although she was often full of grievances and this played a central part in her mental functioning, she saw no cause for her refusal to eat and for her desire to kill herself. On the one hand, Lydia sometimes had a clear picture of her worrying condition and of her desperate need for help, and on the other she was extremely suspicious and ambivalent about any help I could offer. Although she talked to me openly about her irritation, her unhappiness, and her resentment of her predicament, I was made to feel that I had nothing to give her that would be of any help.

My visits, which apparently Lydia had wished for so much, invariably evoked very heavy feelings in me, and left me confused and lost, useless and rejected. I recall a series of arrivals at the hospital in cold and snowy weather, wearing a heavy coat, only to find my patient in a light and smart dress, looking like a graceful Degas ballet-dancer, coming unwillingly but nonetheless graciously towards me as if to welcome a tiresome visitor. I felt that I was the one who needed her, hoping that she would allow me to help her. Lydia showed the same ambivalence towards the hospital, which offered her a safe environment but was to her the cause of endless irritation. The nurses were either unreliable or patronizing: she could not bear to be congratulated when she ate; it was something that anybody could do. Her friends' visits were irritating, too. If they paid too much attention to her illness this made her feel inadequate, different and pathetic; but when they talked about what was going on in their lives she felt excluded and envious.

Finding ways of approaching Lydia was very difficult. If I tried to explore her feelings, she became irritated and said that she hated it when people wanted to know why she was depressed. If I tried to address what was going on between the two of us, she yawned and withdrew. Nevertheless, and this seemed very puzzling, she also complained that our two sessions were not sufficient. Gradually I began to realize that, on the one hand, Lydia wanted a therapist into whom she could project her unbearable feelings of being ugly and fat, unequipped to satisfy the demands that came from the outside world and from within herself. I also had to experience on her behalf her feelings of being needy, vulnerable, and dependent on others, of being cruelly controlled, and fearful that she could collapse at any moment. On the other hand, I was terrified of my possible failure, and she desperately clung on to me.

It was still difficult for me to bear my countertransference feelings, and the hospital environment did not provide a safe-enough emotional containment for either of us. Nevertheless, I began to think that in Lydia's defensive and apparently derogatory request for somebody there was perhaps a confused hope that this "other one" could eventually help her to put the fragmented pieces of her self together.

When Lydia's weight improved, plans were made for her to leave hospital, starting with going home at weekends. During one of these weekends out, while she was at a party with friends she fell to the floor unconscious and was brought back to hospital in an ambulance.

I quote now from the session at the hospital which followed this event:

In a very matter-of-fact way Lydia described how upset she had been before going to the party, because she had felt ugly and fat, unable to find the right dress and the right pair of shoes. She had, however, gone, but she had drunk too much and had become even more upset by seeing some friends who were drunk and who had thrown up. One of her best friends had complained because she had been dumped by her boyfriend, but what could Lydia do about it? She had felt angry with her friends and guilty about not wanting to worry too much about them. She had become panicky, could not breathe, her legs had given way, and she had fallen on the floor unconscious. In a lighter tone, she continued to say that she would leave the hospital in a few days. She was not sure about continuing her sessions, as "all the badness inside her had now come out and she was very optimistic about her future". I was extremely worried seeing Lydia's apparent indifference about the events of her weekend and worried about her doubts about needing further help. I commented on her apparent lack of concern about finding herself without the safety net of the hospital and without therapeutic support. At this point Lydia began to cough violently, as if she was to throw up. I then told her that my words had been perceived as if I was forcing her to swallow something dangerous and disgusting, which immediately had to be thrown up. Lydia's cough diminished, and she seemed to relax. She then recalled that her best friend Rosa had tried to be supportive, but she could not bear Rosa's attempt to understand why she felt so bad. In order to make Rosa happy, she told her the first thing that came to mind. I told her that she was telling me that I should be there for her, but I should not try to explore the reasons for her unhappiness. This, far from being helpful, was only seen as intrusive. At the end of our meeting she agreed to continue her sessions.

This episode shows how Lydia's terror of finding herself divorced from the hospital environment, which she felt had deserted her, was so unbearable that she reacted by projecting her feelings into me. I had to experience, as indeed I did, strong feelings of rejection and worry about her state. Not surprisingly, my attempt to show her that her optimistic expectations were unrealistic had been experienced by Lydia as if I had tried to push her worries back into her. My words had become poisonous and disgusting food. There was no possibility of my giving a meaning to Lydia's bad experience at the party and helping her to protect herself from other distressful experiences. Yet Lydia now felt free of worries. To use her own words, "all her badness inside her had now come out".

What was taking place between Lydia and me could be understood by making a reference to the mechanism of projective identification described by Klein (1946) and later by Bion (1962a). Klein describes the splitting-off of parts of the self in order to project them into another person for purposes of attack and control, and the consequent feelings of chaos and disintegration resulting from the splitting—feelings that she saw as closely related to the fear of death. Bion speculates that all infants make use of projective identification not just for the purposes of attack and control, but as a defence against their primitive anxieties. These should then be mitigated by the mother's capacity to understand, contain, and give them a name. The massive use of projective identification protracted in life shows that the container has been unable to digest and metabolize the infant's anxieties and that they have been returned to the infant as "nameless dread" (Bion, 1962a).

Gianna Williams (1997) suggests that with some patients—and among them severely anorexic patients—it is possible to think that not only the infant's anxieties are returned back in an undigested form, but also that the mother's own anxieties may have been projected into the infant. She stresses that these projecting mothers have no conscious intention of attacking their infants, but that they cannot contain their own feelings. In some cases they have themselves experienced projections coming from their own mothers, thus perpetuating a cycle through various generations, often without the help of a sufficiently supportive partner who could create some space between them and the baby.

Lydia's pathology—her refusal to eat and to make use of the available help, particularly if this involved thoughts and links; her total lack of a sense of herself; her desperate attempt to defend herself from anything that was felt as out of control—made me feel that Lydia might have been an infant who herself had been the recipient of unbearable projections. She had then developed a very rigid "no-entry" defensive system, as described by Williams (1997).

At this time I had only a vague picture of Lydia's parents, particularly of her mother. She was described by the other professionals as caring and supportive, but I also had the impression that she was unable to stand up to Lydia, often giving in to her demands, even if this meant turning a blind eye and ignoring the dangers involved. A significant instance of this occurred when Lydia was discharged from hospital. Lydia thought that her mother needed a rest and convinced her to go away for a few days. She asked a friend to stay at home with her, but at the last moment, after her mother had already left, the friend had been unable to come. Lydia had to stay in hospital for a few more days, feeling extremely resentful and abandoned, although she herself was responsible for the situation. As this episode shows, there was no father around who could intervene and set firmer boundaries, nor was Lydia's mother aware that she was colluding with her daughter's assumption that she did not need her help.

Lydia's first therapy as an outpatient

After two months, Lydia eventually left hospital and reluctantly agreed to continue her sessions at the local Adolescent Service. However, she was adamant that she would only come once a week. She often repeated that she wanted people to care about her but did not want to be understood, since she was not proud of herself and of her thoughts, and therefore it was better to keep them to herself. Sometimes she gave me some clues, which allowed me to formulate some ideas about the nature of her disturbance. In one of her sessions, she said that her father's disappearance from her life was a relief but was also the source of angry and frightening thoughts. She said that as a child she had felt herself to be her father's favourite, but when she grew up his attitude towards her had changed completely: he was no longer interested in her and was contemptuous of her developing sexuality and called her a tart if she wore a miniskirt or makeup. She bitterly said that her mother should not have married her father as they never loved each other, and that she had been the one who had convinced her mother that she should get rid of him. When she was living at home she had found his presence frightening and disgusting; he often drank too much and used to make awful noises particularly when he went to bed. She had never been able to sleep well, and even now that her father was no longer around she often remained fully awake, thinking about noises that had also prevented her from sleeping when she was in hospital—babies crying, a girl shouting, the nurses chatting to each other.

Here there seems to be a real terror of violent and disgusting intercourse, which keeps Lydia awake, her mind full of violence and crying. Deep down, Lydia felt that she had split up the parental couple, out of hatred for the father. She felt on the one hand that he wanted to keep her mother to himself, yet on the other he did not allow his daughter to become a woman. As a result, the couple in her mind was both damaged and persecuting.

How could I help Lydia to begin to understand what was going on in her mind, while she was still so extremely vulnerable and at times even suicidal? Only rarely did she allow me to explore our relationship, which could have thrown some light on her internal world perhaps in a safer way. I quote from one such session, which took place after a bank holiday.

Lydia told me coldly that she had meticulously cut out all the images of her father in photographs where he appeared with his arms around his daughter or his wife. He only pretended to love them, since he never cared about them. She said bitterly that her father was the source of all her problems and that she never had a real father. I then told her that she could not bear picturing me as being together with my husband during the bank holiday weekend, when she had felt cut off from me, and without her Monday session. Unexpectedly, because on similar occasions she usually pretended not to hear or yawned and withdrew, Lydia laughed and said that two days before she had said to her mother, "Roberta must have a bloke because her eyes are brighter! Something nice has happened in her life." She then went on to say in a more worried way that her boyfriend's father, "usually a nice bloke", who usually liked her and found her pretty, had been very unwelcoming the last time she went to their house, making her feel intrusive. Again I took up her feelings of rejection when she felt that a father/my husband wanted to keep her out. I said that the "nice bloke" had suddenly turned into an angry, cold and rejecting figure, who did not want her intruding into his home. Lydia became tearful and said that the day before, while waiting for her boyfriend who was late, she had felt like throwing herself out of the window. That would ensure that she would have nothing to worry about. She added that in a way it had been easier in the past when she was starving herself and had thought only about food: now she was obliged to think about other and more upsetting things.

Lydia brings here her anger and despair at having her mind intruded upon by a united couple; her rejection is double, since she feels abandoned both by a mother who prefers her "nice" husband and by a father who is no longer seduced by his daughter. It seems that, not having the mental equipment to tolerate her distress and to learn more about herself, Lydia's solution is to destroy what she thinks is the source of her troubles, to obliterate the father, as she did concretely when she cut him out from the family pictures. This could not lead to any growing process; it only increased her persecutory feelings, and she felt suicidal.

I came to realize that Lydia's extreme fragility was linked to her lack of a sense of identity. As Waddell (1999) writes, the capacity to construct internally one's own space, "a room of one's own", is based on the experience located from the beginning in the relationship between mother and baby. Not having had, apparently, such basic experience, Lydia lacked this room inside herself: she did not know who she was and what she wanted, and she endlessly tried to borrow what she felt was lacking in herself from others. In this attempt she went from one project to another—university, work, travelling—every time convincing herself that this was what she wanted, and she reacted angrily if I tried to explore her wishes and plans. Nonetheless she slowly began to recognize that our therapeutic alliance had become more secure. Eventually, there were times when she trusted me and was able to tell me about her anxieties rather than to project them into me. She valued our work more and asked me to increase her sessions.

A considerable upheaval took place when Lydia returned after our first Christmas break. I had to ask her to change one of her times by fifteen minutes. Lydia agreed but wanted to drop one of her sessions because she had found a part-time job. I did not immediately agree, in the hope that she would change her mind. She then missed some sessions, and finally I received a letter in which she said that she had decided to stop her therapy. It was exactly a year from the beginning of our work together.

Lydia agreed to come to meet me one last time. She coldly explained that she did not need any further help; she now had a new job, was earning money, and felt in control of her life. If she kept coming to see me, she would never be able to do without a "shrink": either she would have to find another one at university or, worse, she would never be able to leave. When I interpreted her fear of being trapped by me forever, Lydia said, "To be honest, coming here was the most important thing in my life, but it shouldn't be." Now she wanted to prove that she was able to cope without help. Only at the end of the session, before leaving, did she say that she might come back in the future if she needed to.

This was our last session, and it was a very depressing end to a stormy year of treatment, at the very point when Lydia had become more engaged and closer to me. With hindsight, I should have seen Lydia's massive acting out coming and perhaps I could have prevented it. Any break was dangerous, since Lydia did not tolerate not being in control. That particular Christmas break found her more vulnerable and softer, because warmer feelings existed between us, but she felt rejected and betrayed during the holiday and also after her return when I asked her to change her times. Moreover, Lydia hated Christmas, which she thought was for families, while she felt she never had a family; it had been around Christmas last year that her father left and she was admitted to hospital. Finally both her previous therapists had left her, each after a year of treatment. Lydia felt that I was in control of her time, and therefore I ceased to be a supportive and available mother for her and instead became the cold and rejecting father-figure that she wanted to cut out of her life—just as she had cut out the image of her father from family photographs.

The second phase of therapy

Lydia did not contact me immediately afterwards, but I knew from her doctor that her weight had remained stable and she was doing well. It appeared that her year of treatment had helped her to mobilize some internal resources. This encouraging picture changed when a year and a half after the end of her therapy, Lydia again asked for my help, because she was frightened of her self-destructive behaviour. This time she had not tried to starve herself, but she had taken a small overdose of paracetamol and had been admitted to hospital.

Soon after her overdose, Lydia had contacted our service and asked to see me. When we met she told me that she had felt reasonably well after the end of her therapy; she had taken her A-level exams successfully while working part-time, but she had found herself at crisis point when she had to decide whether or not to go to a university outside London at which she had been given a place. Eventually she had decided to go, but a month before the date she planned to leave London, she had taken the overdose.

Lydia described to me what had led her to her desperate gesture, which fortunately was followed by alerting her mother. One evening she had gone to a club with some friends, among them a girl who told her how much she envied her because, unlike her, she had failed her examinations and therefore could not go to university. Lydia had felt extremely bad and guilty and had left the club by herself. Outside it was dark and rainy; she wanted to die, and thought of running in front of a car, but she lacked the courage. She had then gone home and taken the paracetamol. She had been very frightened by her own gesture, and being determined not to repeat it she was asking for my help. At the same time she wanted to carry on with her plan to go to university.

At that moment it was not possible to explore further what lay behind Lydia's suicidal attempt, which seemed to be triggered off by some process of identification with the failing girl, just when Lydia was making an important step towards adulthood by leaving home and going to university. I wondered whether the girl represented an envious part of herself which did not allow Lydia to enjoy her own achievements, since in her fantasy this meant allowing her object to do the same. Attacking her body appeared to Lydia the only way out of an unbearable mental state. I was aware of Lydia's extreme fragility, and I agreed to her urgent request to meet with her every time she came back to London.

Although her university was relatively near to London and Lydia could have come to her sessions more frequently, her re-engagement with therapy was very slow. We began with monthly meetings, which later on became fortnightly and then weekly. Each time I left to Lydia the decision of whether she wanted another appointment. She soon became aware that she was not yet ready for living away from home. She decided to leave university, and she began to think about resuming her therapy.

It is interesting to reflect on Lydia's re-involvement with therapy given her intolerance of any feelings of dependency and of her eating disorders. The use of "a no-entry defensive system" (Williams, 1997), mentioned before, seems particularly evident here. Lydia understood that she very much needed help, but she was frightened that I might exploit her neediness by forcing her to accept therapy—my analytic food—and remained determined to keep her food intake under her own control. Given Lydia's fear of a dependency and her manic use of defences to counteract her fear, it seemed better to wait rather than rush into offering more than she was prepared to accept.

The failure of Lydia's first attempt to move away from home made her more aware of her central conflict. This she described as both a feeling of hope for the future and the many possibilities, and the wish to remain mother's little girl for ever. Lydia realized that if in the past it had been possible to ignore this dilemma by concentrating on food, which at least she could control, this no longer worked.

Lydia was very frightened of giving in to her wish to remain her mother's little girl, because confusingly she felt that at the end it meant giving up her own life and, also, as she said herself, she was attracted to all the possibilities that life offered. But what were these possibilities? Lydia knew very little about herself, and she did not understand how to see herself and how to give meaning to her own life. As I have described before, Lydia's lack of identity, of a sense of herself, had also been very evident in the past, but now the passing of time and the choices that she felt obliged to make for her future forced her to face her predicament more than before.

I now quote from a session five months after she had contacted me again, following her overdose, which gives evidence of Lydia's total lack of a sense of herself.

Lydia came in gracefully, and explained that she had missed her last appointment because she had gone to an interview for a job as an assistant manager in a shoe shop. The interviewer, a very nice lady, had liked her, but she probably would not accept the job because it was for a minimum of one year and she did not want to stay in that sort of stupid job for so long. She had other plans instead. I asked about her other plans. She answered defiantly that she wanted to apply for a nursing course, at a university outside London. Her mother, however, thought that a full degree would open up more possibilities, while her boyfriend wanted her to consider a diving course, like him. She looked at me challengingly. I said that she expected me to tell her what to do, while it would have been more helpful to try to understand her reasons for her choices.

Lydia said she was completely fed up with understanding or questioning herself; she had spent all her life sitting in a chair talking to a therapist about her problems. It was unfair that she had been born like that: it was true that she was still young, but she wanted to move on. I suggested that she felt more aware of the passing of time. She agreed, saying tearfully that she was 20 now—"for Christ's sake"—yet obviously she wanted to be sure that she would manage her nursing course and did not want to have to come back again to London feeling a failure. She was totally fed up that things were so slow.

In this session Lydia struggles to find a quick solution to her huge difficulty of separating herself from her family and her childhood and establishing her own identity: her struggles, however, are far from being ordinary adolescent difficulties towards separation and individuation. Lydia wants to convince herself that it is only a matter of finding the right career. Here she oscillates between completely different choices: she wants to become a nurse or a business manager or else to get an academic degree. Where to go? Lydia is frustrated as she cannot solve her existential problems by herself, and this feeling is made worse by her anxiety about making another mistake, either by separating from me prematurely or by becoming too dependent on me. As she still has very little trust in my reliability and concern for her, she feels that she can only maintain a strong grip on me by eliciting anxieties for her own survival. This pattern was present throughout her therapy. I had always felt extremely anxious about her physical and mental survival, at first about her anorexia, then about her suicidal ideas, and was also constantly worried that she could dismiss me as she had, indeed, done after a year of therapy.

I wondered about Lydia's multiple choices for her future. It seemed that her wishes both to become a nurse and to have an academic degree belong to an identification with aspects of the maternal figure, whereas her attraction to a business career seemed more in identification with her father, and with me, insofar as I am in charge of work with my patients. However, these choices were complicated by Lydia's rivalry and ambivalence towards her objects. Lydia said she was fed up with being the eternal patient and wanted instead to be able to help other people herself; she also said she liked the status conferred by an academic degree but did not have a genuine interest in any subjects. She was herself afraid of the thinness and ambiguity of her choices, which is revealed in her resentment towards my explorative work.

I quote now from a session a month later which shows how easily Lydia could convince herself that she had found the right identity. She had decided to accept the job as assistant manager in the shoe shop and was very involved with her work.

Lydia arrived for her session wearing a very smart business-like suit, which made her look more mature. She told me that she was enjoying her work and that her boss had congratulated her for making so much money. However, she had some problems with her staff: one was not sufficiently motivated and another was "bloody useless", but she did not have the time to sit down and talk to either. She wanted to replace them and had already interviewed fifty people, but none of them was really suitable for the job. She added, with a contemptuous smile, that she had turned down all of them. She wanted to achieve the best in her job and was putting a lot of effort into it. Nothing was good enough for her, but the problem was that she was not sufficiently supported. I said that she was telling me that whatever she did had to be absolutely perfect: anything less than perfection was a failure. Apparently I was the obstacle, since I was not helping her sufficiently to achieve her ambitions and she was warning me that if I did not do better work she would turn me down.

Lydia looked embarrassed and said that she did not expect her therapy to work as a pill and was prepared to make an effort, but she certainly did not want to waste her time. She gave me a defiant look. I replied that she expected my work to be of the best standard: if she did not succeed, it would be entirely my fault. In a more thoughtful way, Lydia said that she knew she needed help, but she would prefer to be able to manage without it. She had already let herself down twice, with her anorexia and the overdose—how could she expect not to be let down by other people? This was the reason why she did not want to be dependent on others. I replied that now that she had herself become a manager she resented still needing help. Moreover, she doubted that I could succeed in helping her when she had been unable to help herself. Lydia agreed non-committedly.

Here Lydia expresses her delusional conviction that she has now found a new identity—the successful manager—and does not have any needs. She has become like me or feels that she actually is me; there are no boundaries or separateness—she sees the two of us as the same. We are both extremely busy: I am managing my numerous patients while she is busy with her fifty interviews. She does not need my help in terms of good, average analytic help to explore herself and to know herself better; she expects, instead, that I will provide a magic formula that will solve all her problems and turn her into a new person. On the one hand, there is a great idealization of both herself and her therapist; on the other, there is a sense of an impending catastrophe, since Lydia somehow understands that she is attacking our work.

She had already let herself down twice: will this happen again and again? How could someone else be of any help? Not knowing how to learn from our work and how to accept my help, here Lydia projects some unwanted aspects of herself into me—I become the useless and rejected staff—while at the same time she becomes the perfect manager by borrowing some idealized aspects of me. Lydia says clearly that she does not have any time left to sit down and to talk to her staff—and indeed, as it appears from this session, for the time being she does not have the time or interest to think, to explore her mind, or to listen to herself or to me.

Reflecting on Lydia's dissatisfaction with herself and on her lack of self-identity, Klein's paper "On Identification" (1955) comes to mind. Klein bases her paper on the French novel by Julien Green, "Si j'étais vous . . ." (1950). She suggests that the novel illustrates the mechanism of projective identification: the protagonist, Fabien, an unhappy and dissatisfied young man, is offered a magic formula by the devil, which allows him to change into anyone he likes. The novel describes Fabien's multiple identifications, as he searches for an ideal identity. If at first Fabien is overjoyed, he soon becomes dissatisfied with his choices. In his quick transformations into new identities, Fabien risks forgetting about the magic formula (which includes his name) that he keeps in the pocket of his discarded clothing, thus forgetting his old self and remaining imprisoned in the other person. In Klein's 1955 paper, there is a passage about Fabien's feelings of dissatisfaction and persecution which describes what drives him to become someone else: "He longs to escape from himself, if only for an hour, to get away from the 'never-ending arguments' which go on within him" (p. 154).

Like Fabien, Lydia tries to escape from herself and from "the never-ending arguments" inside herself, her unbearable conflicts, by dropping her despised self and by jumping into a new and more desirable identity, literally jumping into another person's shoes. However, these processes of identification are mainly accompanied by envious and attacking feelings, and Lydia experiences them as persecutory. The solution seems to reside in dropping her newly acquired identity for another one and so on. Inevitably, the shoes don't fit. I sometimes felt that, as I tried to show in the previous sessions, Lydia had a delusional expectation that, like the devil in the novel, I should provide her with a magic formula that would finally give her the right identity, instead of helping her not to drop her unwanted self and to find the truth about herself.

It was only very gradually, as our work continued, that Lydia began to use my help better and became more interested in finding out more about herself and her past. I found it meaningful that coming back after the Christmas holiday, which she usually hated, Lydia reported that she had finally tidied up her room. She had thrown away most of her old things, but not her diaries, which she had started writing when she was 13. Almost in tears, Lydia described her shock on discovering how unhappy she had felt for so many years. However, she had decided to keep the diaries because she knew that they were a part of herself, and she wanted to remember how she had felt in order to avoid going backwards.

This episode seems to show Lydia's new recognition that emotional and mental growth can occur only by knowing the truth about oneself and by bearing the pain; the sorting out of her room suggests a sorting out of her own mind, with a wish not to destroy or to distort the painful evidence of her disturbances. This had been a constant pattern before: Lydia used to rewrite her own story, thus creating an unhelpful confusion about both facts and feelings, which contributed to her own confusion about her own self. This was a new and more hopeful thinking process, showing the evidence of some reparative feelings. It was consolidated for a time, but was suddenly tested by a new event. Lydia's new boyfriend, a young man who had become more important to her than her previous partners, had asked her to follow him in a round-the-world trip, which he wanted to start in a few months' time. Lydia was both thrilled and frightened by his proposal, and a considerable part of our time together was then spent talking and thinking about this. The decision that Lydia had to take reactivated what I knew were her major anxieties: would I allow her to go and to find her own separate way, or would I want to keep control of her and therefore trap her with me? But in this case, how could she be sure that she would be safe? Was I aware of how potentially dangerous this would be?

I knew from my previous experience with her that trying to convince Lydia to stay or at least to postpone her trip would have ended in disaster. I could only make the best of our limited time in order to help her work through it. Lydia was very pleased when she realized that in spite of my worries I was prepared to let her go, but her relief soon gave way to conflicting anxieties, as is apparent in this session:

> Lydia looked very tired, and after a long silence she said that she had been happy after our last session, but now she felt troubled again. I suggested that she had felt relieved that we had been able to think together about her plans and that she felt I was letting her go. She agreed but added that her relief had not lasted long. She had problems with her work, because there wasn't anybody who could set an example for her. Her new boss was nice, but his head was in the clouds: he never came down to talk to the staff and did not know about their problems. Recently he had accused one of Lydia's staff of being a thief because she had sold one pair of shoes for £10 less. This was probably only a mistake. However, Lydia said tearfully, how could she be sure that her staff did not steal? She could not always keep an eye on them. I said that she felt that I was not aware of her basic and emotional needs. I had allowed her to

leave but I was not aware of how scary this was. She felt that I was only addressing her more mature self, forgetting her more vulnerable one. She also worried that something wrong was going on and somebody was stealing something, but we both did not know: she could not always be vigilant, and I, like her boss, was not aware of the problem, as I kept my head in the clouds.

The moment Lydia felt that I freed her to walk away, she was filled with fears. She has become aware of her own needs and does not know if she has the capacity to walk safely through life, or if she has not yet paid the full price (like the right price for the shoes). She knows that her internal resources have increased, but how far can she go? And if she fails, who is to blame? Is she robbing herself of this capacity because she is leaving her therapy prematurely? Or am I to be blamed because by letting her go I am robbing her of her place with me, and of her identity as my patient? Can leaving me be seen as a theft or only as a mistake? Although she was also thrilled by the possibility of discovering something new and more adventurous by herself, she was also terrified of failure and hated me for not being able to release her from this impasse. These themes of stealing, of "turning a blind eye" (Steiner, 1985), and of not facing problems, were going to return again.

In the middle of this upheaval, our work came to a halt because of the summer holiday. Lydia missed two sessions before the break, leaving me once again in the dark about what was going on and not knowing if she would return at all. When she did come back, she announced that she had just bought her plane ticket for her trip and that she was going at the end of October, two months before the previously planned date of her departure, Christmas.

I quote now from one of her first sessions after she had told me of her decision, at the beginning of September.

Lydia looked pale and said she had fainted a few days before. She did not understand why, because she was eating regularly. She went on to say that she could not stand her new boss; he was extremely lazy and let other people do all his work. She refused to be his dogsbody as his previous assistant had been.

Her boss was also unable to face problems. Recently two valuable bags had disappeared from the shop; a woman had then
brought them back, asking for a refund. Lydia had not wanted
to refund the money because the woman had clearly stolen the
bags, but her boss had lacked the guts to confront the woman,
and he had given her the money. Lydia looked at me challengingly. I said that apparently she felt that I, too, was extremely
lazy since I had left her during the summer break to do all the
work by herself. Moreover, she felt that I had not been able to
face her stealing of our two valuable sessions before the break,
and of two months of therapy before the previously planned
date, Christmas. She knew that this was wrong but felt that I
did not have the guts to confront her. Lydia smiled sheepishly
and said that it was her boyfriend who had wanted to book the
trip, and she had agreed because she was fed up with all the
endless planning and talking. I said that she had clearly refused
to resume her thinking again here about the decision. Now it
was too late because she had already bought her ticket.

Towards the end of the session, she looked around and said that
she would miss our room, the pictures on the wall, and the trees
outside. Next Christmas it would be five years since her first
admission to hospital, and it was precisely two years ago that
she had taken her overdose. Now she no longer had any suicidal thoughts, but it had been a long journey.

In Lydia's rushed decision there seemed to be an indication of her
fear of missing her chance to finally separate from me if she did not
go with her boyfriend. The summer break had apparently reactivated all her major anxieties, fear of dependency, hatred of my
freedom, resentment of my control over her—all had conspired to
make her run away. However, in spite of her acting out during the
break, Lydia seemed more able to think about her self-destructive
behaviour, and she expected me to confront her. Whereas, in the
session before the summer which I quoted before, she did not
know whether there was a thief or whether it was only a mistake
and she felt very persecuted; here she recognized that she was the
thief and seemed relieved when I spelt it out. At this point, Lydia

knew that she was robbing herself of something valuable—her therapy—which meant the possibility of acquiring a better understanding of herself and of finding her own identity, instead of stealing it from others.

I had the impression that more depressive and less persecutory feelings were aroused, and that Lydia now regretted her decision to leave. However, I felt that there were also some positive aspects in her wish to move out of our dyadic relationship and to want to fully live the experience of being in a relationship with a man. These more positive feelings increased as the date of Lydia's departure approached. On one occasion, she said movingly that perhaps if she had not been in therapy she might have been dead by now. She thoughtfully recollected the history of her life—of the onset of her eating difficulties, her father's leaving, her overdose—and ended up by saying that she still did not know why all this had occurred to her, perhaps in these words expressing a wish what might happen, if not now, then in the future.

In thinking about Lydia's eating disorders it is very interesting to note that, together with the lessening of her defences against emotional pain and with the beginning of a capacity to think, Lydia's eating problems had not only considerably improved, but she could also be more open about them. On one occasion, after saying that she had completely stopped making herself sick and that she could now eat in front of other people, Lydia said that one thing that reminded her of her problems was her disgust of any woman with a big belly, and that she would avoid having one herself at all cost. When I made a link between her feeling uncomfortable and pregnant women, Lydia agreed and said that she was disgusted by the sight of a pregnant girl at work and recalled that her mother often said to her daughters that she blamed them if now her stomach was no longer flat. Lydia was not prepared to think further about these problematic aspects, which might have thrown some light on her anxieties about sexuality or her hatred and disgust of the parental couple's creativity. Not for the first time I had to acknowledge the limits that non-intensive treatment impose on analytic work with such disturbed and needy patients, only hoping that in the future Lydia would be more ready to do deeper work.

Ending Lydia's therapy

Lydia was very reluctant to think beyond her trip, but sometimes she could not prevent herself. She would have to come back in a year's time, and then? In her more reflective moments, when she was not delusionally convinced that her experience abroad would change her into another person, free of any problems, Lydia had painfully to admit that she had no ideas about what she would do with her life. Sometimes she would say that she felt as if there was nothing and nobody to come back to, which revealed her painful sense of having no roots and no good experience to return to.

I have already underlined the importance, in the light of Lydia's lack of identity, that shoes seemed to have for her. Lydia too seemed unconsciously aware of this connection. I was always struck by the fact that Lydia always seemed to be wearing new shoes, but in the last months of her therapy I noticed that she wore the same shoes, comfortable trainers. In one of her last sessions, she told me that she envied her friends who appeared to be happy about their choices in life. She, on the contrary, could not wait to finally leave her job in the shoe shop. Lydia was no longer so interested in shoes as she had been in the past, when she had continued to buy one pair after another. She had cried when her mother had made her take thirty-six pairs of her old shoes to Oxfam. When I connected her frustration for not finding the right pair of shoes for herself with her sense of not knowing where to go, Lydia yawned, as she usually did when she did not like what I had said. She then said that the shoes she bought hurt her easily and that her feet were covered in cuts and bruises. I commented that it was painful not to find her own way of walking through life, and to have to discard her old shoes because they did not fit, but that it was also distressing to have to think about it. Lydia agreed: she did not want to have to continue to think—she had done too much, and now she wanted to go and discover things for herself. I was very struck by the discarded pairs of shoes. They looked very similar to Fabien's discarded clothes, which he left in a heap on the floor when he took over another person's identity. Later on in the same session, Lydia very unusually recalled a dream, in which a colleague of hers was photocopying a book he had written about the war and was filing it away in boxes. I said that there seemed to be a wish to file away her own story, which she saw as full of fights, dangers, and pain, like the cuts and bruises on her feet. She did not want to lose it, and I should keep it here for her. Lydia agreed: she did not want to lose what was a part of herself, but nor did she want to come back and find everything as it was.

As her dream shows, Lydia was now more able to reflect on herself, on how she would be, and on what she would find on her return, a very different emotional state from her jumping into new shoes and new identities thoughtlessly. Lydia was very pleased that she had continued to come until the end, and I felt that she was right to be pleased, because she had to tolerate both great doubts and uncertainties about her year ahead and pain at saying goodbye to me now that a much better relationship had developed between us. Lydia oscillated between the fear of still needing help when she came back—an almost unbearable thought—and the hope that, if she did, I would still be here for her.

CHAPTER FIVE

"I didn't want to die, but I had to": the pervasive refusal syndrome

Jeanne Magagna

E maciated, eyes closed to every object or person, she lay on the hospital bed. She refused food and drink and seemed not to notice urine trickling out of her. With her straight dark hair and smooth oval Modigliani face, she looked like a porcelain doll. She was motionless throughout the day and night. When after some time she began to respond, she treated any nurse's touch or word like a mosquito creating a stinging irritation. She looked as though the umbilical cord that held her in life had been broken. There seemed to be no emotional point to her existence.

Diagnosis

Yufang was admitted into hospital in a coma. Her right lung had collapsed completely, her kidneys had stopped functioning, and she needed dextrose transfusions because of hypoglycemia. She was being fed by nasogastric tube and was diagnosed as in a state of depressive stupor. Initially the doctors treated her with psychotropic drugs. When those drugs failed, the psychiatrists decided to give her a series of bilateral electroshock treatments (ECT). I offered to see her, but the consultant said that my time was far too valuable to spend it on her. It seemed that she was slowly dying because of a loss of a wish to live. I was outraged by the doctors' choice of ECT. The ECT would awaken her thought processes, and before her phantasies became restructured, she might appear lively again, even though at a deeper level her internal world would probably not have improved in its capacity to bear distress. After six ECT treatments, the consultant psychiatrist agreed to allow me to see Yufang for supportive help. If she had not improved within six weeks, ECT would be re-administered.

Work with pervasive refusal syndrome

I shall now describe how this child suffered from what the Mildred Creak Eating Disorders Team at Great Ormond Street Hospital have described as "pervasive refusal syndrome", and how she was helped within a paediatric inpatient setting to regain hope to live. Pervasive refusal syndrome is an extreme example of the profound helplessness and hopelessness that underlies many severe eating disorders. It can mask various pathologies, including psychotic depression, anorexia nervosa, and related problems. The treatment illustrated involves work in the transference and use of the countertransference. Attention is paid to the total contextual milieu, and to the mechanisms of splitting and projection, which may involve the therapist herself, staff, child, and family. The therapeutic work involves family therapy, parental counselling, and cooperation of the teaching staff, paediatric nursing staff, and the mother as therapeutic agents working alongside the individual therapist. The chapter also illustrates the powerful impact on the environment of a profoundly ill girl in a near catatonic state, depressive stupor, or a profound Spitzian "conservation withdrawal reaction" (Spitz, 1965). This state provoked the initial reaction in medical and nursing staff to provide medication and ECT. Trust in my work as a psychoanalytic psychotherapist within the Kleinian tradition only gradually developed.

Presentation

Yufang is a 17-year-old girl, the middle one of three children from a middle-class Chinese family, who had recently moved to London from China. She had passed music exams in China and had been accepted for admission to a prestigious London music academy, where she would be studying the cello. Her older brother, aged 19, had been left behind in China, where he was studying engineering. Her younger sister, aged 11, was attending a local fee-paying school. Her father worked full-time as a successful businessman, and Mother had been a housewife for most of her adult life. Yufang was referred to our hospital for admission three months after her family arrived in England. Neither Yufang nor her mother or sister spoke English very well, and for this reason Yufang had been studying English during the first three months in this country. Because of the linguistic difficulties and Yufang's mental state, it was very difficult to know whether or not she understood what was being said to her. A Chinese psychiatrist was asked to see her. He said that she had a lack of self-worth, suicidal ideation, and a strong sense of having done something wrong. She had a psychotic depression. Within the first month of treatment, subsequent to the administration of psychotropic drugs, her condition worsened. She stopped eating, drinking, walking, and going to the toilet. It was necessary to tube-feed her nasogastrically. By the end of this early stage of her admission, she was completely mute, lying motionless in bed. Yufang was so pale and lifeless she seemed nearly dead.

History of the presenting illness

There has never been a very adequate family history. The family lived with Yufang's maternal grandmother, to whom she was very close. Yufang's mother was depressed during her early childhood. Father had left the family home to work in Russia for twenty months just before the family moved to this country. It was felt that perhaps Yufang's grandmother would have a more detailed picture of Yufang's development history than her parents did. Yufang was very close to her grandmother. Developmental milestones were apparently normal. The parents described Yufang as being hardworking and popular, with a wide circle of friends. She was very successful with her music and exams. She was friendly with both her younger sister and older brother. Her brother had been very ill with diabetes throughout his life, and this had absorbed much of the mother's anxiety and attention. While in the English-language school, Yufang met a Spanish boy with whom she became friendly. Both he and her parents made separate trips by air just at the time Yufang's illness began. The Spanish boy returned to Madrid, whereas Yufang's parents were just away for the week-end.

While the parents were away from the house, Yufang imagined she heard her father's voice saying, "I have had an accident." Around the same time, Yufang complained that the doll she kept on her bed had eyes that haunted her and she was afraid of it. She was afraid to go to sleep for fear of being attacked by it. She wrote notes to herself saying that she was stupid and selfish. It was at this time that she stopped eating and drinking and her body developed a waxy "flexibilitas", which meant that she tended to stay in the same position her mother put her in for long periods of time. The staff were aware that twelve days after the ECT, as before ECT, Yufang did not open her eyes to even look at anyone and she didn't speak at all. When I suggested that I, a psychoanalytic psychotherapist, see her for six days a week for supportive psychotherapy, they felt that I was simply offering to pester a very ill girl. This was linked with the notion popular in current British psychiatry that psycho-analytic psychotherapy should be given only after a child regains her normal weight, for it disturbs "very ill" or severely depressed patients rather than helping them. The current child-psychiatry texts also refer to psychoanalytic psychotherapy as being suitable mainly for children who have the capacity to express themselves verbally, use symbolic thought, and do not have too much difficulty in forming interpersonal relationships (Graham, 1986). Yufang had her eyes closed, did not speak, barely spoke English if she spoke at all and certainly did not show a wish for a personal relationship. I was having to struggle to convince the professional network that psychoanalytic psychotherapy provides a way of understanding such a child's virtually wordless communication.

Milieu treatment

I became involved four weeks after Yufang was admitted to hospital, a time when all medication had stopped and when ECT treatment failed. She had been referred to an adolescent psychiatric inpatient unit, but there was no vacancy there for four months. I visited the paediatric unit daily, physically helping Yufang to hobble into the charge nurse's office on the ward for half an hour. I then walked her back to her bed on the paediatric unit. Later in the day, I would meet to discuss her case with the nurses. They felt totally bewildered by a patient whom they experienced as unresponsive and, most of the time, hostile to any gesture of concern or practical care that they offered to her. I encouraged the nurses to play soothing music or read picture stories to Yufang. I suggested that I was not really indicating that they were to do something strange. I reminded them of the fact that a mother generally spends twelve months with her young baby speaking without expecting that the baby respond to the mother through speaking. I warned them that their task would be difficult if they expected a response from Yufang, and I suggested that they imagine themselves to be nurturing her with their thoughts and words until she developed sufficient hope again to respond to people. I encouraged the nurses to talk with her about themselves and to comment on how they thought she was feeling towards them. I gave them examples of how they might comment on how she was moving towards them with a glance or moving away from them with a flinch. They were encouraged to use their intuition to describe the different meanings of her moving towards them or pulling away from them. For example, they might say "you are looking at me, trying to find out just what kind of person I am", or "I seem to be frightening you", or "I seem to be making you annoyed with me".

In these early days, the focus of the nurses' comments was on how they were being perceived and experienced by the patient. I also showed the nurses ways of trying to have a dialogue with Yufang, using her nonverbal responses as the base of their next comment. For example, "I've brought some books for you." Noticing her immobility the nurse would say "You don't seem to feel they're of any interest to you", or, "I'd like to read you a little bit of the story", or, "You seem to like my talking to you." The nurses appeared to feel challenged by this idea of relating to Yufang as a mother would to a young infant, interpreting the child's nonverbal communications. I met with them daily to discuss how their conversations with Yufang were going. The nurses often felt rejected by Yufang, and they were inclined to see so much time spent on trying to communicate as a waste. This non-responsiveness was, I countered, a protection against disappointment. If the world didn't matter, she could never feel disappointed. I asked them to bear in mind that they were feeling disappointed but that it should not lead them into feeling that they were useless in their attempt to foster her wish to be alive. I reminded them that a child can receive their concern without showing if she has accepted it or felt it to be helpful. I shared with the nurses my sense that we were working towards understanding Yufang and had no reason to believe that she would not gradually respond. I held out hope for a better relationship with her in the future.

Parents' roles

Initially, Yufang's lifelessness was directly and urgently linked with her starvation and emaciated life-threatening state. She would not lift a cup to her mouth or even open her mouth. Yufang initially rejected her mother, who also appeared very depressed. With the help of the nurses, I encouraged mother to persist and bring Chinese soup and other liquids, and later feed her Chinese food with chopsticks. After two weeks, nasogastric feeding became unnecessary because mother was so gentle and naturally persistent in feeding Yufang tiny amounts, responding to her rejection, but then trying again with comforting words. In the absence of a psychiatric nurse on a busy paediatric unit, Yufang's mother, with our continuing support, stayed with her from morning to night, often lying in bed alongside her. Mother spoke virtually no English and talked to Yufang in Chinese. She seemed gentle, very timid, depressed, and anxious about her daughter. The father was a competent, successful businessman who dominated the household with his forceful style of organizing family life. He was easily angered if the family members did not obey his orders regarding the way in which they should live. The family was easily intimidated by his loud controlling manner. He remained a solid, not too worried person, who cooperated by giving detailed reports of how he saw Yufang's progress.

Creating a therapeutic space in which to work

As I reflected on this first period of Yufang's hospitalization, I began questioning my aims as a psychotherapist. Why is it that I felt so determined to rescue Yufang? Perhaps I had projected all my violent phantasies into the ECT, so that it seemed to be torture and mutilation of the mind. I was struck by the readiness with which I got angry with the two psychiatrists recommending ECT. It seemed to bring me such psychological relief to locate the violence in them aimed at the ill, dying patient. But for Yufang and in reality, I was still a part of the same clinic team, partnered with the family therapist and psychiatrist managing the treatment. When Yufang met me, she rubbed her hands, looked at the black-and-blue marks on them and fostered my temptation to become cocooned with her against the hostile external world that had given her pre-treatment medication marks linked with the ECT. In this frame of mind, I became too protective, too maternal. The tone of my voice was too soothing. It lacked sufficient strength and thoughtfulness. In order to find the appropriate therapeutic space, it was necessary for me to acknowledge that I had been part of the therapeutic team that had permitted ECT to take place. I also had to accept that I could not evade my disquiet and guilt by evacuating it into external figures. I knew that it was essential to be linked with the psychiatrists, in order to maintain a therapeutic space for thinking about the team and family dynamics surrounding Yufang's individual therapy. The continuation of the therapy and development of my strength and insight as a therapist were dependent on reintegrating my projections.

As the weeks passed, the nurses and I became aware of how much we expected some response from Yufang. Each day I listened to the nurses and shared comments relating to the slightest responsiveness from her. "She looked interested in the music." "She cried." "She looked at me today!" When there were days without much of a response, when Yufang simply lay in bed not wanting to move, it was easy to feel irritation or even anger with her for "not trying". During the third week of her hospitalization, Yufang's music teacher expected her to sit with the cello between her legs. When he was disappointed with her failure to try, he immediately became a persecutory figure from whom she turned away. The cello became a bad object, although she had loved music since she began playing at the age of 5.

Our task as a team was to create a therapeutic space for thinking about how Yufang felt in her relationships with us each day. We could offer music, stories, and conversation and think about how she responded, but if we began to expect a response from her, she perceived us as horrible demanding figures. This had repercussions in the countertransference. Yufang's withdrawn state could leave us feeling hurt and deprived by her! Yufang's role as patient was in danger of being compressed into the gratification of our need to feel helpful and not destructive in our roles as nurses and therapist. We felt frustrated and impotent. There was a phase when all our comments seemed to be imbued with a sense of superiority, barely perceptible, but present, as we professionals searched for weaknesses in the family. A tone of blame and irritation in our comments about the family concealed the team's annoyance with each other's differing points of view. Our comments included many hypotheses about the damage done to Yufang by her family.

Present in the team seemed to be a thwarted wish to be angry with someone: the father, the family, the doctor, the referring psychiatrist. The theme of "who is to blame" seemed to permeate the team's informal discussions. Scorn was barely concealed—Why had the doctor let things go for so long? Why did he let her get so emaciated before referring her? Why did he pump her with chlorpromazine, whose side-effect made her even more stuporous? This attempt to place blame somewhere was shared by the family. They were impatient with our lack of progress and lack of certainty about a healthy future for Yufang. Why hadn't we given her the right medication? We didn't seem to be making her better—rather, we were hurting her and she was beginning to cry! To make very critical remarks among ourselves and about each other seemed an easy, common outlet for our ignorance and impotence—something shared by the treatment team and the family. Blaming also hid, however, the need to accept our inability to quickly relieve the despair in Yufang. Blaming also interfered with the more free exploration of the dynamics. These could only be understood, not through textbooks but through patient curiosity, as well as through understanding the complex interactions involving loving and hating feelings in Yufang, the family, and the team.

In retrospect, I realized that blaming the family was preventing us from looking at the hostility present within Yufang and her family. The professional network was in fact unwittingly re-enacting an unconscious process, not yet understood, within the family dynamics (Britton, 1981). It was more difficult to create with the family a "containing framework" for bearing paranoid anxieties and living with Yufang's despair inside us. Blaming exempted us from sustaining the painful hope that if we could nurture Yufang with our understanding of her feelings, she might be drawn to life, to a figure who understands and provides hope for life.

The family met weekly with a child psychotherapist to assist in the task of supporting Yufang and managing the situations that might interfere with or support her progress. When Yufang was able to sit in a chair, she joined the family meetings, even though she was mute and withdrawn. During these sessions the family members shared their worries about Yufang. The family tried to understand Yufang better and find ways of supporting each other during this family crisis. They also talked about the deep sense of loss of their home and Chinese culture. Customs, housing, and food was so different in China. They described how they also worried about the life of their oldest boy, aged 19, who suffered from a severe diabetic condition. The loss of the maternal grandmother was discussed in great detail. The entire family was sad about separation from all that was familiar and a source of happiness in their lives.

Yufang was the extreme version of the family's reluctance to take in, feel, and accept the sadness and resentment about separation from all things loved and familiar. The family had lived apart from the father for eighteen months and had little control over the father's decision to come to London. The business had dictated the move. Each family member had to accept passively the transition to London in order not to lose the father on a more permanent basis. They were unable to take into account the adverse emotional aspects of moving to London without the English language to smooth their entry. Work with the family helped contain their anxieties; they became more able to allow themselves to own their own sad and conflictual feelings previously projected into Yufang, and to support Yufang in her individual therapy. It is a matter of great controversy, but, as demonstrated in Yufang's case, it is essential in my opinion that individual therapy for any severely ill child is accompanied by family work or parental counselling.

Individual therapy
and accompanying therapeutic work

I think that any child—whether speaking or non-speaking, psychotic, borderline or neurotic, intelligent or not very intelligent— should be considered a suitable candidate for psychotherapy at any stage of his or her illness, as long as there is the appropriate inpatient or outpatient network of professionals and parents who jointly support the treatment effort. Two significant issues are the choice of therapist and the modification of technique.

I viewed my task in working with Yufang as similar in some respects to that of the parents and other members of the therapeutic team. I needed to be attuned to the emotional experience of being with Yufang in the present in the session in order to give meaning to her communications. This is a task similar to the parents of a small child using their own emotional experience, coupled with their thinking, to make sense of the child's projections of physical and emotional states. Confusion and lack of integration in Yufang could be linked with a mismatch in communication in her primary experience with her parents. For this reason she needed me to consider her primitive experiences, including sensations and the movement or stillness of her body, before she could put these experiences into a symbolic form for communication. An integration of her body and psychological self could then occur. Deep inside, Yufang was hungry for understanding, even though initially she could not eat, talk, or even open her eyes.

I would like now to describe some particularly difficult aspects of my dialogue with Yufang, using her non-verbalized cues as a focus for my communication with her. I used my countertransference responses as the basis of a dialogue with her feelings that

could not be verbalized. I sensed that initially she had little awareness of many fragmented parts of her personality, which were
isolated, lonely, and out of communication with everyone including herself. Following the technique recommended by Herbert
Rosenfeld (1987b), I met with her for half-hour periods six days per
week. I saw her for four months in a nurse's office in the paediatric
inpatient unit. As an illustration of how I worked with Yufang, I
shall draw on sequential selections from our sessions during the
treatment. As I joined with the hospital team, supporting the
nurses and talking with the psychiatrists, I was able to share many
feelings with them. For long periods of time, both the nurses and I
felt continually rejected when Yufang remained mute, immobile,
with an incredibly sad, vacant look on her face. It was difficult to
bear Yufang's rejection of our offers of help, and this made us feel
useless or annoying. The following session is from the second week
of Yufang's treatment and is typical of the early sessions:

> Yufang holds onto my arm to come to the room. She can barely
> walk. She sits down and keeps her eyes closed. She hears the
> sound of the ventilator. She looks frightened. Opening her eyes
> she searches for the door. I say she does not like the sounds in
> the room. She would like to get out. She does not like me
> speaking. When I look at her briefly, she looks into my eyes for
> a second. As she glances down again she struggles to mouth the
> word, "go". I speak for her with a tone of being in a frightened
> state, saying "Let me go. I don't want to be here." Yufang
> hesitantly nods in agreement. I talk about how she is so uncer-
> tain about what any sound means. She isn't certain if I can be
> trusted to keep her safe here in the room. Yufang seemed to feel
> claustrophobic in a hostile world. She was not only disturbed
> by the sound of the ventilator. She wanted to get out of my
> room, out of my presence.

Yufang at times viewed me as a dangerous enemy threatening
to break the protective shell of non-feeling, of depersonalization, of
unintegration, which shielded her from acknowledging what she
experienced. However, for a moment she was able to meet me with
fleeting acknowledgement that I understood how frightened she
felt. Yufang seemed in "a shell", like children Spitz (1965) de-

scribed, or like Jewish refugee orphans who, having no emotional link with someone, gave themselves up to death. Being invited into the therapy-room seemed to intensify danger for her. Yufang viewed me as a dangerous enemy, threatening to break through her "shell" protecting her against alive feelings.

It was nine months later that Yufang let me know that there was a malevolent force condemning her to starvation and death. This sense of being a passive victim of imposed cruelty is a main problem in girls with severe eating difficulties. Yufang described her initial experiences: "When I was ill I had to starve myself. I had to die. I didn't want to die but I had to. I starved and became unconscious. I felt I was dead." She added, "When I was ill, I could not look in a mirror. I could not look in a mirror because I did not know who I saw. I could not see myself. I saw another girl. I thought I was someone else. I felt I was a girl (a friend), who had difficulties with her parents. I felt strange when I couldn't see myself in the mirror. I worried about other children looking at me, because I was afraid that they could see through me." In these descriptions, Yufang suggested that she had lost a sense of her *self*. She did not feel her ordinary self, but was depersonalized. She felt she was a passive victim of a malevolent force which she did not experience as part of herself. This split-off destructive part of her personality dictated how she must treat her *self*. Most significantly, Yufang said, "I didn't *want* to die, but I *had to*."

Helplessness

It has been pointed out that a sense of helplessness (Garber & Seligman, 1980) leads to a picture characteristic of post-traumatic stress disorder (PTSD). The features illustrated include numbing of responsiveness, reduced involvement with the external world, pervasively diminished interest in the normal activities of daily life, and severely constricted emotions. Those were followed by exaggerated startle responses. These symptoms, shared by PTSD patients, brought the team to assume with virtual certainty that such a global avoidant response must certainly be linked with a traumatic event such as physical or sexual abuse or else the witnessing of threats and violence at home. In this context, it was very difficult to maintain a psychoanalytic stance and be open to Yufang having experiences that were different from those of a helpless, frightened child. Ken Nunn's work (Nunn & Thompson, 1996) suggests a more complicated understanding of pervasive refusal. He maintains that separation anxiety is a prominent feature. This is accompanied by social withdrawal and depression. The patient feels, and may be actually experiencing, that it is impossible to control situations relating to health, safety, and happiness within the family. He suggests that hopelessness occurs in these situations and prompts the emergence of the pervasive refusal syndrome in certain children. As the team was so influenced by those ways of interpreting the pervasive refusal syndrome, it was very difficult to maintain a psychoanalytic stance, as I said before, to just use my countertransference in order to find the understanding of clues to Yufang's unique experiences.

Denial of destructiveness

It was difficult to imagine or notice Yufang having any destructive, jealous, contemptuous, omnipotent impulses that could contribute to the causation or perpetuation of her depression. Intellectually, I was aware that it was impossible to facilitate Yufang's development without ridding myself of the notion of her being a "helpless victim of hostile external events". I knew that I needed to experience *all of her*; yet even when the supervisor suggested to me that Yufang's giggle might be contemptuous, I still found it difficult to accept. Yufang's central psychic defence was a massive denial of conflictual feelings, projection of aggression, and fear of real or phantasied persecution from the external world. How could I *dare even think* that she had some destructiveness in her? If so, would it be cruel and damaging to talk about it? There was also a deeper task, which was to recognize that both in her and in me there might be personal responsibility for evoking these responses of contempt. It was difficult as a therapist to see contempt in Yufang's giggle, but even more difficult to realize that I might have provoked a contemptuous reaction to my words. For example, my being repetitive in my interpretations, without much depth of feeling, could provoke disdain for the meaning of what I was saying.

Silence as deprivation

There are other points that I would like to refer to when talking about this phase of the work. I did not think it was helpful for Yufang to come into the room and sit in a motionless, severely depressed silence for more than five to ten minutes. My impression was that if I did stay silent, she felt I had invited her to be in a room to be deprived by me, deprived of my attempts to nurture her through sharing my thoughts and feelings with her. At other times there was between Yufang and me a prevailing desire for a static space devoid of feelings, because feelings were so disturbing to her. It was sometimes very tempting to succumb to her feeling of dictating that no life should exist. Members of the hospital staff had tried asking questions but Yufang had remained mute most of the time. My own questions would feel intrusive and demanding if I did not balance them with descriptions of my thoughts about Yufang's experience.

What seemed most important was my talking about Yufang's experience in the room and generating in her an interest in her emotional life. I tried to identify with Yufang, using her physical posture, glance of her eye, expression of her mouth and hands, to describe what she was feeling. At times I spoke as though I was Yufang talking. I might at some point describe things as I would to a very young child, such as describing what Yufang had been doing during the day. Then I would think in more detail about the experiences that Yufang had. She lacked capacity to observe herself, but observations were provided by the staff's daily descriptions of her day. These observations were simply part of "the setting" provided each day for Yufang.

Meanwhile, the focus of my thinking was on the developing relationship at that moment between "the-little-child" in Yufang and me. I described a mood that I felt in the room on each given day. I would comment on how she greeted me when I met her. Each nonverbal response she made or did not make became a possible opportunity for dialogue. For example, I would say: "You looked up when I came into the room. You have been looking into my eyes, listening with interest some of the time I have been speaking. Now, when you are leaving, I know you can nod good-bye, but you have chosen not to." Yufang giggled when I said this.

I then said, "You giggled as though you agreed that you could have nodded goodbye. Perhaps I should feel the neglected one."

My aim was to meet Yufang's most immediate emotions present in the therapy. This involved "listening to her mood" as one listens to music. As she remained immobile, I had to allow her mood to enter me and then name it. My idea was that internal change in Yufang could best be facilitated through comments that met her immediate feelings and her anxiety in the room. When Yufang became "verbal", I would rely on her to talk about whatever was on her mind, as I would with any other patients. In the initial phase, however, Yufang was lifeless, mute, and as there was no conversation it seemed necessary to help her gather her *self* together "to be present" in the room. My words were vital to evoke her apparently disintegrated emotional and mental functioning.

Using dolls for stories of
the patient's family and experiences

I sometimes brought out a set of dolls and told Yufang about her family and herself. I would tell her about anything I knew about her day in the hospital, her background. For example, I used the dolls to dramatize the story of how Yufang's mother came to visit her daughter and how for a moment they greeted each other, looking at one another. Initially, I told the story in the third person, more emotionally distant, sitting slightly to the side of Yufang. I was deliberately leaving her free to ignore all that I was saying. I then said that if Yufang touched one of the family dolls that she wanted me to think about, I would say something about that person, telling her about what I knew about that member of the family. Sometimes I used toy animals to tell stories about her life on the ward. I talked about the frightened rabbit, closing her eyes, wanting to run away from everyone and everything that touched her heart.

Later, however, I spoke more directly to Yufang—for example, when she touched the father doll, I said that she seemed very frightened of her father. I would describe how her father seemed to dominate the family. Sometimes he became very angry, and she didn't know what to do then. She was quiet and then cried silently. At another time when she touched the mother doll I said her mother also seemed sad; she too seemed frightened of father and needed to obey him. On another occasion, I used the dolls to show the whole family crying. I said that Yufang's parents, particularly her mother, were sad about being in this new country, sad to have left Yufang's brother behind in China. I described her needing the protection of her mother in hospital and how she had begun to accept it. I did not ask many questions.

Within this framework of enacting family issues through play, I was able to comment on my sense of our transference relationship, a confusing experience in which Yufang both distrusted me as a frightening figure and depended on me as a nurturing figure, one who tried to understand her experiences, working through her conflicts related to me, as well as to family and staff. Part of the success of this therapy was reliant on our very frequent meetings allowing us to keep the scattered shifting views of me and others in mind within a steady caring context.

Thoughts about the patient's transference relationship to the therapist

The work described is only partly a talking cure, for that which cannot be spoken or conceptualized by the patient can nevertheless be conveyed emotionally and physically to the therapist. As well as describing shared, obvious, external family issues such as the loss of grandmother, brother, and homeland and the frightening anger of father and sadness of mother, I focused much of my effort on understanding Yufang's present emotional experience with me in the session. The following sessions illustrate how I observed an attempted to use Yufang's non-verbal movements to elucidate her relationship to the internal parental figures as represented by me in the transference relationship. It was through a detailed experience of the transference that I was able to grasp Yufang's relationships to internal parents and siblings. This enabled me to comprehend some of the factors contributing to her depression and pervasive refusal to eat and live.

Illustrations from sessions

The following session excerpts of selected experiences illustrate
how I worked with Yufang; some comments are also given on my
technique and interpretations.

From a second-week session

Yufang is silent. She is picking away at the skin of her thumb in a
very aggressive way. She looks at me attentively, not moving any
part of her body. In the following session, she is sobbing with a
tremendous flickering of her eyelids; it feels like a convulsion of
sadness erupting from her.

A fifth-week session

Yufang sways precariously from foot to foot as she wanders to the
session. She cannot seem to find her balance and appears like a
toddler beginning to walk. I know she is not under the effect of
drugs, but her giggling makes it look as if she is. She tells me she
has a dream about her brother and then begins sobbing with a
pained grimace. She doesn't speak, but she is reluctant to leave. In
a session later that week she says "brother dead", "must die"
(implying, I think, she must die because she killed her brother).

A sixth-week session

Yufang spends the whole week with a pain in her leg, with no
apparent underlying physical difficulty. When I talk about the
pain, her whole face moves from being expressionless to being
contorted with pain, with her eyelids flickering rapidly as she cries.
Her nose is also dripping. As usual she makes no effort to wipe her
nose or her face, covered in tears. She bites her lip, then turns
towards me, opens her mouth and then turns away. When it is time
to go, she hangs onto me, not wanting to separate when I leave her
at her bedside. One day after this session, Yufang played the cello
for the first time since she became ill. She played monotonously for

five continuous hours, without her usual skill. The music seemed to be a way of dealing with the discordant emerging feelings of separation from me, but Yufang could not bear to tear herself away from the cello either.

A seventh-week session

Yufang arrives looking cheerful. She doesn't speak. She appears bored and yawns while I am talking to her. She appears to be completely out of touch with being in the room with me. She inaudibly mouths some words, yawns, going blank. She moves her lips again and begins to cough. She coughs several times. When she leaves, she acts as though she is falling back-wards. When I put my arm out to stop her, she leans back as though she is going to fall over. After this session, Yufang virtu-ally stopped drinking and eating for four days. She also stopped talking for four days.

Comments on the second to seventh week

During this time when Yufang picked her finger, I commented that she was punishing herself or someone, in her mind, perhaps me. Later when her fingers were very red from her picking them, she would insist that she was not picking. She did not want to accept any responsibility for any destructive impulses and cat-egorically denied them. During the fifth week, her sobbing seemed to be related to comments about her brother, to whom she had been close. (Her new Spanish friend at the language school may have been an internal substitute for her brother, whose permanent de-parture may have precipitated her breakdown into her psychotic depression.) He had remained in China. He had also been ex-tremely close to mother, who was always anxious about the seri-ousness of his diabetes. His remaining in China caused Yufang to sob with an overwhelming sense of loss of an important relation-ship. However, Yufang's own wish to possess mother more com-pletely for herself and push her brother out of the way made her feel guilty. She felt that her jealousy of her brother's closeness with her mother had killed him. Her punishment was that she should die in identification with the "dead internal brother".

At other times, the crying seemed to contain a multitude of feelings that had found a primitive form of expression; crying gave expression to a cluster of undifferentiated emotions. I felt I was to be present to *simply experience* and *contain within myself* this flow of feeling emanating from Yufang. By the fifth week, Yufang seemed to be walking in a way that created anxiety that she would fall. Her reluctance to leave the session suggested to me that she now felt she had become attached to the "thinking space" with me and that being out of the sessions and leaving the sessions left her feeling "dropped" by me. I wondered if her leg pains were linked with her anger with me about parting which got directed to her own body. She attacked my legs walking away from her and identified with me and my damaged legs. I postulated that her attack on her relationship with me was directed to her own body, first her thumb picking, now the pains in her leg, and later her chest and heart hurting when we parted for the Christmas break. Yufang's growing dependence on me aroused a protective, distrustful part of her opposed to talking with me, so she bit the lip that had been trying to talk with me. These non-verbal behaviours around our parting suggest a split in her developing transference relationship. By the sixth week, she hangs on to me, not wanting to separate at all lest she begin to fragment and fall apart entirely.

Subsequently, Yufang struggles with two different physical/emotional responses: on the one hand she keeps coughing as though trying to rid herself of some noxious "substances or experiences" inside herself, while on the other, she moves into a state of obvious boredom, going blank, yawning. As she becomes more able to use me as a "refuse dump" for "her unpleasant physical/emotional" experiences, she has to struggle with this part of herself that runs away from distress through going blank, yawning, cutting off the sound of her words. There seems to be an increase in the force within her against sharing her experiences and thinking about them with me. At the end of the seventh week, Yufang acts as though she will simply collapse. Occasionally she falls down in the corridor. Now, at times, this falling seems to be a dramatization of Yufang's feelings. She is no longer feeling completely helpless. The falling is a dramatization of how the child in her feels dropped if I do not hold her in my mind all the time. If I don't, she falls down again and again. If she begins to depend on me, the dependence feels so limitless that it affects both her body and her mind.

An eighth-week session

It is the last session before the Christmas holidays. Yufang does not speak. She yawns but seems to be in a manic, excited state. After she has given me a wrapped present of a little tin of cherry tea, I talk, as many times before, about my Christmas break, which will last for ten days. Immediately, Yufang seems to see something dancing before her eyes. She begins to giggle. I feel that she is in a dizzy, confused state. Later she turns to me and makes some very ugly smiling-monster faces, three or four times, and then laughs. They are shockingly frightening and grotesque faces. When I take out the family dolls and describe how she will be going home for a few hours during the holiday, she says, "My mother is a very, very good cook", adding, "I like my mother's food." When I put the dolls back into their container, she comments for the first time on how the dolls are being flattened. Later in the day, the doctors are called to investigate her severe chest pains, but these have no physical basis. When the doctors examine Yufang, she becomes sexually excited and temporarily manic. I feel she is again dramatically feeling, in her body, her emotional experience of being flattened by my departure, my putting her away.

Comments on the eighth-week session

I described to Yufang how she was telling me how she conveyed the thought of separation from me by describing a picture in the room of dancing, happy figures looking down in a very cruel way at the "child-Yufang". She identified with these cruel figures, imitating their faces, while I was to be the terrified child left with monstrous faces. She was apparently hallucinating these faces initially. I also commented on how there existed a very good mother who made good meals for "the little girl Yufang". Alternatively, perhaps she first identified with me being away having a high, exciting fun time on holiday, but underneath she felt I was cruel and leaving her behind. Yet she also wanted to thank me at Christmas time for the moments of understanding that I had given her. I added that I thought she appreciated her mother's good meals but was using her meals to foster jealousy in me. I was to feel that her mother's good meals were far better than the meals I gave her which stopped so suddenly at Christmas time. Later I talked about how, when I went away, she felt I gave her no space for having her feelings understood by me. When we parted for a break I recalled feeling flat inside, so I said when I left maybe I left her feeling flat inside. I think that Yufang felt very hostile towards me for leaving and interpreted my leaving as squashing her flat, squashing the life out of her, as shown by her squashing the dolls back into the box. The pain in her chest/heart suggested once again that the object is attacked for being uncaring by leaving her. She identifies with the damaged object and feels heartache.

A ninth-week session

When I return from the Christmas break, Yufang cries profusely. She feels her stomach. I say I see her tears. She says, "Not crying." She is silent. After a long time she asks "What is the difference between belief and trust?" She then cries more profusely. I wonder if she can trust me enough to tell me what she is feeling. Her lip trembles with the incredible sadness and flow of tears. She mumbles some words. After a long while she says, with a hint of pleasure, that her brother is coming in the spring.

Comments

I described to Yufang how she is crying but wants the crying and sadness not to exist. I suggest that she may have been very sad while I was away. I explored how she may have had difficulty holding onto a belief that I was returning, and she didn't know whether she could trust me to have her best interests in mind, since I went away. I add that now I am to feel that I have faded into nonexistence for her, with her brother now being the hopeful person important to her at that moment.

Assisting the nurses and mother
in working therapeutically

As I worked in individual therapy with Yufang, I also was helping the nurses work through various stages of therapeutic work with her. Initially, they were talking with her about her need to find a safe place in hospital with them. They later talked about how she felt that being curled up in bed felt good but outside felt bad. Subsequently, the nurses were encouraged to comment on Yufang's interest in being with the nurse and her mother. The nurse and mother, when present, were beginning to be experienced as good figures, and Yufang was looking forward to mother and nurse being present. Nurses and mother were encouraged to tell Yufang about when they would be away and when they would be returning. They then were encouraged to describe in detail to her when she felt distressed or angry because they were late, were away, were talking to others, or had misunderstood what she experienced, or when things were sufficiently tolerable for her at that moment. If she became annoyed with silence or too much talk, this was also commented on. Mother and nurses were encouraged to speak on behalf of Yufang if they thought that her facial expression was expressing the slightest conflict or pleasure. Gradually, Yufang began speaking for herself.

An eighteenth-week session

The time came for Yufang to go to the inpatient psychiatric unit. Her medical condition had improved, and the vacancy on that unit had finally become available. Yufang and her parents, in conjunction with the consultant psychiatrist, decided at that point that she was actually well enough to be cared for at home. The decision was partially based on the fact that the psychiatrist felt that she was making good use of the individual therapy. It was decided that

Yufang would have psychotherapy three times a week and begin two cello lessons per week in order to put some structure into her time. After two weeks as an outpatient, coming to therapy three times a week, Yufang arrived wearing a new white silk blouse, looking as elegant as a woman in *Vogue* magazine. She had missed the previous session and had called me saying she thought the appointment was later and asking for another appointment that day, which I told her was impossible for me. Now she apologizes for the missed session, saying she had decided to write some thoughts in a notebook. She describes what she holds in her note-book. During the four days we have not met, she has written a haiku-style poem:

> Night, star, moon, wind
> noise, light, shine, whisper
> sound, a hint, a code
> be fragrant, silent
> warmth, asleep
> the moment of silence
> hanging on the air.

She reads the poem dramatically, one word at a time. She has also drawn a cartoon-style picture of her beloved grandmother, who is in China. The next picture is an aeroplane, and she links it with a film she had seen the day of her missed session. In the film a plane is searching for a man who has fallen near Mt. McKinley. Someone is calling out from the mountain, "Noemi, Noemi". The man dies near the foot of the mountain. On her last page of her notebook she has written:

> If I had a scoop of melon,
> the world will be all right
> If all the houses are upset
> but tree won't move other place
> Space is all round, round and round
>
> I can hear the voice from other space
> I have to do something, my mind go fast
> I broke the window
> That is mad but not mad.

There is an empty white space on the sheet, which Yufang says is a glass window. She talks about breaking through the glass window, throwing herself out of the window. She says she had wanted to do that when she was ill.

Comments

Many interpretations were possible with this rich material, but the most important focus was my emotional experience of Yufang feeling dizzy with emotions. I strove for simplicity because, with her "mind racing" with too many thoughts, it was difficult for Yufang to understand and digest too many. I described how she had missed the session, which was very unusual for her. She had felt the silence of the missed session, felt very lost. When I couldn't see her she had begun to try to find some ways of taking care of herself. She found a notebook, writing down her thoughts. I also described how terrible it felt inside when she let these feelings get too big and take her over. In saying this I was aware that she was quite confused in her "grown-woman identity"; but I felt that she had been trying to find a way of "holding herself together", and she was continuing to do so. For the moment, this was very important for such a very ill girl. At a later date I would talk with her about slipping into an identity of a "fashionable mother".

Session in the twenty-second week

Yufang arrives with a little nest holding three tiny toy bluebirds. Some feathers are scattered around the nest. She tells me she has had a dream in which *"military officers from two countries were hiding behind trees. It was midnight, the men were shooting at me. I was a boy. In the dream, I was thinking, 'What was the best way to die?' I thought fast firing by guns was better than dying slowly. There were many children with their families in the dream."* Her associations were: "In primary school there were three children who were angry with her and she didn't know why, and when she was in China she was angry with her mother."

Comments

In this session Yufang seemed to be expressing her conscious wish to preserve the babies of the mother (the toy birds in the nest). There is a hint of compassion, suggesting the development of a good, loving, and sensitive aspect of herself—necessary for reparation of the internal figure. She also seemed to be aware that there was a destructive force inside her from which "these families with children" required protection. Yufang is beginning to have a notion that she experienced anger and jealousy towards the mother with her other babies. This leads to an incredibly violent punitive guilt—represented by the military men killing her. She seems fascinated by the killing—"slow or fast killing?" she asks herself. In her therapy with me now, Yufang was starting to find an emotional space to symbolize her inner conflicts. These inner conflicts augmented the weight of any external trauma she may have experienced, contributing significantly to her state of "near-death".

* * *

The treatment continued for two years. Sadly, it was then stopped by Yufang's parents, who felt that there was no reason to continue therapy when she was so much better. She had developed more capacity to contain her feelings rather than project them and she was able to take care of the "child within her". Successful in her new cello studies at an excellent music academy, Yufang described how she loved her music and was playing with more feeling than before. With some shyness, but much pleasure, she was socializing with British and Chinese friends. Yufang still had, however, a very fragile capacity for thinking with any emotional depth about her very passionate feelings.

Further considerations regarding the treatment

There is a question of technique when faced with a child severely traumatized by internal and/or external destructive events. George E. Gray (1983), writing about his own severe depression, says, "The results of a session should be carefully assessed. If it makes the patient feel worse rather than better, further sessions should be suspended. A patient should be allowed to sit quietly in the corner for as long as he wants or needs to." I have heard quite a few psychiatrists say, "Let the patient be, don't intrude with psychotherapy. Such a severely depressed patient's ability to think and concentrate is dramatically impaired. Therapy will only make her worse." I know there is research on this subject; however, as far as my practice is concerned, I shall try to remain true to what I have learned from my own experience. I know that out of the ten pervasive refusal syndrome patients I have seen, Yufang has made the most progress, in the briefest period, in integrating with her family and peers and resuming her studies successfully.

Not separating her from parents during the illness and intensive psychotherapy seemed particularly beneficial to the patient during her inpatient admission. During her hospitalization she was encouraged to think about what she wanted to do with her time. This element of choice was important as long as it was compatible with what we felt would be good for her. She received physical and emotional "nursing" undertaken daily by her mother and a few hours of hospital schooling with other children. The paediatric nurses supported the mother and fostered her relationship with Yufang. Family therapy was concurrent during the acute phase of her illness. Yufang was seen every day for brief periods of supportive psychoanalytic psychotherapy. During the sessions, I tried to avoid creating a situation where she would be traumatized or invaded by overwhelming feelings. At the same time, I tried to delineate, provide, and open up the space for her to feel and eventually acknowledge both her good and her bad feelings and thoughts.

My desire to offer psychotherapy to subsequent patients with similar difficulties is based on Yufang's remark: "I didn't want to die, but I had to." The implication of this remark is that, regardless of whether or not there has been an external traumatizing factor, the healthy part of pervasive refusal patients is overwhelmed by the impulse to die. In this context, it seemed callous not to help Yufang struggle with the cruel forces that attacked hope and propelling her towards death. When perceived in the transference as the embodiment of the destructive tormentor (from external or internal reality), I found it extremely difficult to bear the staff's belief that I might be taking the child into the room to torment her with psychotherapy. This particularly applies when one experiences oneself as "the witch" during some of the treatment. This inevitably occurs in the countertransference because I think it is inextricably paired with this bad, painful, emerging negative transference. During this phase of the treatment, it is difficult for the therapist to maintain a belief that if Yufang walks to therapy, part of her may be experiencing relief as well as the inevitable pain that mainly derives from unfreezing and facing denied, un-nameable dreaded feelings.

When confronted with anxiety about psychotherapy being useless, I hold on for dear life to a formerly silent patient's written words: "Even if I don't talk, it doesn't mean that therapy doesn't help." I would now add that even when she did not talk, it did not mean that we were not communicating. When the child has virtually given up life or is rigidly protecting herself in silence, therapy is essential to help the child to reassemble her sense of self. My words and emotional acceptance of the nonverbal communication seemed vital to evoke and gather together Yufang's disintegrated emotional and mental life. Yufang deserved the experience of being deeply understood as well as being given gentle encouragement to participate step by step in the ordinary activities of life. The pleasure and relief in being understood created the possibility of psychological growth. Yufang's development in this regard was facilitated by various therapeutic endeavours of the team and the half-hour individual psychotherapy six times a week, and also the daily five to seven hours of mother's protective and supportive presence within the context of twenty-four-hour nursing care.

Theoretical conclusions
regarding the pervasive refusal syndrome

I have subsequently worked with nine other children, aged 9 to 19 years, who arrived in hospital not walking, talking, eating, drinking, or caring for themselves in any way. They had become unresponsive to any social stimuli and failed to indicate pain. As they became slightly better, they began to withdraw when spoken to or touched. I now work in the psychiatric inpatient unit of a paediatric hospital, Great Ormond Street Hospital for Children in London. As I said before, our team there had decided to describe this syndrome as the "pervasive refusal syndrome". A psychodynamic view of pervasive refusal syndrome involves taking into consideration the external situation of the child as well as the child's inner world. The inner world of the child is peopled by aspects of figures first loved and hated in life and also contains aspects of the child itself. These inner figures exist in phantasy and are engaged in apparently independent activities "as real, or even more real and actual to the child in his unconscious feeling than external events" (Riviere, 1955). Internal figures are not exact replicas of the external world but are always coloured by the infant's and child's phantasy and projections (Segal, 1979).

The external world of the child is affected by the pervasive refusal syndrome, characterized by separation anxiety, social withdrawal, and depression. The child has no control over the external events, and this might often incur a sense of hopelessness. Uncontrollable events may include family relocation, including migration from another culture, the loss of grandparents or other loved ones, and severe illness, often a viral illness in the child or mental illness in the parent. Abuse, as a form of inescapable trauma may be another contributory factor. These uncontrollable events may occur against a background of parental overprotectiveness but, more importantly, of parental helplessness and hopelessness. To an outside observer such as a teacher, the child may appear to be achieving both academically and socially. However, internally the child is failing to meet personal developmental expectations (Nunn & Thompson, 1996).

The external family of these children had a weak psychic structure, too weak to contain feelings of an intense nature, with a marked tendency to deny hostility in day-to-day situations. In some families this may then lead to explosions of hostility, which can take the form of parents throwing pots and pans, resorting to sleep as a flight from anxiety, sobbing uncontrollably, and relinquishing parental responsibilities. Sometimes, the denial of hostility is accompanied by hostility directed towards internal family figures. This leads to destruction and the breakdown of the child's already fragile psychic structure, coupled with depression and persecutory guilt due to the damage of the internal family figures. For example, Yufang thought that she had "killed her brother" and that her father had "died in an accident". Her dreams conveyed a feeling of the whole world destroyed by an earthquake. In this context, it is notable that, prior to the onset of their illness, the ten children whom I have seen denied conflict and were unable to express any hatred or anger directly towards their parents. In some families, this was understandable since one of the parents was feared as a potential retaliator if a family rule was broken. This fear was partly evoked by the fiery temper of one parent, but it was also linked with the projection of aggressive, hostile feelings towards one or both parents, making the parents feared figures. Lacking an inner psychic structure for dealing with the pressure of emotional stimuli driving towards them from internal and external sources, the child retreats from the external world and all stimuli emanating from it. The child is in a kind of "claustrum" (Meltzer, 1992). Some children have reported afterwards that they could gradually begin to hear and understand when in this state but were initially very confused. They said they felt that they *could not* speak, even though sentences or phrases might be forming in their mind in response to what was being said to them.

When the child ceases having any emotional link with anyone and gives him/herself up to death, not eating, talking or walking, hospitalization is then required. The separation of the child from the parents is extremely traumatic because the child lacks an "internal parental figure" for protection to help with living independent of the external parents. The child feels that it is essential to cling for dear life on to the external parents and feels deeply hurt and rejected by them when the hospital requires the parents to leave the hospital. After an initial phase of crying for the parents to stay, many children give up crying and break the loving emotional link. Although they are simply following hospital instructions to leave the child in the care of the hospital unit, the parents are perceived by the child as bad and abandoning. Nurses may approach these children, but they, like the parents, are ignored and then viewed as dangerous enemies. The children do not want, or are not able to take in, anything from them, as they have become persecutory figures containing projections of the child's violent rage. Such children often end up in hospital, and because of their frequent life-threatening physical state, they cause deep concern and confusion in the paediatric ward. Their emotional needs are often overlooked because their bodily needs are so great. Staff often overreact with either passivity, or avoidance, or impersonal invasive overactivity because of the parental denial and the urgent and confusing countertransference reactions they are experiencing. It is extremely difficult and demanding—but absolutely essential in some cases— to hold in mind the child's and the family's total emotional situation and needs and to sustain an empathic, cooperative psychological intervention. As I have mentioned, pervasive refusal syndrome represents extreme forms of the instinct of self-preservation and of passive surrender. Usually there is an underlying psychotic process, of a catatonic nature.

Characteristically of this syndrome, the child's expression of emotions takes several forms initially:

1. *Overwhelming sobbing*: This feels as though it will never end. One can experience in the child's sobbing a panic about the overwhelming nature of any intense feelings, and at times it is often linked to separation from and loss of loved ones.

2. *Identification with the aggressor*: This feels very cruel to the therapist or targets of the aggression. The child seems to take delight in hurting other children and staff. The child appears to be identified with a cruel internal mother who enjoys the suffering of the "baby". Although the child hits people or pushes them away (as they have become bad, terrifying objects), when the mother goes away, the child may still feel abandoned by someone cruel.

3. *Hallucinating a monstrous "male figure"*: This figure functions as a kind of concentration-camp prison guard. It promises protection to the child as long as the child obeys it by withdrawing from any kind of human contact. When the child attempts to eat, and therefore to depend on the nurturing figures, the hallucinatory male figure threatens punishments. This is work of the destructive part of the personality against life, hope, and dependency. The monstrous hallucinatory figure is at times turned to as a king or "companion".

The trauma that these children have experienced varies from child to child. In the present emotional climate, where sexual abuse is more prominent as a cause of disturbance, clinicians feel tempted to investigate sexual abuse as a matter of course. My own feeling is that unless the child has first re-established a trusting link with a family member or a member of the nursing staff, investigation of trauma can itself be traumatic. In the throes of a severe breakdown of the personality resulting in somatic symptoms, the child cannot bear emotionally intense issues. The first step is not to talk about the trauma, but to build a link for the child. This link will give the child the necessary protection to become reacquainted with the trauma that is at the origin of the pervasive refusal of life.

Summary of treatment
for the pervasive refusal syndrome

In individual therapy, there is often a sequence of emotional developments that occur within the child. In the most severely ill children, the child is at first almost completely immobile, as though overwhelmed by a destructive force against which the child is unable to struggle. The child's eyes are closed and the body has a kind of waxy flexibility. There is no observable response to either positive or negative stimuli. The child may be suffering from a painful physical illness such as Crohn's disease which causes extreme pain in the gut, but the crying out in pain normally accompanying an illness of this kind does not occur when the child is suffering from pervasive refusal syndrome.

When the child begins to flinch, hit out, or moan to avoid a persecutory situation, one feels that the child is regaining life sufficiently to struggle against something negative or destructive. Occasionally, the child has retreated from intimate relations with people in the external world, but there may indeed be other relationships taking place: the child may be involved in listening to or seeing hallucinatory figures.

Gradually, if the environment is sufficiently containing, the child begins looking at and listening to people but will retreat immediately if anyone notices. Subsequently the child may regain a relationship with the self when "deeply touched" emotionally. The emotional response of the child is then uncontained and overwhelming, taking the form of copious crying, uncontrolled hitting, or mania. Any "uncomfortable" experience suggesting emotional pain or conflict is followed, at times, by a massive withdrawal, sometimes through immediate sleep. In time, however, there is clear evidence of the child being able to enjoy pleasurable activities. This heralds the beginning of a possibility of intimate relationships, as long as they are relatively conflict-free. The child is usually able to draw, tell dreams, or write in a private diary before being able to discuss difficult issues with a therapist or key worker. Conversations including the child may occur if daily events that do not have too much emotional intensity are discussed. The child might make sparse replies such as "no", "yes", "good", "feeling left out". Finally, the child may be able to begin to discuss conflictual events that may have contributed to his or her difficulties. It is in this latter stage of treatment that the child can describe how paralysed around speaking and eating he or she felt initially even though able to hear what was being said.

This work is important for the understanding of severe eating disorders, for it presents an extreme version of the child's withdrawal from the intimacy of human relationships and food and drink necessary for life itself. Withdrawal into a "claustrum" away from any experience of the stimuli of food or human contact can be seen as a life-protective mechanism saving the self from further encounters with adverse emotional experiences. Such withdrawal is similar to that of the predicament of foetal development when the foetus is totally helpless, unaware of the self and of feelings. The child may sometimes comment on missing the "old experience" when all needs were met and he or she did not have to do anything.

If the therapist provides an experience that is enlivening, interesting, nurturing, and pertinent to the child's present emotional life, the child may begin to turn to the therapist and become dependent on the relationship for an understanding of his or her emotional life. The introjection of the goodness and strength of the therapist gradually will facilitate psychological growth and hope to live again in the world outside the hospital.

CHAPTER SIX

Some reflections on the processes of projection and introjection in eating disorders

Emanuela Quagliata

In conjunction with clinical work with patients suffering from severe eating disorders, I am going to discuss certain typical processes of splitting, projection, introjection, and identification leading to characteristic forms of pathological projective identification often evident in these patients. Projective identification as described by Bion (1962a) is a central aspect of normal development, contributing to healthy identity formation. Patients with eating disorders employ a pattern of projective identification more akin to that described by Melanie Klein (1955). It leads to a disturbed mode of omnipotent functioning in their object relations that prevents development of a sense of healthy identity and interferes with a sense of boundaries and capacity for tolerating limits and frustrations. These patients feel that they project into their object in a violent and intrusive way, and this leads then to an equally violent introjection and incorporation, very different from normal identification and identity formation. These underlying processes are experienced consciously by the patient as hostile derivative phantasies and are communicated graphically to the analyst. Klein introduced the concept of projective identification in 1946 and defined it as the prototype of an aggressive object-relations:

> These excrements and parts of the self are not meant only to injure but also to control and take possession of the object. Insofar as the mother comes to contain the bad parts of the self, she is not felt to be a separate individual but is felt to be the bad self. Much of the hatred against parts of the self is now directed towards the mother. This leads to a particular form of identification. I suggest for these processes the term Projective Identification. [p. 8]

The infant forcefully introduces into the mother, or caregiver, parts of his self with the aim of gaining control of the contents of the mother's body or of dominating her. Klein considered it "a phantasy far from consciousness" in which certain aspects of the self are placed elsewhere. She added that the child has phantasies of projecting both "positive" and negative feelings. When, however, the process is "excessive" this results in an emptying and an enfeebling of the sense of identity as the self is depleted by the constant process of evacuation of the bad or dangerous parts. Klein considered projective identification to be a defensive measure against the infant's most primitive anxiety. If excessive, it could ultimately reach the point of depersonalization. In a subsequent paper (1957) she observed how envy was deeply connected with projective identification, describing it as a forceful intrusion into another person with the aim of destroying the best attributes.

Developing particular ideas of Klein, Bion brought the mother or clinician, more into the fore in his conceptualization of projective identification processes:

> Projective Identification makes it possible for him [the patient] to investigate his own feelings in a personality powerful enough to contain them. Denial of the use of this mechanism, either by the refusal of the mother to serve as a repository for the infant's projections, or by the hatred and envy of the patient who cannot allow the mother to exercise this function, leads to a destruction of the link between infant and breast and consequently to a severe disorder of the impulse to be curious, on which all learning depends. [Bion, 1959, p. 106]

According to Bion, what made a distinction between a normal form of projective identification and a pathological one, what distinguishes one from the other, is the degree of violence present when the mechanism is put into effect. The pathological form is characterized by extreme violence and a feeling of omnipotence. The two main aims marked out by Bion in the use of projective identification are, according to Hinshelwood (1989):

(i) . . . to evacuate violently a painful state of mind leading to forcibly entering an object, in phantasy, for immediate relief, and often with the aim of an intimidating control of the object;

(ii) . . . to introduce into the object a state of mind, as a means of communicating with it about this mental state. [p. 184]

The first of these is often referred to as evacuative projective identification, the second as evocative projective identification. Many authors, in particular Rosenfeld (1971), have contributed to the elaboration of this ensemble of what O'Shaughnessy (1975) calls "distinct but correlated processes". They have pointed out the different underlying phantasies and functions that affect the analytic relationship. Rosenfeld described how the object is no longer independent; instead, a fusion between the object and the self occurs. This is used as a defence against separateness, need, and envy (Rosenfeld, 1964). Projective identification is currently considered to be a "term which embraces a whole group of processes and is used to describe normal ways of communicating as well as extremely pathological manoeuvres, and even permanent pathological states, which are the root of certain personality traits" (Sodre, 1995, p. 2). I shall return to these ideas by presenting clinical material from the treatment of a bulimic girl just before and after summer vacations during the second, third and fourth years of her analysis. This material also illustrates the therapeutic modification of these pathological processes, both at an intrapsychic and an interpersonal level, during the course of the analytic work.

Assessment

Deborah was 19 years old when she began treatment. She was the third of four children, all rather close in age. Her parents ran a business in their home town, about sixty kilometres from Rome.

Everyone in the family cooperated in different ways in this business, except Deborah, who moved to Rome about a year and a half before beginning analysis, with the intention of becoming an actress. At the time of referral, Deborah was bingeing two, three, or more times a day, followed by self-induced vomiting. According to her, she took to driving to her mother's several times a day to make herself vomit in order not to be discovered by her flatmates. At her first appointment with me, she arrived accompanied by her mother, wanting her to be present during our meeting. Indeed, she seemed to want to delegate everything to her mother and wished for her to tell me about her problems. In the latter part of the meeting, I asked Deborah's mother to leave us so that I could remain alone with her daughter. Deborah seemed at that point totally unable to speak about herself and, instead, inundated me with a detailed list of her show-business "contacts" who fascinated her. I was struck by the difference between mother and daughter: mother was overweight, had a limp, and seemed weak and depressed. Deborah flaunted herself, as though living excitedly in a world of unreal career phantasies. I did not perceive in her any feelings of pain or anxiety. At the end of the session, I suggested that we continue meeting a few more times to try to explore her difficulties together. Deborah's assessment lasted several months. I suggested weekly meetings, which she often cancelled, sometimes letting me know in advance. Elusive and inconsistent, she seemed to lack any idea of why she was coming to me, and she never spoke about her problems or feelings. She occupied the time instead by relating encounters with directors or talking about work projects (probably mostly imagined, I thought) and about her secret relationship with a very famous elderly actor-director. She often came to her sessions accompanied by girl-friends, who were generally very beautiful. Deborah herself was neither beautiful nor fascinating but was distinctly thin despite the very rounded shape of her bottom. Her appearance was made striking by her provocative clothes, extremely high-heeled shoes, heavy make-up, and excessively groomed hair. Deborah's choice of eccentric shoes has often been a focus of our comments during the course of her analysis. She used expressions such as "to come down from her heels" or "to look down on people" also to refer to her mental state. "To come down from her heels" meant feeling downcast, and "to look down on people" meant feeling like "a star". She told me without the slightest emotion that for many years she had had a boyfriend called Mario and that this relationship ended a year and a half ago, although maybe not forever. Mario was much older than Deborah and very handsome. Next to him, Deborah said she felt like a naïve little girl. Affected by a serious form of alopecia, Mario had begun to lose his hair, and Deborah, frightened by this, left him, under the pretext of having discovered him with another girl (this was a relationship she knew about all along). A few months later, her best friend, who was also called Deborah, committed suicide by jumping out of a window. This friend had always been a reference point for her: at school, for example, she had always been much cleverer, and Deborah would copy everything from her. A few months after these traumatic events, Deborah decided to come to Rome and become an actress.

Initial exploratory phase

During the course of the initial exploratory phase of analysis, Deborah began each session saying she would not come any more, and that she intended to find someone else: it was first a craniotherapist, next a homeopath, then a psychiatrist who would give her medication. She was very frightened by the idea of the time-consuming nature of analysis. However, her bulimic symptoms compelled her to seek treatment because they dominated her life so totally that she could only be away from home for short periods of time before she was suddenly seized by the need to eat and vomit. When at home she spent most of her time in bed with a hot-water bottle, withdrawn and drained of energy. It was evident that Deborah found it extremely difficult to be a sick, dependent person in need of help. She tried in every way to avoid her role of patient with me, trying desperately to draw me into her exciting, fast-paced life of money and success—a world with little interest or time for addressing her profound and threatening feelings of inner emptiness. Instead, she created the naïve and false mask of an aspiring young star, which enabled her to feel desirable and full of promise, in order to try to make up for her total lack of identity. Initially, of course, I took care not to demolish this pseudo-identity, which served vital defensive functions. I began by accepting her with warm but restrained interest as we explored her activities and her stories. Whenever possible, I directed my interpretations to occasional glimpses I caught of her suffering and need.

Beginning psychotherapy

After about three months, Deborah convinced herself that her problem was of a psychological nature, and she agreed to begin psychotherapy. At this point I proposed just two sessions per week in order not to threaten her. Deborah agreed and was also prepared to lie on the couch. With severely eating-disordered patients, it has been my experience, along with others (Williams, 1994), that a long exploratory phase and then beginning work with just a few sessions is often very useful because of the patient's underlying fears of intimacy and dependency. Deborah continued to arrive late for her sessions, looking provocative and even cheap. She had the habit of parking her car in absurd ways, probably distributing seductive smiles to the various caretakers of the buildings whose entrance she might be obstructing. All her actions revealed a lack of any sense of boundaries and limits. In her relationship with the elderly actor, she imagined herself to be his only woman, knowing very well that he had also a wife and children and affairs with a flock of young actresses. Over the following months she continued to do nothing very constructive, spending her days in bed with the hot-water bottle. Eventually Deborah felt the need to be active. She thought of signing up for a training course or possibly taking a screen test, but when she had such thoughts she found herself *"seized by a terrible anxiety which took my breath away"*. As we discussed her reaction, it became clear she felt flooded by the urge to do "ten things at once, to do everything". Being flooded and overwhelmed by sudden impulses to socialize was similar to her characteristic bulimic symptoms. Eating for Deborah meant eating anything and everything. At such times she would arrive smoking and chewing, driving a car full of candies, chocolates, and so on. Food was the pivot on which her identity, her day, her whole life, all turned: continuous, unlimited, filling, and comforting food. The only alternative was, of course, the opposite—complete fasting, abstinence, and social withdrawal.

For each minor difficulty Deborah encountered, she turned to her mother, who immediately hurried to her side, as though they were somehow joined together. This tendency was reflected in her early transference to me. I was not a distinct object, but, rather, I fitted in with her unconscious phantasy of being totally merged with her object. I was a warm and protective shelter, like her hot-water bottle under the blankets. In the countertransference, I felt the pressure of her expectations of my facing her problems for her and preventing any type of frustrations. Deborah was asking me to accept that I enter a collusive conspiratorial alliance to deny our separateness and the painful feelings associated with such an awareness.

The parents

During the course of this initial phase of work with Deborah, I met her parents once to gain their support for our continued work and their assurance of financial support for her analysis. Her parents lived separately but in the same household, and they did not intend to separate legally. Their relationship was full of conflict, ostensibly due to economic issues. During our meeting, the husband, a man of humble origins, accused his wife of spending too much money and of giving too much to the children. The mother appeared to be a weak woman unable to impose limits on herself or on the children. She never took a stand during quarrels, especially those that took place between Deborah and her elder sister. The elder brother and the youngest sister seemed to have a good relationship with Deborah and to support the mother. The mother's excessive availability and extreme tolerance stood in stark contrast to the father's impatient criticisms, violence, and drinking. Thus, the parental couple seemed to be made up of two opposing elements that could not be integrated.

I have found in other patients with eating disorders that the presence of a fragile mother and a barely present father results in a double problem: the mother is unable to contain her child's anxieties, and the father is similarly unable to contain those of the mother. Bion (1958) suggests that a child's emotional development is greatly damaged by a mother who will not allow the entry of projections and their emotional content. In Deborah's case, as in others, I think that the mother's inability was somewhat different: it was not so much a difficulty in receiving projections, but more of processing them and giving them meaning. The difficulty centred around providing boundaries and limits around the child's aggressive or hostile projections, and in particular around envy and greed. This difficulty will be perceived by the child as a misunderstanding of an important part of his or her emotional life, even though it does not take the form of an actual rejection. The mother's failure in containment and lack of boundaries leaves the child lost and confused within an amorphous relationship with the mother and strangely alone with his or her more dangerous feelings. The catastrophe is a consequence of the mother's failure to accept, to metabolize, and to give back to the baby his or her projections in an improved and more digestible form. Bion (1957) felt that the failure of this essential maternal function, which he termed the alpha-function, can give rise to "nameless dread" in the child who experiences mother's refusal as hostile defensiveness, and the child may increase his or her hostility in an attempt to communicate with her. The mother is also perceived as being hostile towards his or her desire to get to know her. These failures represent an obstacle to the creation, in the child's inner world, of an apparatus able to "digest" emotional experience, to perform the alpha-function and to receive healthy projective identification. "Feelings of hatred are thereupon directed against all emotions including hate itself, and against external reality which stimulates them. It is a short step from hatred of the emotions to hatred of life itself" (Bion, 1959). On the other hand, Bion (1962a, p. 73) felt that if the mother has the capacity to receive and modify the child's projections, the child introjects this healthy containing maternal function and identifies with an internal object capable of perceiving, understanding, and knowing.

From psychotherapy to analysis

Six months after the first meeting, Deborah began to get out of bed and explore life a little, but she became anxious in the process. She agreed to increase the sessions from two to four times a week because she felt so anxious. Perhaps she felt the need for a relationship to help her contain her many uncomfortable feelings and to "start thinking" instead of acting out in order to evacuate them (Waddell, 1994). In practice she continually tried to re-establish a more fused and dependent relationship. In the course of the second year the bulimic attacks continued but were reduced to about one a day and were not confined to her mother's house; they also occurred in the new flat that Deborah was sharing with a friend and his girlfriend. The bouts seemed to occur in the afternoons when Deborah was at home alone, and they served the purpose of filling an inner void or emptiness that was the consequence of a fragile, dissolving sense of identity. At other times, the bulimic attacks seemed to represent an anaesthetic, or an emotional modulator, one that moderated Deborah's feelings of being overwhelmed as she became active with people socially and at work. At about this time, Deborah began a relationship with a politician, Ugo, twenty years her senior, who proposed a *ménage-à-trois* with her friend Anna. The two girls agreed, thinking that this man, who was politically influential, might benefit them in their profession as actresses. Quite soon, however, the friend Anna disappeared, leaving Deborah with Ugo. Once again, Deborah believed that she was his only woman, although he only saw her secretly late at night. She found herself very attracted by his power and money, which he obtained through corruption and intimidation, and by his use of cocaine, which fitted in with her philosophy of how things could be obtained magically.

Summer separation: the second year

With this background in mind, I would now like to present in detail the clinical material related to the impact of the summer breaks of the second, third, and fourth years of analysis. As the summer break approached during the second year of analysis,

Deborah decided to join a drama workshop held by an American teacher called Jane in which Deborah was asked to enact her own emotions in order to create her role. She became Marta, "a bulimic girl, a bit of an oaf, who's a bit funny but really wants to die; she feels a bit of a monkey but is also full of anger inside". At times Deborah got stuck during her drama lessons and felt unable to portray this character, while at other times she managed to play the part successfully to general acclaim. It was difficult for Deborah to work in analysis on the feelings associated with our approaching summer break. Any potential anxiety about our separation quickly got transformed into a new idea for one of Deborah's drama-class roles. Such roles would become a vehicle for manic success, where Deborah and her instructor became a mutually idealizing pair and I became a denigrated maternal object over which Deborah triumphed.

Upon my return from the summer break, I found several messages from Deborah on my office answering-machine. The first ones (left in the middle of August) were desperate. She did not want to go on holiday with her mother and siblings, deciding instead to remain in Rome alone. She also left a message about analysis only being able to help her up to a certain point. At that moment, she did not know whether to have done with it by committing suicide, as she saw no way out. With cynical detachment, she described the people around her who established relationships with her based on personal gain, and these included me. In messages left towards the end of August, the tone was different and, at times, even manic. Deborah spoke about screen tests she would have to face in September, one of which was with a very famous director. The break over, she came to her first session in a super-sexy dress and very high heels. In an aggressive and provocative tone of voice, she told me she had preferred to stay in Rome alone, eating and vomiting continuously. However, she added that at a certain point she had a "brilliant insight" and she decided to write a script that will no doubt be received with great success. The story was about a bulimic girl who had resolved her problems and had become a famous actress because she was very talented. Then she talked about Ugo and the wonderful sexual relationship they have and how he was getting very fond of her. She ended by saying that analysis was of no use and that from

September she would come only once a week because "in life you have to get by on your own and nobody can help you". Deborah was, of course, describing her way of dealing with our analytic separation. She was swinging to and fro between extremes: either she was empty and downcast or she was feeling full and triumphing over everyone and everything. Initially she chose to stay in Rome alone, graphically becoming identified with a child, abandoned by the idealized mother, and refusing to go anywhere. The desperate messages were aimed to make me worry and thus spoil my holidays. She admitted she had wished to give me a shock with her first suicidal messages. In the latter part of the analysis, she defended herself from perceiving the absence by way of manic triumph through projective identification. She tried to expel her feelings of rejection and rage into me by denigrating me and thus freeing herself from all painful feelings occasioned by abandonment and anxiety. In the second phase, she switched over to an identification with an active independent mother/analyst/director who cured and dominated other people.

According to Klein, during the first few years of life and also later in the deep strata of the adult mind, extreme fluctuations between good and bad feelings occur. An attempt is made to keep them separate so that they do not contaminate each other internally. Through splitting, the object may be felt to be excessively good or bad: persecution and idealization alternate. In this way the infant tries to organize his or her chaotic experiences and safeguards the good objects on which survival depends. The ego is thus afforded a primitive structure and the infant defends against the very intense anxieties that threaten his or her integrity. This initial mode of functioning is termed by Klein the paranoid–schizoid position. A defence used comprises splitting (idealization or denigration of the object), projective identification, and denial. As Segal (1957) observes, these defences have tremendous power over thought processes and one's ability to symbolize. Klein also talks about excessive splitting, where the self is weakened by constant efforts to evacuate unwanted or dangerous parts of the self. The breakdown towards more primitive splitting processes is particularly pronounced if envy prevails. In the face of severe separation anxiety over the break, my bulimic patient, because of her particular primitive defensive organization, relied heavily on narcissistic defences and omnipotent phantasies, falling back on paranoid–schizoid levels of splitting and denial. Her narcissistic defences were mobilized against the experience of separation and loss. Her efforts to deny the experience of separation were evident in the many messages she left on my answering machine, as if I were constantly there at my office or at home. In her omnipotent phantasy she wanted to continue a dialogue that was, in fact, a monologue. Thus, she was relating to me by denying the limits of time and space. At this stage in her analysis, she was not able to contain, work over, or digest her feelings through an internalized relationship but, rather, "vomited" them into the answering-machine tape. During the initial phase of my absence, she experienced herself as small, rejected, and empty, with an intolerable rage aimed suicidally at herself, but also clearly at me. In the second phase, she talked in an excited, rather manic manner about her project for a script, saying that she was going to direct it and that she would include me in the show, clearly incorporating me subserviently within her grandiose omnipotent phantasy, while at the same time attacking me and reducing our working relationship to once a week.

Deborah missed the next session without giving me any notice. The same thing happened the following day. Finally she arrived for the last session of the week, again wearing her very high heels. She proceeded to talk about the script, saying that she was scared somebody might steal her idea, and this led her to think that she must take out a copyright. She also related a dream she had had a few days before: *"There was a tiny little kitten who didn't want to eat and was dying of hunger, even though all the people around him were desperately trying to feed him."* This helpful dream seemed to express the need to grow and establish ties to survive through dependency and yet, at the same time, to show an awareness of the risk she was running by preventing the establishing of such ties. Deborah reacted to each interpretation regarding her suffering, needy self as if she felt that it was a narcissistic wound; she attacked thinking about such things and the analysis itself by repeating what others had said against psychoanalysis and giving many examples to demonstrate its uselessness. She began to say that she would get treatment in other ways and with other people. At this stage in our work, there was a significant risk that analysis might be brought to a premature end. For the first time Deborah was beginning to realize the type of work we were doing—namely, that psychoanalysis involved a transformation of her defences and approach to life and did not offer the immediate solution she so desperately craved. Nevertheless, Deborah kept trying to use all her familiar defences to free herself of all painful feelings linked with separation and the absence of a wanted object. While waiting to meet me again after the vacation, or between our less frequent sessions, she projected her distress into her active dramatic roles, "curing herself" by identifying with a caricature of an analyst, thus triumphing over me.

According to Klein, projection is a way in which the ego faces anxieties, freeing itself from danger and hostility—the intrapsychic equivalent of expelling dangerous substances from the body. The infant projects damaging contents—as well as good parts—into the mother and, in the same way, projects those parts of his or her mental apparatus with which they are connected. The mother is identified with the bad and good parts of the self. She processes them and gives them back to the child in a tolerable form. Splitting and projection therefore form an important way of interacting with the other person. Deborah was undecided about carrying on with analysis, which she felt was directing her towards a new approach to life. The struggle she was going through in this respect was particularly notable during the fourth week after the summer holiday. On that Monday, Deborah cancelled the appointment with a message stating simply that she had an eye infection and could not come. On Tuesday, she left another message saying she had to go to the ophthalmologist and then see a psychiatrist to get a prescription for sleeping tablets. On Wednesday, she left yet a third message announcing in an excited and haughty tone of voice that she would not be able to come because she had to go and give Roberta a hand with "those poor psychotic boys at the X clinic". After a long pause, she changed her tone completely and, in a depressed voice, added that she didn't know if she'd be coming at all because she wanted to stop analysis, that she was feeling so tired that she didn't want to think any more. On Thursday, she arrived punctually, dressed as usual in provocative clothes and high heels. In a detached tone of voice she told me she had received the offer of a job on television for forty million lire (about £13,000).

She then talked of her friend Ugo, who stayed up until three in the night talking with her and giving her advice—and she reciprocated.

Unsure how to approach her in what might be our last session, the thought of the hungry kitten came to my mind. I tried to create a connection between her eye infection and her difficulty seeing her own needs that might allow us to feed that kitten part of her. I commented on how she chose instead to climb way up on her "high heels", moving rapidly away from sensing any painful feelings linked to her frightening loneliness and dismissive anger at me for leaving. In particular, I pointed out how she could not tolerate the importance of my role for her, taking on instead my function herself or giving it away to others—for example, the opthalmologist, the psychiatrist, and Ugo—and diluting the intensity of her needs and my significance for her. She replied that she knew she wasn't well and felt confused these days. She then talked of mistrusting everybody. She felt that the producer was a pig, because all he wanted was "to take her to bed". She added that Ugo was also a pig. Anna told her some terrible things about Ugo. She called him in tears, asking him about Anna's allegations, but he put Anna down in a way that she found particularly disturbing. He said, "She's just a poor thing, someone who doesn't know what she wants from life . . . but you're different, Deborah! Just think how tragic to be like her, always in the grip of some tremendous anxiety." As a result, Deborah felt guilty and threatened by getting in touch with her own difficulties, finally saying to me, "I want to eliminate everybody! Ugo, Anna, and even analysis . . . you all think about your own bloody selves anyway!"

Deborah projects intolerable parts of her self (Klein, 1935) into Anna, but she can only see these aspects of herself through contemptuous eyes. She experienced each of my interpretations in this manner, only allowing briefly some room for my interpretation about the kitten, which temporarily brought her down from her high heels and made her forget momentarily about the forty million lire. As a result of this climbing down, she began to feel "downcast", like a despised and rejected child—a persecuted state of mind she found difficult to stay with for very long. I asked myself who I was for her at that moment. I represented different aspects of her, a part of herself that despises whoever is suffering from loss or the absence of another, and, at other times, an ideal-ized greedy, successful part of herself looking down contemptu-ously at me from her high-heeled manic position. When Deborah was faced with perceiving her need for the object, and experienced at the same time the object posing frustrating limits through ab-sence or interpretation, she responded by experiencing the other person as having everything and she nothing, as though she was worthless, depleted, and empty. If she was not the star, then I was the star, and a star with feelings of superiority and contempt towards her abject neediness and dependency. She found it impos-sible to be fed by such an analyst who exults in her interpretations and speaks to her from on high. These projections that turned me into an intolerable object created a serious problem for her capacity for introjection and healthy identification with my empathy, pro-cess of thinking, and nurturing analytic function (cf. Bion, 1956). Her evacuation of these unbearable feelings into me, which ren-dered her empty, left Deborah feeling that she had nothing inside or outside to hold on to, and this stripped her of all hope. She was so driven to empty her mind of her afflicting thoughts that it made her feel unreal and suicidal.

Deborah's profound distrust of her own greedy neediness, cou-pled with her own compulsive urge to eject everything bad, found physical expression in her repeated bulimic vomiting. Deborah regularly emptied her stomach of all its contents after filling up with fruit, vegetables, and liquids. After vomiting she felt unreal and exhausted. Eating food more solid required active, aggressive use of her teeth which was not possible, suggesting anxiety about nourishing food that will be absorbed, as well as suggesting her oral aggressiveness towards her objects on whom she depended. Neither real food nor analytic food could be absorbed, kept in, or integrated as nourishment for cohesive identity formation. Her envy and greed led her to perceive each limit as a frustration and torture coloured by tantalizing feelings. She also felt an object of contempt. Under these circumstances, Deborah seemed to indicate a use of excessive and pathological splitting. According to Deborah, eating something she really liked was more prone to give her very bad cellulitis. She was quite certain about this. She seemed to feel that being full equalled becoming bad or contaminated inside and eventually covered with cellulitis; being empty equalled being clean and beautiful. And in the same way, analytic food was experienced as something threatening and bad to ingest, running the risk of the mental equivalent of cellulitis or identificatory contamination. The nourishing object could not be accepted, because it would be identified as a foreign body, something separate from the self, with all the attendant risks of feeling tantalized and feeling that intolerable and painful limits were imposed on her. For Deborah, those who did not set limits on her but let her gorge and vomit were good people. This included her real mother and Ugo, who gave her the illusion that this excessive behaviour could lead to money and power. Excessive splitting was linked to the problem of massive projective identification, which was based on the omnipotent phantasy of becoming the object or a particular version of the object. This could be seen in Deborah's excessive splitting of herself and the analyst or others into grandiose or denigrated figures, filled with extreme good or bad qualities occasioning powerful feelings of greed and envy, admiration and contempt, for herself and others. Deborah was at times identified with me, when she wanted to treat psychotic patients or when she went to auditions feeling that she was already a celebrity and came away complaining, "How could they dare ask me what I can do! As if in the hospital they would ask you, 'And what can you do, doctor?'"

These states of pathological identification, in which the self becomes the object, imply an excessive use of violent projections as well as concrete pathological introjections. They have as their basis an unconscious phantasy of literally and concretely incorporating the external object into the internal world. Normal identification with an internal object takes place because of the capacity to introject symbolically, while allowing it to have a separate identity. Patients like Deborah tend to think more through "symbolic equations" (Segal, 1957) than by symbolizing.

Two dreams from this period highlighted the type of object relation that bulimic patients often experience. On a Monday during the same period following my absence, Deborah told me this dream: "Ugo was showing her the cocaine that he kept in a sideboard. It was in the form of a transparent stone that she took in her hand. It crumbled, turning into a white powder, like cocaine." Deborah hastened to remark that the dream was not important and "didn't mean a bloody thing". She attempted to keep us both mindless and to strip the dream of any meaning. The food that Deborah wanted from analysis was cocaine-like food, food that would take away pain and tension (Abraham, 1916–17, p. 264), making her feel well immediately and automatically. Deborah then said that she wanted to go to the seaside and sunbathe, and she did not intend to look for work! She refused to do menial jobs, disdaining the idea of staying in some shop all day in order to earn a pittance. Talking about taking a course that would prepare her for joining her parents' business, she said: "Why should I tire myself out? . . . I don't want to get stressed!" In this phase of her analysis, Deborah acted as if analysis might go on forever, without having an active thought, without any participation or commitment on her part. Facing psychological reality and doing emotional work were avoided through her omnipotence and megalomaniacal narcissism. As I have indicated, her mother aided and abetted her in this, imposing no real limits or expectations on Deborah regarding her future or any real responsibilities. Under these circumstances, with inadequate parental input, it was difficult for her to tolerate any minor imposition of limits on my part, or even to conceive of my having limits myself. My interpretations received replies such as: "I refuse everything, doctor! I couldn't care a fuck about anything! You haven't understood that your words don't even get to my brain!" Once more I asked myself who was I at that moment, and what made it so impossible for Deborah to be able to think about what I was suggesting. Deborah seemed to feel that interpretations entered her in order to damage, not to nourish. That which was intended to nourish exposed her to feelings of envy (the other person has something she does not possess), feelings of greed (what someone gives her is not enough), feelings of dependency (she needs the other person too much), or feelings of mental and emotional fatigue (she has to make a contribution). In my countertransference, I was overcome by a feeling of impotence and aimlessness: sailing without sails, at the mercy of the wind. Even Deborah's language reflected this detachment from emotions and feelings. Everything was expressed in terms of "bullshit" or "great stuff"—that is, manipulating feelings with the aim of emptying them of their meaning and eliminating any link with me.

The second very interesting dream during this same period highlighted her unconscious phantasies concerning wishes and fears of being able to parasitize the object and suck out its vitality and strength: "*I have to expel a tapeworm from my mouth. I pulled it out with my hand and threw it in the toilet but I realize the head has remained inside.*" She told me that when the head is left, the worm will reproduce itself. She went on to talk about Ugo, saying she had called him but he was busy, so she started reading some notes she had written during a drama workshop with Jane before the summer holidays. She had underlined, however, only the compliments given her by her teacher during her rehearsal, and she had eliminated the criticisms. She had thus created an exclusively self-complimentary monologue and recited it while waiting for Ugo to call her back. When he did call, she explained to him—in a maternal tone—that it wasn't necessary for them to be in touch every day, saying, "What's important is for you to know that I'm here whenever you need me." The dream seemed to express clearly Deborah's awareness of a parasitic aspect of herself that sucks exclusively the good compliments, money, energy, and effort from her mother, and from her analyst, while trying to protect herself from her fear of continuously reproducing her parasitism or, worse, becoming the victim of parasites all around her (Bion, 1970; Rosenfeld, 1971).

This complementary monologue illustrated the tortuous route and extent to which she would go to avoid anything causing pain and the effort involved in making contact with the feeling of being abandoned. She avoided the thought of not being called back by a mother-analyst who was too busy with other things and soon ready to leave her to go on holiday. It was difficult for Deborah to feel normal and to have normal feelings, especially painful ones. I pointed out how she set up this situation even with me, making her feel intolerably lonely. She feared I would gain control of her by engendering a feeling of dependency by my interpretations, and so she abandoned me when I left her, only to appropriate my role externally by taking care of psychotic patients. Whether host or parasite, she was alone: the tapeworm is solitary,[1] and her

---

[1] The Italian for tapeworm is *verme solitario*.

parasitism seemed to be connected with her feeling and fear of loneliness.

As Deborah embarked on writing her own script, she was unaware of the personal and autobiographical parallels. This provided us with the possibility of clarifying certain aspects of herself emerging as she wrote her fictional characters. These enabled us to reflect on them in the session. Increasingly she permitted discussion of these parallels, indicating that there was no longer a total dis-identification of her projected parts (Sandler, 1988). For example, in the new version of the script, the main character falls into a state of depression despite her success, because she "wanted to have everything". She even noted about the character that, "Even if analysis was helping her, she decides to have done with it." The possibility of thinking about this very greedy, insatiable, and highly dependent part of herself increased. In analysing her script, I had to be careful not to fall into a moralistic role and thereby run the risk of derailing her creative project.

A change began to emerge at this point. This was heralded by the patient's increased ability to stay in better and more sustained contact with those aspects of herself that she had hitherto been projecting. Moreover, I sometimes began to get the impression that her extensive projections were beginning to have a different aim. They were not used so much to evacuate painful feelings but more often to serve an evocative communicative function, helping me to understand how intolerable it was for her to feel excluded and left alone with her worries. I noticed a parallel shift in my countertransference, since this was exactly how I felt: concerned for her but at the same time ignored by her, as she boasted of her non-existent victories. I experienced a lonely but not so empty hope. Deborah had a dream in which she seemed to be taking in nourishment, something like food, but in the form of suppositories. Those were linked with injections that she said she wished to have in order to firm up her buttocks. This made me realize that intrusive phantasies were present and that they were connected to Deborah's pathological projective identification into an unhealthy maternal object—one who lets herself be invaded and taken over by Deborah's distorted projections. I had become the maternal object, which showed characteristics that Deborah perceived of her real mother, who reacted to projections without modifying them but by being indulgent and without boundaries, thereby representing a particular perversion of maternal nurturing (Meltzer, 1966).

Deborah's telephone calls and her repeated answering-machine messages were ways of invading my life, freeing herself instantly of her problems, without the pain and effort of thinking or feeling. There was no need to wait, no possibility of waiting—yet. All this fits with a primitive way of communicating. Her way of turning to me or her mother had the aim of making us hasten to her, give her money, listen to her as if she were saying: "If you put me up against any kind of limit, if you don't give me everything, everything for nothing now, I'll kill myself." Joseph (1984) points out that one objective of projective identification is to induce in the analyst compliance with the unconscious phantasy of the patient. According to O'Shaughnessy (1989), a certain degree of acting out on the part of the analyst is always present before he or she becomes aware of the patient's projective identifications. Bulimic patients repeatedly demonstrate a characteristically greedy urgency, disdain for limits, and poor frustration tolerance. These engender intense emotional states and acting out on all who care for them. This can often result in unwitting caretaker compliance, if not collusion or capitulation, and even premature or excessive prescription of medication by analyst and psychiatrists.

Despite her constant search for "contacts" Deborah did not manage to get an acting part, except as an extra—ironically, as a mentally ill person. However, her frenzy to get everything without giving anything lessened a little over time. Deborah began to earn money in her parents' shop to help out the family, since they were beginning to be in some financial difficulties. She also managed to get a part-time temporary job in a similar type of business in Rome to pay at least part of her expenses. Though only occasional, this job allowed Deborah to appreciate the fact that she could manage and be somewhat responsible; she enjoyed her new-found capacity to understand simple administrative problems, and she socialized more comfortably with the other shop assistants and customers. She allowed herself to try mixing with ordinary people rather than with lofty stars from the top of her high heels.

Summer separation: the third year

Predictably, close to the summer vacation of the third year of analysis, when Deborah received the offer of another small part in a film, these small gains dwindled to nothing. And typically, Deborah wanted to change the part entirely to her liking, intending to astound the director with her creative proposals. "You see, doctor," she said with a resentful voice, "I'm never going to put myself in a position to learn!" She couldn't think of creating a project together with another, perhaps just adding a little something of her own or simply taking what was being offered to her. The moment she was confronted with reality and had to face a concrete test, her envious, manic side became mobilized: she then wanted to astound, desiring the mother-analyst to fade away and the father-director to beam at her, holding her in the spotlight so that only she could shine. Of course, she would in fact be directing herself, thereby robbing him too of his role. The only alternative to being a dependent parasite on her object was to separate totally in manic triumph. The victory was always felt as something gained in opposition to the analyst-mother and not together with her in a spirit of cooperation. The victory carried with it the ever-present risk of powerful persecutory anxiety, and the expectation of vigilant counterattacks against projected envy.

Deborah began at this point to attack analysis, trying to make me feel jealous of other, "better" colleagues. On other occasions, she would employ other tactics, complaining that she was fed up with thinking, that it was better to be a whore. On one particular occasion, referring to her Strasbourg drama-workshop, she turned the tables on me. She said, "If I feel anxious I'll do as Jane says: put all the anxieties into your part ... you'll become an anxious, bulimic, and provocative secretary ... you'll be a great success!" Unfortunately, her sudden massive attempts at expelling everything bad led to dramatic consequences: as a result of an episode of excessive projective identification, Deborah suddenly felt in a bottomless void and felt completely depleted. Impoverished by her refusal to take anything in, and her evasion of a more mutual give-and-take relationship with me or the director, her massive avoidance of identification and introjection had led to feelings of persecution by the analyst-director whom she unconsciously attacked and offended so violently. Her characteristic grandiose, omnipotent phantasies had once more backfired. The way she plunged into her permissive, self-indulgent Strasbourg drama-workshop style, and the self-absorbed hours she spent talking to Ugo on the telephone, led me to feel that she was being recruited to action by some destructive inner aspect of herself, by some inner enclave or "gang" of the kind Rosenfeld (1987b) describes. I felt that there was a powerful tropism at work under the direction of a narcissistic structure (Rosenfeld, 1987a, p. 111).

Deborah's feelings of frustration, deriving from her first steps towards autonomy by earning a little money and her feelings of insecurity, were once again intensified by the approach of another summer break, which was, unfortunately, to be even longer than usual. Her small acting part was to take place during this period. Predictably, through projective identification, Deborah repeatedly acted out in primitive ways the phantasy of "archaic object-rela-tions" with me and the director for a time (Feldman, 1995). Unlike the previous year, however, Deborah was finally able to perform the part well, the result of eventual cooperation with the director. She came back to the session to tell me about it and showed me an article concerning her, but she confessed that even if she is satis-fied, she "doesn't feel a celebrity". She talked about her family's financial problems, and her own newly experienced feelings of guilt, as well as a desire to take on more of her own responsibilities. Depressive feelings linked to the fear of losing the object were emerging more strongly. Also, as my summer break approached, Deborah described a situation developing between Ugo and a woman friend of hers which stirred jealous feelings. But this time, through our work, she was able to recognize that her jealousy was a consequence of her own view of the situation, and gradually it became clear that it was related to our separation due to my approaching summer break.

On a Monday, Deborah arrived at a session slightly early, which was unusual. She told me that during the weekend she had felt tired and heavy-headed, but she made an effort to do what she had to. She could not understand why on Sunday evening she felt the need to eat and vomit even though she did not feel like it. She added that she was worried because her symptoms persisted, though they were less frequent than before, and then said that after having vomited she felt relieved; it was a way to lighten her tension. She went on to say that she had paid a visit to the old actor and told him about what she now calls "an idea of a story" instead of a script. She became aware of the fact that she wanted to make his wife jealous, but she managed to hold herself back and behaved properly showing true gratitude to both of them. We talked about the symptom as a way to free her head from thoughts, violently emptying it of meaning, as well as a way to prevent painful feelings from being digested. Deborah was now aware she had to fight her parasitic tendency. On the other hand, she was also aware she had to fight her only way out of the parasitism—that is, a mental state in which she becomes the object (analyst-actor's wife) and triumphs over it. With my help, she was able to hold feelings of jealousy and exclusion inside, not acting on them, and eventually to express them within the analytic relationship, allowing us to work on her jealousy about someone or something taking me away from her. She also became more resolved about finding a better job after the holidays in order to contribute more towards the family expenses. She was also becoming increasingly aware that her relationship with Ugo was preventing her from growing socially and professionally, and she finally said: "I felt really terrible because it's awful not being able to be genuine with him. ... I now ask myself what are the positive things and the negative ones [she was crying], and I feel I have to make a definite change and talk to him. I'm not interested in judging him, I wanted to be a whore too at times, but then I just couldn't. I want someone who can help me to grow." She reflected on the fact that Ugo cannot give her anything, "because he is the sort of person who resolves his problems by smoking marijuana or sniffing cocaine, instead of facing them by looking inside with all the pain this implies".

It was clear to me at this point that a substantial change in the analytic relationship had occurred. Deborah was beginning to employ more normal splitting in the form of an evocative use of projective identification, with reduced violence in her projections and an increasing capacity for healthier introjection. I found I was able to think more clearly and coherently during the session and was no longer overwhelmed. Nor did I feel altered by massive projections as I had been in the past. I felt that Deborah was beginning to move more solidly into the depressive position. She was much more willing to come to the sessions and more punctual. Her telephone messages were much less frequent and had a different quality to them. They no longer felt like an evacuation of anxiety into me, no longer simply venting her feelings mindlessly. Instead, they seemed to express the need to pursue a thought, with messages such as: "I realize that my illness is a way to stop me from living and I can't take it any longer. . . . I know I'm feeling bad because you are leaving and I'm here on my own and I'll have some difficult times . . . but I'd like to be able to become a woman and prove it to myself as well as to others." And to my surprise, the next day, after the last session before the holidays, Deborah left me a very warm, genuine message, with no hint of veiled venom.

Deborah was providing us at this stage with a glimpse of her movement into the depressive position (Klein, 1935), in which she is more able to integrate experiences and make distinction between her self and her object, between the real object and the ideal one. The object is now more fully perceived as whole. Any ambivalent impulses no longer lead to pathological splitting of the object into good and bad parts, but now are more fully directed towards the same object. During the summer holidays of our third analytic year, Deborah stayed at home and worked in the family business; this led to tension with her elder sister. On her return to analysis, she looked very sad, often crying during the sessions. In the countertransference, I felt her anxiety of facing a new and as yet unexplored way of living. She was approaching and experiencing the world differently somehow. My interpretations and my tone of voice conveyed the wish to be close to her and sustain that part in her that wanted to grow. Deborah wanted to leave Ugo but was very frightened. She was able to tell me: "I am aware that the problem is not Ugo nor work. The problem is me. . . . Today I was anxious to come here. But apart from you there is nothing else in my life." She was thinking of joining a professional course relevant to her family business, but was scared of the effort, even acknowledging her concern about how she would compare with others. She was also thinking of applying for courses in the faculty of psychology, but was afraid it would require a great effort.

She admitted she was afraid of giving up what she called "the enchantment" of her relationship with Ugo, who managed to get her parking fines cancelled. She was aware, even a little terrified of the realization that the time and money involved in studying might mean stopping lesser investment in beauty treatments. Deborah's lavish attention to her external body seemed to represent a way of controlling her fear of breakdown, of falling apart. Now, as she began to invest in her inner world and value the functioning of her own mind, we were more able to deal with and contain her anxiety and fear about disintegration within the analytic relationship. A significant change was taking place in her inner world as her emptiness began to fill in and take shape—no longer stripped and impoverished by her defensive use of excessive pathological projective identification. No longer so anxiously driven to disown her sad and threatening parts, she was now beginning to reclaim her fuller self in relation to her significant others.

Such progress is fragile and is never linear. It is prone to setbacks, retreats and collapses. Entering the depressive position means owning one's aggression and guilt. During the weekend she caused her mother great anxiety. She told her she wanted to commit suicide. Then she wanted to sleep in the same bed with her and wanted mother to hug her. "I realize I am not making any effort . . . I have no will-power." The problem seemed to have reverted to the familiar one of her greed, urgency, and difficulty with limits rather than to be related to the anxiety of entering new territory. When she anticipated studying a language, Deborah could only think of registering simultaneously for French and English classes and learning them both in a few magical months, but then, in the end, she naturally would give up. It was so difficult to choose because any choice implied giving something up, making great effort, and accepting one's own limits. She was finding it difficult to shift from primitive forms of projective identification to a confrontation with reality distorting her efforts to actually try her dreams on for size. She found it hard to achieve a different frame of reference, for her trial identifications around career choices and courses of study. The attempt to ask herself what she liked doing—and more importantly, what she was really inclined to work towards—was sobering, painful, and fatiguing. Rather, she was inclined to fall back on her old way of thinking, centred on how to make a grand impression on others, so she could bask effortlessly in their doting eyes.

As the time approached to register for the professional training course, Deborah suddenly joined another brief drama workshop, which meant giving up the course and being absent from analysis for two weeks. She left me a very disconcerting telephone message in which she asked me imperiously for a referral to another analyst who would be willing to give her four sessions per week free of charge. She ended by announcing that she would not come any more. Needless to say, I felt suddenly attacked, flooded with feelings, and dropped again. Clearly, Deborah was swinging violently back towards the paranoid–schizoid from the depressive position. Such violent and frequent swings would characterize our further work for some time to come, with her swings slowly moderating.

A critical moment in the depressive position arises when we are confronted with having to relinquish control of the object. The paranoid–schizoid mode, which aims at possessing the object, has to be changed radically so that the depressive position can be worked through and the object given its freedom and independence. These processes imply a severe conflict that we associate with work on mourning, causing anxiety and mental pain. I was relieved that Deborah was willing to come back and talk with me about the current situation. We were able to discuss the anxiety-producing implications of committing to the more serious longer-term course compared to a brief, easy workshop. This led us to the difficult topic of facing change, choice, and commitment in general: managing competition, cooperation, and responsibilities, feeling inexperienced and inadequate at the start, and accepting the pain connected with looking at what has happened.

At the end of the month, for the first time Deborah paid part of her own analytic bill, from the fruits of her own work. The very next day she missed the session and left a series of violent insults on my consulting-room answering machine, including a threat to commit suicide. I decided to phone her and leave a message on her answering machine, asking her to resume her sessions. I thought that Deborah needed to feel that I was willing to continue working with her even when she became more destructive. However, I persisted in keeping a stable setting and in interpreting the negative therapeutic reaction caused by her omnipotent and envious feelings. At this moment in our work, Deborah was precariously balanced on pointed toe, seemingly ready to leap ahead into the unknown, only to fall back violently into her paranoid–schizoid position, rejecting the mental pain of progress, and instead succumbing once again to self-destructive acting out. I noted this tended to occur after she began to "take in" or introject a perceptive, containing object, which evoked feelings of concern prompting her in the direction towards the depressive position. Meltzer (1967) notes that when a patient is on the threshold of the depressive position, he has a need to put the object to the test: trust in the object is undermined by enemies. In my view, with patients like Deborah, the problem does not only relate to a transformation of inner objects, but also to the emotional acceptance of the change. This involves developing the capacity to acknowledge and tolerate the accompanying affects. Deborah, for instance, indicated that she was very alarmed by this new space in which there was room for thought and feeling, for acknowledging others and collaborating, rather than denying, exploiting, or "parasiting". This new space was perceived as something unfamiliar and dangerous (Feldman, 1995), and her projections seemed like desperate attempts at restoring the old, familiar, dramatic scenario. She began to swing between telephone calls where she was telling me I was the only person who could help her and other calls implying I was inadequate or worthless, declaring she was giving up analysis for Buddhist meditation. One day she would buy the newspaper to look for serious work, only to announce the next day that she wanted "a mug" who would keep her and shower her with gifts. During this precarious and risky period in our work, a scandal erupted when a young woman offering sex in exchange for a television job subsequently reported the person who had not fulfilled the promise. Deborah initially reacted by saying, "it is I who must take responsibility" (i.e. find a job), but shortly thereafter she began pilfering products from the parents' shop and selling them to her friends for the proceeds. But shortly after, she begrudgingly acknowledged in a session: "It's not that I'm sorry, but that I feel a shit—that's different!"

Her frequent calls continued, and I finally decided the time had come to be firmer and put some limits on them. She was furious. Eventually she realized she could not continue to be so arrogant, taking everything from me and others and without even asking permission. As Riesemberg-Malcolm (1995) observed, necessary developmental situations missed or not adequately experienced with the mother are often repeated in the transference. I sensed Deborah's partial acknowledgement of the licence she was taking by calling me one year after she stopped doing it. This happened at the time when she had had a telephone conversation with a male friend. As she was reporting it, we could both hear the irritating noise of repair work taking place in the street below. Finally, Deborah said: "Fortunately, he became exasperated and put the phone down on me . . . I cannot continue to be like this . . . like a drill!" The friend had set a limit on her just as I had, and Deborah was finally able to recognize that it was an appropriate and constructive thing to do. Around the same time, after one screen test she felt for the first time she was not that good after all. Slowly recognizing some of her imperfections, she began to tolerate, accept, and integrate them into herself, and she began to give shape to a more complete and realistic sense of herself. She was moving towards a new identity derived increasingly from work in the depressive position. She talked about her parents and the difference between them—mother was everything, father nothing—although she was beginning to acknowledge the efforts made by her father, given his humble origins. She talked about their ill-health in connection with her own problems with eating. But at first she had denied any possible connection. She was now beginning to realize that there was one: "Because I was not living in the real world," she said, "because I denied everything about myself, I didn't realize that I might die if I carried on the way I was. And, of course, I ignored the fact that my parents were old and ill." She now realized her effect on them, including her not facing the prospect that they might die soon, exhausted by her incessant demands.

An unexpected separation

Through our work she recognized her underlying fear of losing the object and was beginning to develop a deeper stability. Unfortunately, my sudden absence for two weeks, due to an infection, brought fresh doubts about everything. Deborah stopped contributing to the cost of analysis, threatening to reduce the number of sessions to three. She bought a mobile phone (this helped her to communicate with everyone else, from a distance, whenever she wanted!) instead of paying her telephone bills at home and her share of the cost of analysis. Upon my return, she came back to her sessions in provocative new clothes. At that moment, I felt that there was a great risk of Deborah breaking off the analysis. Though stimulated by my unexpected absence, I thought that her increased awareness of her destructiveness towards me at this stage caused the near collapse of the analysis. Attacking a bad object was different from venting one's destructiveness on an internal object now perceived as more benevolent, helpful, and needed. According to Steiner (1992), there are variations within the paranoid–schizoid and depressive positions. I observed these in Deborah, as well as in other patients with eating disorders, during the crucial transitions from fear of losing the object to an actual experience of its loss (Steiner, 1992). Because my absence was sudden and unexpected, but also because there was some uncertainty about the timing of my return, Deborah's anxiety and anger were significantly aroused. After we weathered this storm and worked through it, I continued to try to get her to think of the distortion she herself contributed each time she experienced a limit or loss with me— how I immediately became a frustrating and mean person, not letting her participate, but excluding her from all privileges and riches. At the same time, however, I realized the need to keep myself at some distance in my interpretations, reminding her of her readiness to recognize that this was no longer entirely a personal, head-to-head combat. The perception of our separateness and the development of her own autonomy through her freely chosen training course underscored that; whatever her choice may be, my life was independent from hers. Deborah became increasingly aware that the sentence she often repeated to her mother— "Mummy I'm going to die with you"—did not have to be true any more. Despite her swings and provocations, I tried to stay aligned with her emerging, growing, responsible side, pointing out that she seemed like a little girl unable to bear a difficulty without falling into the embrace of her internal narcissistic part. I tried to keep calm, allowing her to choose, but also to be responsible for her choices.

Summer separation: the fourth year

For every analysand and analyst, each time summer approaches, the issue of whether the absent object can remain a continuously good object presents itself. Of course, other less positive prospects also begin to emerge. In a session not long before the summer break, Deborah informed me that her homeopath had given her some pills and told her that they would make her feel well. She had, however, thought to herself: "Sure! Tell me another one!" With this, I felt she was beginning to discriminate enough to be suspicious of this kind of seductive magical statement. At the same time, she told me she was very tempted once again to try to get Ugo to buy her clothes, pay her bills, and get rid of her fines. She was, however, also scared of this type of relationship, which she felt was no longer "right". She also recognized the progress she was making in her analysis in overcoming difficult moments, saying: "I made an effort to refuse the clothes; I did some thinking, I thought about what you told me; there's something not quite right in depending on these sort of things." At the end of the session, she got up and her mobile phone fell noisily to the floor. Looking at it, she said resolutely "It's broken!" and to my surprise she smiled. The next day she came wearing green shoes with very high heels. Lying down, she asked me if I thought they were ugly. I asked her why she wanted my opinion. She said she thought I was a "refined" person and she a "bumpkin". In the course of the session, she said, "I'd like to work hard and put myself to the test." She also wanted to try to show her parents that she was capable. She cried and said, "I'd like to be thought well of." But she admitted that although the things her elder sister said to her made her feel bad, they were true: everybody in the family but she had made a contribution to the family business, and she had stolen beauty creams to sell just for herself. "I don't want to be considered a sick person any more. I want to take responsibility and contribute. Yesterday I ate and vomited, and for the first time I burst into tears and I felt terrible. I can't bear destroying myself and other people any more." At this stage in the work, Deborah was acknowledging desirable qualities in the analyst, such as her being "refined". Such thoughts were linked to a deeper appreciation and "object esteem" (Williams, 1983). As a consequence she was showing appreciation for more refined things, things less gaudy and visible, internal things. She also wanted to be respected. I could sense in the countertransference the presence of a good internal object taking shape, one that needed to be protected and maintained. I felt that Deborah had a great need to be acknowledged, which I tried to respond to indirectly. Though this was a turbulent phase, I was able to contain and sustain her. Deborah returned to work in Rome, if only occasionally during the week, and she even worked with her parents during weekends.

Unfortunately, though perhaps predictably, there followed a new wave of aggressiveness and bulimia, provoked this time seemingly from without, by the family's financial difficulties. And once more somebody was blamed for putting limits to her freedom by asking her to cooperate. At times Deborah successfully held on to her internal shifts, managing to observe and think about her feelings, while at other times she was not able to do so. She left several messages for me; one of them said: "I felt a shit but I was able to eat and not vomit. I wanted to ask you to help me. Thanks, sorry if I called you at home, have a good day." She read me a letter she had written to Ugo, in which she had changed the tone of the words I had said to her. She was not pretending she had thought those things, but she seemed to be letting me know that she remembered them in her own way. Even when she took the initiative, I felt somehow acknowledged.

As the summer vacation of our fourth year approached, Deborah seemed more stable and integrated. During the second to last session she told me, "I painted a picture frame with Alberto [her flat-mate], and then I cooked with a friend. I then went to a musical event and met one of your patients, C____, who greeted me. I was happy. I felt this is what I want to do. I realize that until now I have lived as if I was saying 'fuck all'. Then I worked this out; I don't think I can write a script. Some people spend a lifetime studying how to write them." She went on to say she felt well even though she cannot tell how long it will last. "The more I fill my life with good things and feel good with other people, the more I fill myself with food. I even told my mother, 'Mummy, I won't promise I'll never vomit any more; it might happen . . . occasionally . . . but I feel good'," and this made her happy. I feel like I'm beginning to live! If they had read my old script they would have thought I was ill and that I wrote about my neurosis. My writing, it is really only of use to me." After the holidays Deborah started dating a very affectionate and easy-going young man. She also made a serious decision to register for the professional course, even though she did not totally want to give up the idea of becoming an actress. She was very torn, and she alternated between sessions in which she was lucid and integrated and sessions where she attacked me, altering me once again in her mind. She managed, however, on her own, in one and the same session, to become aware of her attacks and even to apologize. I distanced myself from her decisions and made her feel that I did not expect her to do either one thing or the other. It was clear, though, that the two years' professional course would give her the possibility of reaching competence and financial independence. It would also enable her to have different "contacts" with new and more reliable people living more normal lives. Clearly, it meant following the reality principle rather than the pleasure principle. She would be giving up trying to evacuate anything unpleasant (Bion, 1959; Freud, 1911). Finally, as she herself put it, she would have to "educate her brain" and "allow the teachers to feed it". On the last possible day, and certainly not without conflicts, Deborah managed to register for the professional course. The next day, she arrived punctually for her session and exclaimed, "Today is my first day at school!" She said she felt restless and sad but then added that she also felt happy. "Perhaps it is not so difficult. Everybody works hard and so will I". She told me she actually spoke to the director of the course about her eating problems and the difficulties she had had registering in years past. The Director of Studies was very understanding. Then she added: "In the past, I used to dream, now I don't want to give up my dreams. But I want to live in reality." She told me she had gone past Ugo's house. She hadn't been to see him for several months, and she saw the blinds shut. She felt excluded and realized that he had not been calling her for some time now. After reflecting a moment, she said, "He's like the sick part of me that wants absolutely everything from a person or else it destroys you!" This sobering recognition on her part showed, I thought, an awareness of the extent to which certain psychotic aspects of her personality could make her feel primitively destructive, even on the side of death, wishing to destroy and eliminate someone she had cared about. She felt tempted to destroy him at that moment, but she tolerated her longing and loneliness, her sense of exclusion, and her rage at him. I also felt she may have been anxious that I might close the shutters on her, if she were to become healthy and successful, by ending the analysis.

In any event, she went on past Ugo's house, returned home, and wrote him a letter, which she was able to keep herself from sending. Instead, she brought it into this analytic session and read it to me. As she began reading it, she cried. I was so moved I could only recall few sentences in it:

> "Your desire to grow is big but your sick part stops you from doing it. . . . When you feel you need something, ask and be satisfied. Even if you say you don't need anybody, fight this part of you which makes you empty. I wanted to give you what my analysis gave to me. . . . My growth inevitably makes me look for full plates not empty ones. . . . Sorry for the heavy stuff of the last period, but entering everyday reality was difficult for me. . . . It's difficult to say what I have thought and worked through in many years. . . . I hope you too want to fill up this bleak life and surround yourself with healthy people. . . . I needed to choose you to relate to a part of myself."

I felt sincere pain in Deborah's tears, which seemed linked to the perception of letting go of a dream, the dream of a little girl who wants to be mother (and mothered) in an omnipotent way—a girl who even dreams of overcoming mother completely, turning against her need to destroy. Instead, she has come to accept that for now she does not have the throne. Giving up this dream has become, during the course of our analytic work, more and more tolerable, while before it was only a source of hate and envy. Separation meant being excluded from the world of privileges and having to make efforts for oneself. Finally, embarking on her professional course represented the external concrete expression of a deep, hard-won internal change. She was finally letting go of her childish self, her childhood dream, her narcissistic birthright entitlement of being a privileged omnipotent object. Now she was settling on the more realistic and arduous course of aspiring to become herself through hard work in the real world, with all the risks, limits, and opportunities that reality imposes.

At this point in our last session to be reported here, since the work is still ongoing, Deborah recalled a dream she had had the night before: "I see Ugo with a woman and a child enter the main door of a building. I feel a great pain and feeling of exclusion but I think this is how it should be". This dream seems to capture both Deborah's progress to date and her internal state of affairs. According to Britton (1989), we resolve the Oedipus complex by working through the depressive position and resolve the depressive position by working through the Oedipus complex. Deborah seems to have entered this higher and more complex, dangerous terrain fairly solidly now in our work. And as Britton indicates, this work will involve letting go of an ideal world, settling for something that can be realized in the material world, with acknowledgement of the distinction between aspiration and expectation, between what is tangible and what is emotional. "Otherwise, the relations with the outer world can be used only as a stage for a persistent inner conflict whose function it is to deny psychic reality, the reality of the Depressive Position and the pain of the real Oedipal situation" (Britton, 1992, p. 45). Deborah now seems better equipped and able to begin facing the problem of mourning. As Steiner (1990) observes, "if this is worked through successfully, it leads to separateness between the self and the object because it is through mourning that Projective Identification can be reversed and parts of the self attributed to the object can return to the ego. In this way the object is seen in a more realistic way and no longer distorted by the projections of the self and thus the ego is enriched by repossessing parts of the self which it had previously given away" (p. 54).

Deborah now feels she must allow the object to go, even if she feels she cannot live without it, whereas before either she tried to deny loss by trying to possess the object and omnipotently identifying with it or to destroy it, or she became quite depressed and bulimic, devouring and ejecting parts of it. At the present stage, faced with the double threats of loss through growth and loss through separation, Deborah seems more able to come off her high pedestal, no longer towering above everyone on her "high heels". At the same time, she does not descend precipitously into "downcast" depression or self-destructive acting out. Faced with these challenges, she seems able to avoid violently devouring physical and psychological nourishment from others, no longer compelled to eject or spit it out secretly. Rather, she seems better equipped to take in and learn through mutual experience. She is standing more solidly with her feet on the ground, willing to proceed more in a more cooperative fashion with her analyst and others in her journey through life.

Conclusion

Based on my analytic work with patients suffering from eating disorders, and illustrated in particular through the case of Deborah, a bulimic patient, I have described certain typical processes of pathological projective identification frequently seen in these patients. Characteristically, they employ a severely distorted mode of omnipotent functioning in their object relations, preventing development of a sense of healthy identity and interfering with their sense of boundaries and capacity for tolerating any limits or frustrations. The hostile nature of their projections is experienced as violent intrusion into their objects, leading to violent introjection and incorporation, rather than healthy identification and identity formation. Pathological forms of splitting, projection, introjection, and identification are characteristically employed. These underlying processes, so characteristic of these patients with severe eating disorders, are experienced consciously by the patients as hostile derivative phantasies communicated graphically to the analyst and others through words and actions. By centring my discussion around a series of separations always at the time of summer breaks, I have illustrated these points in great clinical detail. I have paid particular attention to the patient's evolving transference and my parallel countertransference, as well as to her experience outside analysis and acting out. By presenting this in an unfolding fashion, I have tried to provide the basis for understanding my patient's internal world and its dynamic internal and interpersonal functioning over time, following the progressive changes occurring through our analytic work.

CHAPTER SEVEN

An anorexic girl's relationship
to a very damaged persecutory internal
object and its impact on her illness

Hélène Dubinsky

Julie, an intelligent and sensitive young woman, was referred to me by her GP because she suffered from anorexia nervosa and severe depression. This chapter is focused on the first two years of her therapy. She was 19 years old and was training to become an occupational therapist. I arranged with Julia's GP to have her weighed every other week.

When I first met Julie she struck me as being painfully thin, relatively tall but waif-like in appearance. On her extremely pale and somewhat expressionless face, framed by very short black hair, the only splash of colour was her bright-red lipstick. Her legs under her trousers looked like two matchsticks. She did not remove her jacket, because, as she later explained, she worried I would find her fat. Although she talked a great deal, her voice remained distant and cut off; her words, however, conveyed a searing pain, which stayed with me long after she was gone. She almost completely avoided eye contact. Over the course of the therapy, whenever she greeted me or said goodbye at the end of a session, her eyes would glance vaguely in my direction, quickly sliding past my face.

Julie dated the beginning of her anorexia to her sixteenth year. At that time she was preparing for her GCSEs, and she was frequently quarrelling with her mother. Her mother reproached her for not seeking a job, as she herself had done at Julie's age. Julie described her childhood as having been very happy, despite her mother's ongoing and severe obsessional illness. The father was, and always had been, a fully supportive presence within the family. Both parents were of Greek-Cypriot origin and came to England as children with their families, fleeing the war in Cyprus. From her descriptions, Julie seems to have been a well-behaved, pleasant, conventional child. Her present misery was often contrasted with idealized recollections of family holidays by the sea, romping about in the sand with her two younger brothers, sharing family reunions and wonderful meals alongside peaceful moments of contentedness captured in happy snapshots of Julie smiling forever. . . .

Beginning of therapy

From the very start, the sessions were shaped by Julie's incessant and rapid talk, never leaving a moment of silence between us. Her talk essentially revolved around her two main obsessions: food and friends, with all possible links between the two. She proved to be overwhelmingly preoccupied by what her friends at the university halls of residence thought of her. Indeed, she spent a great deal of time wondering why a given person or group had not spoken to her on a specific instance, or why nobody had knocked on her door at teatime for a chat. She immediately concluded that they were angry with her, or possibly they shunned her company on account of her excessive weight. In Julia's mind, fat was equated with despicable ugliness. Such ruminations, all linked to her massive fears of rejection, led her into deep depressions and feelings of persecution often accompanied by suicidal fantasies. Her constant need for attention and reassurance was reinforced by crippling self-doubt, itself fuelled by guilt: "I want the attention of my friends all the time, and then when I get it I feel I don't really need it, or that I took it away from someone else."

Julie repeatedly rehearsed persecutory scenes in her mind (what she called her "paranoia") linked to her weight. In such scenes her friends talked behind her back the minute she left the room, most likely laughing at her because, she said, "they had tricked me into becoming fatter than they were". In fact, at some level Julie was engaged in a covert and constant competition regarding weight, jealously trying to maintain her position as the thinnest person amid her circles. She had had a couple of boyfriends a few years earlier, but she had broken up with the first one when he started talking about building a future with her. She often said that she couldn't even conceive of a future. Julie broke up with the second boyfriend when he attempted to "fatten her up". She added: "I didn't like myself so I didn't think they could truly like me." Julie often repeated that she didn't deserve the therapy, that she was just fat and only wanted the attention.

At the onset of treatment, Julie's daily intake consisted of one or two crispbreads for lunch, plus a few lettuce leaves, followed by some chocolate for dinner. She described spending the best part of the day plotting her meal strategy, worrying about when and where she was going to eat and, quite crucially, in whose company, given that she feared any intervention that could potentially induce her to stray from her daily allowance, quite literally counted to the calorie. At that time, Julie weighed five stone.

She experienced relief when I suggested at the very start of our work that her eating disorder was in fact a symptom of considerable emotional difficulties. The following excerpt, a few weeks into her therapy, gives a vivid picture of her internal world.

Julie seems even more distressingly thin than usual. She mentions having been very low the previous Sunday, really suicidal. She had gone to a party that weekend. Her stomach had been bloated, causing her tremendous physical suffering, but the pain had subsided and she managed to enjoy herself after all. On Sunday she felt very "paranoid", and this had continued until the time of her Wednesday session; people were watching her. "Perhaps they think I'm too thin, or perhaps I'm too fat." She says she cannot stand the idea that people are looking at her and not telling her what they think, as if they are judging her all the time and not conveying the "sentence". I point out how she fears that I also will judge her too fat and greedy. She agrees and returns to the subject of her uncontrollable tears over the previous few days. She had kept thinking of a recent spate of bombings in London, and she says that it would be just her luck that she wouldn't be able to come back to the clinic. She goes on to describe how that Sunday she had gone to the canteen at work where she had had an apple. She bumped into her friends there and worried that they hadn't bothered to knock on her door. This immediately triggered an overwhelming sense of persecution, centred as always around being looked at or watched. It had caused Julie to break out into tears right there and then, in the canteen and in front of her peers. We continue to address her feelings of depression, and I suggest that Julie has been terribly worried at the possibility of not getting her sessions with me. Perhaps she has also wondered what my feelings for her are, and whether I keep her in mind in between sessions. Would I be at all concerned if she didn't come to her sessions? Or do I think when I see her that she is bad and greedy for wanting a session? A little later Julie adds that she thought she would ring me up, if she were unable to make her session, and that she had in fact been very worried about letting me down. Soon after she mentions that the friend with whom she usually ate had not been there over the weekend, and that she always binged when her friend was absent. I ask her what she means by bingeing. She explains that she would just sit in front of the fridge and eat whole spoonfuls of ice cream out of the container. On this particular occasion, however, she had decided not to binge and had gone to the table to sit down, with the food already set on her plate.

Towards the end of the session, Julie says it is her mother's birthday soon and she had thought a lot about buying her presents. For instance, she asked herself what she would do were she suddenly to win £1,000, imagining all the presents she would like to get for her mother. I comment on her wish to mother me, to buy things for me, and on her concern about letting me down should she miss a session. I also mention her fear of potentially hurting me if she allows herself to have strong feelings within the session. She readily agrees and talks of how easily she herself gets hurt and can't believe that anyone could withstand the intensity of her feelings.

After a silence, she alludes to being so "paranoid" when she goes shopping. Indeed she worries that people are observing her constantly because they suspect her of shoplifting. As a consequence, she keeps her hands in clear view at all times, in order to show that she isn't stealing anything. I point out her confusion to her: she needs food to live, but she somehow accused herself of stealing it. I linked this with her feelings about the therapy. "Yes," she replies, "I feel as though I'm attention seeking and that all my problems are not really serious." She turns to her childhood: "When I was little I used to eat so much!" She continues that her mother used to buy lots of sweets and there was always delicious food at home; then, when Julie reached adolescence, everything changed. Her mother would present her with her food already served on her plate and say, "This is for you." But, in Julie's words, "I started to take control and would say, no, I don't like it." She goes on to remember that when she was little she would buy cakes in order to come home and enjoy the pleasure of sharing them with her mother.

Julie is curled up in a foetal position. There is a brief silence, after which she reveals that she was thinking about her stomach pains. It transpires that she hasn't eaten that day. She had had a friend accompany her to the clinic because, she says, "as I get closer to you, I'm getting more upset when the session finishes". I relate this to the cramps caused by her self-starvation. I describe the end of the session being experienced as a painful emptiness in her stomach, to which she replies: "Yes, it's as if now the hurt is coming out." After another silence, she speaks of not being able to imagine a future for herself. I allude to her fear that I will forget her in between the sessions, that she would cease entirely to exist in my mind. Julie replies that it isn't right for me to think about her because she really doesn't deserve it since she isn't ill. She seems to be in considerable physical pain. When the session ends, she gets up, avoids my glance, and says, almost under her breath, "I'm sure when I walk in the street the pain will be gone."

Over the course of her therapy, Julie conveyed at length the endless torments of a daily life wholly dominated by compulsive thoughts. A more complete picture of the utter bleakness of her internal world started to emerge: overriding feelings of worthlessness and depression, deep inner fragility and an inability to withstand any strong feelings, crushing social insecurities alongside deep suspicion and persecutory fantasies. All this combined to produce Julie's desperate attempt to control her every need. Julie feared I would not recognize those needs and would instead accuse her of taking too much from me. It became clear that, at times, she saw me as fragile and envious like her own mother and felt she needed to feed me with reassuring words. One can see in this session that Julie's obsessionality was aimed at placating a harsh superego—a bargain had been struck: if she starved herself, it would stop the incessant accusations and demands from within. She then attempted to put an end to her suffering by imprisoning her infantile part and all its needs.

A few weeks after this session Julie started making herself eat very low-calorie meals. This fundamental change in her eating regime initially caused her unimaginable suffering; she said that it was the lowest she had ever been and she felt so depressed that she wanted to die. She described feelings of "going cold turkey" as she stopped her dieting and resumed more normal eating patterns. Julie was beginning her battle against the addiction to control and deny her needs, manifested in her through her addiction to starvation. It was like opening a dam, and she felt overwhelmed, terrified, and desperate about her "human needs and emotions". She was, I thought, engaged in a struggle against a destructive part of her self that strove to maintain omnipotent control over her body and her thinking via obsessional control and limitation of her food intake.

Only very gradually did it dawn on Julie that it was her emotions of which she was most terrified, rather than eating and putting on weight. At this point, she often referred to how her thoughts would stray to food when even trivial questions came to her mind, or she thought about her difficulties. She would, in her words "switch off from people into her safe world". A pattern was emerging that we could begin to think about together: perhaps her anorexia was not only a manoeuvre to placate her superego, as we had previously seen, but also a refuge from the overwhelming anxieties associated with her growing awareness that staying alive meant having emotional needs and being dependent on her internal objects.

Linked to this, in a session that took place six months into therapy, Julie managed to ask me whether a little plant on the window-sill might be dead. It emerged that she had been wanting to raise this question with me for weeks but had not dared to for fear of hurting my feelings. If one takes the little plant as standing for Julie's infantile self, one wonders if she felt that the therapist-mother could not, or did not want to, nourish the baby enough to keep it alive, but also whether the therapist can bear being reproached for her shortcomings without retaliating or succumbing to excessive feelings of guilt.

Changes in her external life

Julie managed to stick to her three meals a day, despite bouts of deep depression. As a result she gradually gained over two and a half stone and was no longer at risk. Her whole physical appearance had changed. She now looked attractive and feminine, although her face retained a guarded, tense expression. As her obsession with intake and schedule of meals decreased, Julie was more able to lead a "normal adolescent life", with weekend outings, socializing, and so on. She had many friends now. In fact, it often seemed that she threw herself somewhat desperately into the swing of adolescent life, as if she hoped to make up for the lost time and also manically repair the previous harm done to herself and her objects. This state of mind was evident in her fantasy about getting married. She very much wanted to get married now, and she imagined herself in a white wedding gown with everybody looking at her, this time not because she was bad but, rather, exclaiming, "Isn't she lovely", admiring a lovely young woman dressed all in white; the pain, the dirt, and the damage somehow all would be erased.

Remembering how she felt as a little girl

For many months, Julie persisted in describing her childhood as idyllic, especially in contrast to her subsequent miseries. In time she started to remember other parts of her childhood, schooldays mainly. She recalled a feeling of constant doom at school, having to sit next to another girl at all times for fear that the other children would think she was bad and had no friends. She remembered her tremendous need to be liked by everyone, and how she was constantly giving presents to the little girls around her. She also recalled how she would wait all morning for the school lunch, and how once the meal was over she would be overcome by a sense of loss at the thought of having to wait for so many hours until the next meal, lonely and friendless. She remembered always thinking that she was going to die. Her thought was that she was just going to last through the holidays, and then die.

As she remembered aspects of her childhood that did not coincide with the idealized version, she also became more in touch with how threatened and terrified she was by her mother's unpredictable outbursts. Any sense of well-being and happiness might suddenly be shattered or snatched away by her mother's violent reproaches. Julie now recalled a childhood dominated by her own obsessions. She went through phases where she absolutely had to swallow five times, matching the number of people in her family, and she felt that if she failed to do so, something very bad would undoubtedly befall a family member. As such memories emerged and cast a shadow over her past, she at times resented and feared the therapy for darkening those images of childhood to which she had been able to cling throughout all her subsequent unhappiness.

Fear of criticism, "paranoia"

The slightest comment that could be construed as a criticism festered inside Julie's mind. At night she would go on and on ruminating: "I did something wrong, I'm a bad person." She would get agitated if people did not say goodbye to her; she imagined colleagues at work talking behind her back and saying: "She's mad, she's a bad occupational therapist." If someone was ill-tempered around her, she thought: "How shall I cope?" The slightest neglect on the part of her friends was experienced as abandonment. For instance, when friends didn't reply to her letters immediately, her reaction was: "I feel so fed up with life. They don't like me any more."

It was very painful for Julie to realize that she had been mainly engaged in a struggle for self-survival and was not the selfless person she aspired to be. She started to wonder if she really cared about her job, or if she was just doing it for her own gratification. Whenever she gave something to someone, she needed the person to reciprocate promptly or else she felt "funny, neglected, unloved" and "took it out on herself". We talked about this infantile part of her that was at once greedy and demanding, but also feeling deprived and depleted so that she could not bear to give something away. She commented that she did not feel strong enough to recognize, let alone accept, this anxious, greedy child within herself.

Ambivalence and persecutory guilt

Julie had tremendous difficulty acknowledging her angry feelings, her ambivalence, and her competitiveness. She did not seem to have the equipment to tolerate such powerful emotions, so she immediately turned them into means of self-punishment. She mentioned an old friend who failed to meet her as arranged. Initially, Julie felt relieved not to have to see this girl who, like Julie's mother, monopolized all the attention. Subsequently, Julie was besieged by doubts about how she may have harmed this girl and was plagued by the idea that her friend might viciously turn against her. She stayed up at night wondering if she should write to this person. Once she had gone out with some friends, got drunk, and behaved in a somewhat silly way. Later, it all kept coming back to her as she repeatedly reconstructed the events in her mind—what she had said, how the others had seemed to react, wondering whether she had been stupid and whether her friends had laughed about her, and so on. In her therapy she had to be constantly vigilant with me, censoring herself in order to spare me from any sign of her demandingness, anger, criticism, or neglect, which may cause me to die or turn into a persecutor.

A year into therapy, Julie related the following dream: "*I was in my nan's house. I was calling her and went to the back door and she was lying in the garden next to the washing line. I screamed, I panicked, then I saw her moving. I woke up and went back to sleep and dreamt that I was at the pub with friends. I went to ring my nan and tell her I'd be late.*"

The dream reminded Julie of how her grandparents were alone, out there in Cyprus, and how it would be entirely her fault if anything were to happen to them, because she should be there with them. I commented that when she had a good time at the pub, she felt guilty because her mother, her grandparents, and myself were lonely without her. We had all been abandoned by Julie, who was engaged in being young and having a good time while we were left to suffer through her fault; this made sense to Julie, and she added that she had had a number of nightmares over the course of an otherwise enjoyable weekend. Julie punished herself for any feelings of ambivalence towards her objects, whom she omnipotently felt she had to keep alive.

Obsession with teeth

A month or so after starting to eat "normally", Julie's main anxiety shifted to a fear of losing her teeth. Indeed, she felt that her teeth had undergone irreparable damage as a result of her self-starvation. When it became a daily preoccupation, she felt the anxiety was driving her mad. She thought her life would be ruined if she lost her teeth, for people would undoubtedly mock her ugliness. She came into sessions with a pinched face, her mouth shut, concerned lest I notice the bad state of her teeth. She was convinced she had seen me looking right at her mouth from the very outset, ready to criticize her.

A year into the therapy she spoke of her fear that she would never be able to lead a normal life or meet someone, on account of her teeth. She told me, for instance, that she went out one night and saw a few girls at the pub chatting with the lads. She too got talking to a young man when suddenly she thought: "Oh, he's going to see my teeth!" She continued: "It's like a permanent torture, and I ended up having to leave the pub because otherwise he would see something." I brought to her attention the spoiling of her pleasure in talking to this young man. She replied: "Yes, I can't talk, I can't smile, I can't be happy because of my teeth". She added: "Nobody will want me, everybody will laugh at me."

Julie was showing how frightened she was of her own biting aggression and the damage this had done to her teeth. She feared she would inevitably be punished for it. But while the obsession about teeth receded after a couple of months, the anxiety about her biting/devouring self and the horror of bingeing remained. At this point in Julie's life, bingeing was defined as the ingestion of a bowl of cereal and perhaps a few chocolate biscuits, all of which were safely within the amount of calories allotted to each day. The bowl of cereal was usually consumed on the spur of the moment, late at night, in addition to the three regular meals. Small hurtful events in Julie's life seemed to drive her to this type of clandestine eating. However, at times she had her bowl of cereal for fear of feeling deprived, or because of an anxiety that there would be no more eating until the next morning. She also ate because she was simply not certain that she had filled her daily quota of calories. She always felt that she was a bad person after a "binge", and she hated herself intensely. Her self-disgust was not only for having given in to "greed" but also because the "binge" sometimes left her feeling bloated and she feared she may have to pass wind.

The child part of Julie sought comfort in those private meals before going to sleep. However, the "sweet" turned bad, for it was stolen from the maternal object. The stomach bloating and gases, "sweets" turned bad, were punishments for her rottenness, anger, greed, or secretiveness.

The following session suggests that the cruelty of her internal object was coloured by her rivalrous attacks against her mother.

Julie relates having spoon-fed a paralysed, brain-damaged woman, thinking: "Why didn't she die? Who would want to live like that?" She goes on to wonder: "Who would want to live like me? It's so degrading, I hate myself so much."

She then talks about a visit to the dentist, which was scheduled for later that day. "If he says to me 'All your teeth have to come out', I will kill myself." I wonder about the daddy-dentist taking all her teeth out and the sense that she would have to kill herself. Is it perhaps that these bad teeth are a sign both of her own self-destruction and of her destructive attacks on her parents? Julie replies that when in the past she and her mother had an argument, her mother often used to storm out of the house in a terrible state, leaving Julie to feel horribly guilty. When she was little, she went on, she used to be very close to her cats, and whenever one of them disappeared or died, she would be totally devastated. "When I was 15 and had arguments with my mother, I would turn against my cats; I started to reject them. Since I started my therapy, I feel close to them again." I suggest that perhaps the cats represent the needy, soft, but also scratching, biting baby and that possibly when she reached 15 or 16 she got rid of the baby and its dependent relationship with the mother.

She goes on to talk about her games with Sindy dolls when she was about 12 years old. She was in the habit of playing with her Sindy dolls for hours, after having locked herself in the bathroom. She sometimes even did her homework in the bathroom, locking herself in so as not to be distracted and so she could be in peace. She adds that although, at the time, she was still a 12-year-old child playing with Sindy dolls, she had started a job at a newsagent's on Saturday where there was an attractive manager she fancied. I comment on the little girl's wish to be a pretty Sindy doll/mummy and have daddy all for herself, while pushing mummy away by taking possession of the bathroom. She would become mother in a fantasy of taking over her internal space, probably represented by the bathroom. It emerges that she would also bring food into her secret games in the locked bathroom and would play with the dolls' house. Julie continues, "I was rebellious and sneaky, bringing the food upstairs, which was not allowed." I speak of the little, competitive Julie who wants to be a pretty Sindy doll/mummy and sneak forbidden food out of mother's kitchen and take charge of it in her own secret domain. She adds that she used to make up stories in her mind in which everybody would feel sorry for her. She imagined being the victim of an accident or a rape. At school, they would hold a memorial for her but she would then reappear, alive, and the cries would turn to cheers, all for her. We reflect on her wish to be not only the prettiest, but also the most special and damaged one, the heroine of some tragic story. She responds by remembering how she used to cut up her dolls or maim them by cutting their hair or legs, indicating that the dolls had been in some imaginary accident. She adds that it is weird, that all these feelings that had been shut out were coming back now. She is remembering them and feeling them again in the session.

This session shows, I think, Julie's horror at what she felt she had inflicted upon her object and herself, which were quite undifferentiated. The brain-damaged woman and the toothless girl give us a picture of Julie's internal landscape and help us to understand her. She described how she used to care for her cats, standing for the mother–baby relationship, trying to save them from disappearing or being run over by a car, in the same way that she felt responsible for her mother storming out, threatening suicide, and running wildly in the street after an argument. When she reached adolescence, she got rid of it all—the fear, the reproaches, the projections—but also, by the same token, she repressed the needy part of herself that wanted to be looked after. Talking about her oedipal rivalry with her mother, she displayed the two split sides of her personality. One side bit this reproaching, unavailable mother and her arguments and plotted to steal both father and food from her, which then led to Julie's persecutory guilt and fear of punishment. The other side of her tried to look after the mother and the baby but could not really stop the damage. Her superego, the father-figure represented here by the dentist, exacted punishment for her aggressiveness and competitiveness by resorting to the same violence that she herself had mobilized when she was attacking her objects, condemning her to be deprived of all pleasure—indeed, to a life hardly worth living.

A dream Julie that recounted in a subsequent session, rehearsing the same theme of irreparable damage, helped to identify an envious part working from within her, envious of her own happiness, and allied with her destructive object.

She started the session by stating that she had been all right that past week, but that she is feeling quite "down" this morning. There had been several deaths at the hospital that week. An old patient with cancer whom Julie was fond of had been discharged to die. This led to a nightmare.

Julie remembers her dream: "*I had cancer, it was such a shock, it was so real. I felt anger and jealousy so strongly because now I knew I would never have a boyfriend, marriage or children.*" She comments that upon waking up from the dream, it had taken her a few minutes to realize that she did not truly have cancer. She feels, too, that the dream had been useful in that it made her realize that she has to make the most of life. I suggest that the dream perhaps also refers to our relationship, that she feels I am damaged, that I may die of cancer because of some harm she might have done me. Now Julie has this very ill psychotherapist inside her and is herself very ill. She then feels full of rage, jealousy, and envy towards my other children, who, she feels, have all the things she longs for. In the dream she is, as usual, deprived of all the good things in life because she is being punished for her "badness". Julie agrees with the second part of my interpretation and says that these were indeed powerful elements in the dream—the feeling that she would never get all these "normal" things, such as a husband and children. This leads us to discuss her need to always enquire about her parents' health whenever she spoke to them. I comment on her need to check, for fear that she might have harmed them in her anger, and I suggest that this particular fear and need for control are present in all her close relationships. Julie replies "Yes", with emotion, and confirms that it is indeed happening all the time. She mentions that when she concludes a letter to a friend with the standard "I hope to see you soon", or "I will see you soon", she then worries that she should not have written those words, for fear that something bad may happen to the person. I reflect on the underlying magical thinking: her words may have the power to make something bad happen. Therefore, to say "I hope to see you" is equivalent to tempting fate. Julie acknowledges that in her view she feels it would be her fault if something bad occurred.

We proceed to thoughts about her psychotherapy and her feelings towards me. She explains that it is not that she has doubts about coming, but more that there is "enough worrying me already to come here. It's the journey that is the chore, but not the hour that I'm with you." She goes on to say that she perceives everything in her life as a chore. She feels all these battles going on inside her, and while the little child in her wants to go off and cry, the more grown-up part of her will not allow it, pushing her to resist, cope, and work. She tries to understand why every day seems to loom before her like a string of chores, even when she feels happy and is enjoying her work. We think about a side of her that is relentlessly accusing her, draining away all the pleasure from her life. I add that this side of her attacks anything she invests in and with which she becomes emotionally involved, be it relationships or work, for fear of the potential pain of closeness. Julie immediately adds that while she is often depressed on her way to therapy, when she leaves she feels some light inside her. I suggest that the good feelings cannot be maintained and held on to over the separation but seem to get spoiled or lost. Julie responds sadly: "Well, there are so many bad things over the week, people dying or someone being in a bad mood with me." She mentions looking at herself in a mirror before going out to a party and thinking: "Oh, I do look nice tonight." She adds: "Later, when I came back from the party, I felt so cross because I didn't meet any men and then I think the whole evening was awful." She further adds that lately she has been trying to remind herself that she is enjoying herself more with her friends. She says she knows she is getting stronger in some areas, but when she feels down, she thinks it will go on forever.

Comments

In my opinion, the cancer in Julie's dream represented a destructive and punitive aspect of her personality. This part of herself was in projective identification with a damaged maternal object (see chapter 6) who enviously robbed her of marriage, husband, children, and life. The cancer might simultaneously have represented a punishment inflicted upon her by this internal object for having a healthy appetite for the good things in life and, at an infantile level, for having snatched them away from her mother. At a certain point in the session, she alluded to an incident in a club in the course of which a man had mockingly mimicked her way of saying hello. Despite her attempt to neutralize this incident in her mind, an identification with an attacking object echoed her own self-denigrating voice, and she could not help but find herself allying with it. One can likewise understand her feeling that "everything becomes a chore"—for instance, the journey to therapy or having to write a letter to a friend lest the friend felt offended—by seeing that for her these activities primarily served the function of placating a damaged, envious object whose expectations she could never fully satisfy. It seems to me that this session illustrated a split in Julie's internal maternal object: one side of the object was bent on destroying her, and made her suffer, but there also appeared to be another, more benign and constructive side. It is this latter part that, I think, kept her in therapy and was frequently allied with me as her therapist. She then perceived me—and the therapy—as supportive and sustaining, and the negative feelings were not able to dominate her relationship with me.

Conclusions

Julie's relation to her maternal object and the dual function of food within this dynamic

Julie did not have an internal or external mother who was in touch with the child's needs, who could process anxieties, help her to understand them, and enable her to feel nurtured and contained. Her internal mother did not seem able to tolerate the needs of a hungry, demanding child, with needs of her own. Rather, she perceived the child not only as an extension of herself in which she can project her own needs, anxiety, and persecution, but also as a threatening rival. A parent that cannot allow for separation may impair the capacity for symbolization; perhaps Julie's turning to food in moments of stress, of persecution, and of depression can be understood within this context. Food serves the function of comfort, concretely re-evoking the sense of the feeding bond between mother and infant. This food is taken in with desperate greed in an attempt to blot out distress and acute emptiness, which might derive from an underdeveloped sense of self. It is "stolen food", which she gave to herself with no recognition of a maternal source (e.g. the food she hoarded in the bathroom when she was a teenager). Food taken in such a way turned bad and could not really sustain her. It became persecutory because she felt bloated and full of smelly gases. The feelings of fullness reminded her not only that she had lost control, but also that she had stuffed herself without even feeling hungry. She once told me, "I could just eat and eat or starve and starve." In other words, she felt that there were no natural limits to her eating or her starving. This seemed to indicate that there was not a "father" in her internal world who set limits and might have helped to establish boundaries between mother and baby.

When in adolescence Julie started to say "no" to food, she was in fact saying "no" to the power and control her mother exerted over her, "no" to the fear of her mother's unpredictable moods, and projections (see Williams, 1997), and "no" to accusations of being bad or never being good enough. Her rejection of food was, at this point of her development, certainly the expression of a need to separate herself from her mother by gaining some control over her body. However, as I said before, it was also a way of punishing herself for her "unbearable shortcomings". This violent way of separating herself away from her mother also separated her from the dependent baby part of herself which needed nurturing. When she turned her back on food, she turned away from that which is life-sustaining: omnipotent control over herself and her objects took its place; she became an addict. To summarize, Julie's attitude to food was twofold: she saw it either as an irresistible and despised comforter to which she succumbed or as a means of exerting omnipotent, obsessional control over her needs, which threatened to overwhelm her.

The impact of such a maternal object was expressed in Julie's dream of succumbing to a cancer, which deprived her of everything good in life. At times she suffered it, at others she seemed actively to allow it to spread and take over her life. Only very gradually in the therapy did she become able to internalize a more containing object that would allow her to live her life.

Obsessionality/psychic retreat

Julie's obsessional calorie counting, checking of her weight, and controls over her body and food were ways of cutting herself off from her emotional life. As she said in an early session: "I count calories and I think obsessionally of food because I am scared of life." Because she did not have the equipment to deal with her feelings, all emotional life—conflict, love, sexuality—and also any change in her daily life not under her omnipotent control threatened her with disintegration. Julie faced the basic dilemma of all anorexics: any impulse that may loosen omnipotent, deadening control may feel life-threatening.

The manic–depressive aspect of her mood swings

a. When Julie was in what she called a "positive" state of mind, she felt compelled to look after others and rescue them. She fed and repaired the internally damaged mother and her damaged babies in an omnipotent way. She projected all her own needs into this mother and her babies in order to relieve herself of the mental pain of dependence and feelings of need for the object.

b. When she was in a depressed state of mind, she heard the damaged, angry mother attacking her, reproaching her for having robbed her, for being bad, worthless, and inadequate. Since childhood, this feeling seemed to have always been with Julie: a deep sense of worthlessness and a desperate need to please, to be reassured by her object that she was not as bad as she felt she was. The only way that she felt she could get this reassurance was by starving herself to the point of endangering her life. Only if she was extremely ill would she get the attention she was craving. If she was the "poor Julie" that everybody felt sorry for, then she could not be so bad.

Self and object

A part of Julie's personality was envious and resentful of her enjoyment of life, of food, and of relationships. This aspect allied itself with a destructive, envious, reproaching object. When she punished herself, the part that carried out the attack was in projective identification with an envious object. This part-object identification was reflected in the cancer described in Julie's dream, from which she was doomed to die. The cancer, which deprived her of everything good, had an immense grip on Julie's emotional life and a lot of work in the therapy was focused on trying to help her distance herself from this diseased part of herself.

Transference

Julie's therapy was very important to her. She acknowledged her intense need for help and often said that she felt she trusted me. Her sessions were used to pour out incidents, hurts, and disillusionments, but she was also prepared to think with me about the meaning of her actions and feelings. There seemed to be a need for a safe space to think with me about her problems, but she was still frightened of relating to me in a direct, more personal way, perhaps for fear of discovering an aspect of her destructive, maternal object in me and/or of some intolerable aspect of herself. She often said that she had had a bad week, so she knew how much she wanted to come to her sessions to get relief and some peace of mind, but she did not refer to our relationship. It was interesting that our eyes only ever met briefly meet or sometimes not at all. I felt that this tenuous connection might be Julie's defence against experiencing her dependency and a need for the child to get to food from an object that might unpredictably turn against her and throw her into an abyss of despair and rage. Another way of thinking about this tangential transference could be that I represented a slightly different version of "the father" with whom, in the outside world, she had weekly telephone conversations. She told him about her difficulties, very often practical ones such as, for instance, her panic when her car broke down. He listened and tried to help her in what seemed to be a kind, concerned way, and he seemed to have been experienced as a benign person.

Lessening of control—beginnings of hope

It seemed extremely important to Julie that I was not seeing her purely for her anorexic state, but because I believed that her anorexia was a sign of her emotional distress, and that I made it clear that we would continue meeting for however long she needed to feel better within herself. I mentioned that within three months of beginning her therapy, Julie started allowing herself to have three small meals a day. I still wonder what happened in this initial phase. In her words, she told me that she had decided she no longer wanted to get attention from her friends by starving herself, making herself ill, and having them look after her to prove that she was not as bad as she felt she was. Was it perhaps that she was allowing herself a "tiny meal" of my attention and that this in turn fed the beginning of the hope that she did not need to be so desperately ill to deserve the attention of her friends? Two and a half years later, Julie no longer had a "weight problem" (she had achieved an average weight). However, whenever life became stressful, she had to fight against compulsions to control her food intake and to get stuck in calorie counting again. On the other hand, she was aware of other ways of coping with pain and conflict, by either writing in her diary or by talking to her friends about her feelings. Although she was still fragile and basically quite depressed, there were clear signs that she had begun internalizing a thinking space from the therapy and that she could, at times, make good use of it to hold herself together.

She was longing to be in a loving relationship with a boyfriend, which seemed to me to be a sign of her growing hope that life had something good to offer and that she might be able to have a share of this for herself.

CHAPTER EIGHT

Fantasies concerning body functioning in an anorexic adolescent

Diomira Petrelli

Whe I first got to know her, Ivana was 20 years old. For more than two years she had been suffering from anorexia: she had been refusing food and was vomiting (although this was not associated with episodes of bulimia). With the onset of amenorrhoea, which had been preceded by an irregular menstrual cycle, there occurred a marked decrease in her weight.

Ivana's analysis, which lasted for eight years, was undertaken on the basis of four sessions per week. The sheer volume and variety of material relating to the analysis, the intense nature of both the transference and countertransference, and the multiplicity of the themes—which opened up a variety of potential interpretations of her condition—demand an extensive and thorough report. For present purposes, I intend to concentrate on a particular period in the treatment and on the dreams and fantasies that emerged in the middle and last phases of the analysis. In this way, I feel I can better illuminate the dynamic features, not only of Ivana's case, but also of other cases of anorexia. I shall limit myself to a short description of the patient's history as it emerged during the course of treatment, noting a few significant features of the first years of analysis.

196   DIOMIRA PETRELLI

Notes on the patient's history
and the first years of analysis

Ivana is petite with dark hair and has a lingering, intense, but somewhat sidelong gaze visible from beneath slightly swollen eyelids. She appeared extremely feminine and meticulous in her dress-sense. At times, she walked swaying a little, almost as if she were not touching the ground. At other times, as she walked she seemed to stiffen her legs as she placed her feet firmly on the ground, her low heels making a clicking sound. In contrast to her appearance, her voice was that of a much larger person—strong and serious, as though issuing from a cave. Over the telephone it sounded rather masculine.

She told me during the early months that she believed that her anorexia had started when her mother (whose favourite she had been) had experienced a period of severe depression after the marriage of her only other daughter, who was six years older than Ivana. In fact, the mother, who "had always taken charge of everything", had since childhood been for her "the major point of reference", while the father appeared a shadowy figure, weaker and "passive", incapable of dealing with the "practical" side of life or of "material things". He was an intellectual, highly sophisticated, and cultured but "always somewhat lost in his own world of imagination", she said. Her relationship with her mother was described as very intense, albeit ambivalent; that with her father appeared to have a peculiarly negative character: "My father eats a lot and very slowly", she said, "he spends hours at the table, he annoys me . . . I feel uncomfortable with him. From the time I was little he was a kind of idol, cultured, and intellectual, he'd talk to me about his brilliant work." Now she regarded him as "a weak man withdrawn into himself". He had taken early retirement some years before and now depended for everything on the mother, who is active, over-protective, and self-sacrificial. In this first stage of the analysis, the father was conspicuous by his absence and for the disappointment caused her by his transformation from an idealized figure of childhood to the tired individual, who only aroused in her feelings of irritation and hostility. This image of the father gave further confirmation to Ivana's image of her mother as sad, alone, and without real support.

Her mother's depression had unleashed in Ivana not simply a deep bewilderment but strong feeling of anger and jealousy. She said she felt as if she had spent her life trying to hold on to the role of the favourite daughter by being good, while her sister had always given her parents trouble with her "crises" and her emotional vulnerability. Even though she had felt she was the favourite, the onset of the depression seemed to destroy this. The helpless rage that her mother aroused in her was experienced as an overwhelming desire to "shake" her; she would had have liked "to have given her an electric shock", she said, "to jerk her out of her immobility".

From another standpoint, Ivana's anorexia was also, paradoxically, a way of giving her mother "something to battle with", and therefore a reason to live. About her mother's depression, Ivana said she had thought, "If I go away too my mother will die." In this way there emerged an omnipotent sadomasochistic link, which, frequently expressed in the patient's fantasies, served to keep both her and her mother alive. Her earlier successes—for example, at school—now seemed to belong to another person; she now seemed false and ingratiating, forced to meet the needs and what she perceived as self-serving demands of the mother, and her successes had quickly been given up to make way for a deep and painful sense of emptiness and impotence.

In the stories her mother told her about her, there emerges a picture from early life of a "decisive character: my mother tells how I always went to sleep with a dummy, then one day I suddenly decided I didn't want it any more and that was it; she didn't want to teach me to read and I taught myself, one letter at a time, and very fast". This is in contrast with the memories she had of herself: "I remember being weak and shy, frightened of everything. If they told me off at school, I got upset. I felt hurt by everyone, didn't manage to stand up for myself. I disliked being the centre of attention; it frightened me." She remembers finding it hard to stand up to her strong and resolute mother and to resist doing what she wanted, so that "When I have to decide to do something I avoid telling her so she can't influence me." She would recall with anger how, as a child but also as an adolescent, her mother would dress her and comb her hair, "as if I were a doll", pretty only insofar as she reminded her mother of herself when she was young. Ivana enjoyed a subtle and malicious feeling by undoing everything her mother did to her and going out without make-up to show her "ugly looks". This docile, defensive adaptation was soon apparent in the transference. Even though Ivana came diligently and punctually to her sessions, declaring herself to be more and more "connected" to the analysis, I felt her participation to be largely on the surface and somewhat formal. She rarely failed to accept my interpretations and agree with them, but her acceptance was docile and defensive rather than felt. Often she would talk about herself in a detached, distant manner, as if she were talking about someone else. Every now and then, in the middle of this docility, she would betray signs of her mistrust and of a deep intolerance of anything that wandered even slightly away from what she expected. I sensed in her a strong need for control and a deep inner resentment that was carefully concealed.

After a while she admitted that she hardly ever managed to remember what had been said during the sessions. It escaped her, "as if I were trying to grasp something without managing it", she commented. The oscillation between docility and sudden outbreaks of anger (often not verbalized but expressed through agitation) characterized our relationship for a long time. Outwardly she seemed to accept what I said, but inwardly she stuck to her position, although sensing that any eventual change might be no more than a narcissistic gratification on my part: "the gratification from solving a difficult case", as she would say. For her part it was simply the prelude to my abandonment of her. An apparent improvement in her symptoms during the first year and a half brought a rapid increase in weight followed by a suicide attempt in the second Easter holiday of the analysis. This revealed her tremendous anger towards her inner parents and, in the transference, towards her analyst. The anger was rooted in deep feelings of jealousy and of exclusion. Her relationship with me seemed to be characterized by a powerful narcissistic defence, which drove her to barricade herself behind a docile self expressed via the behaviour of a "model" patient. At another level, the way was gradually being cleared for her to begin to realize that in the transference she sought a relationship of reciprocal control in which staying ill would keep the analysis going for ever. She regularly fantasized about how we would grow old together, trapped in a kind of paralysed equilibrium. The therapeutic relationship came to be experienced as a symbiotic sadomasochistic one in which both sides had to remain ossified, implying that no growth or change was possible. When I offered this interpretation, she replied that she could not imagine any relationship that could be strong and permanent other than one based on the suffering and care produced by illness. It became clear, through subsequent associations, that this notion followed the pattern of her early relationship with her mother. At around age 6 months, Ivana had contracted a life-threatening bronchial pneumonia. The mother, who had stopped work when Ivana was born in order to breast-feed her, nursed her diligently during this long, painful illness. During the illness, her mother had to stop breast-feeding her. Mother often told Ivana of how she had had the task of giving her "huge and painful injections", and how she had felt herself overcome by the tension and suffering involved. This nursing relationship, accompanied by fantasies of a sadomasochistic type, was gradually being re-lived in the transference.

During the analysis, Ivana had at times to be fed intravenously. Sometimes in a session she would take pleasure in the bruises left by the needle in the vein in her arm and would examine them at length, as if attracted by them. Often she would talk at length and with considerable distress about her various physical discomforts, as if the display of her physical and psychological suffering would be a means of strengthening the relationship between us. Behind this lay the risk, which I always felt to be imminent, that I might be transformed for her into a mother-nurse figure who was attempting to provide a cure that was perhaps effective but was essentially extremely painful and intrusive. I became aware during this period, mainly through the countertransference, of the need for some caution in offering interpretations, so that she would not experience my interventions as "painful injections" that she had to endure in order to keep my attention.

In the course of the second year of analysis, following the suicide attempt which Ivana had come to see as a violent attack on her father and the "paternal" aspects of the analysis, the importance her father's illness had had for her became clear for the first time. He had suffered from a form of epilepsy the details of which were cloaked in secrecy within the family so that, even in the analysis, it was not possible for her to talk about it. Since early childhood the father's illness and the hypochondriacal anxiety that went with it had led him to appear to Ivana as a kind of "huge child-rival" whose delicate state meant that he claimed for himself her mother's worry and attention. Behind the closed door of their bedroom, where, during "crises", the mother nursed the father, and where nobody else was allowed to go, Ivana imagined that "secret and terrible things were going on". She heard sounds of gasping that gave her the impression that "something dreadful and terribly painful was happening to her father which also involved her mother". In this primitive primal scene, the father was experienced as a kind of monstrous "super-child" who appropriated by way of his illness all her mother's attention and energy. She said that "her father made her extremely angry because, even though he ate a lot, he'd always been noticeably thin". Her anorexia had been, at another level, also a way of keeping up with her father's state of illness, and thereby getting attention and care from her mother. It also reproduced with the mother, as in the transference, a symbiotic relationship that she considered indissoluble insofar as it was based on the nursing of illness and on suffering.

During these first years of analysis, I often had the sense of needing, during the session, to make considerable efforts to establish an exchange with Ivana that was more real, but once the session was over it was as if everything evaporated again. Each time, it seemed as if she and I would have to start all over again from the beginning. The repetition of this process was enervating, and in the countertransference it gave me a deep sense of impotence and discouragement. Analysing these processes with her, which went together with the difficulties of separation, allowed new and meaningful aspects of her infancy to emerge. After the bronchial pneumonia as an infant, her character, previously tranquil, had undergone a sudden change. Feeding problems arose, as did nightmares and sleep disturbances. It was during that period that the vomiting began to occur, put down at the time to her coughing. As her mother had recounted, immediately after eating Ivana would cough and vomit, and her mother had to begin feeding her all over again. Everyone around her, especially her mother, waited anxiously for what would happen once she had fed while trying to distract her so that she would not cough. Subsequently, during early childhood, she had always eaten only a little and very slowly, thereby keeping her mother by her side. She remembered keeping food in her mouth for hours, passing it from one side to another "so that the meat on the plate, by now cold, became disgusting". Vomiting and a kind of persistent regurgitation featured among her present symptoms. It was clear that there persisted for Ivana an insoluble dilemma. On the one hand, she could not endure even the slightest separation or differentiation; on the other hand, she experienced a state of fusion that was highly idealized but intrinsically suffocating and deadly. This inner state in which she was trapped found expression in recurrent fantasies and dreams in which she yearned to immerse herself in the sea but was always confronted with obstacles. She told me that, as a child, she had read and had fantasized about the fairy stories her mother had read to her. One in particular had captured her imagination and filled her with emotion: "The beautiful little mermaid, sea creature, on whom the wicked witch had decreed that, if she wanted to follow her beloved prince on to land and become a normal woman, she'd have to walk over sharp blades feeling at every step the pain of her feet being sliced in two. This was the price to pay for earthly love." Or, as I thought, the other side of the loss of omnipotence. Often during the analysis I felt like a witch, or like the prince for the love of whom she had to face the painful process of re-working her state of fantasized omnipotence and isolation—a state in which she lived alone, de-humanized, and as though hidden in the depths of the sea, far from earthly feelings. Hers was a fantasy of omnipotence and refuge within a mother who was enveloping and suffocating at the same time. At other times the analysis itself could become this sea-refuge—sometimes cold, disappointing, and dirty, or else a warm and welcoming escape from life.

The central phase of the analysis:
un moviemento in due tempi

I refer here to a point in the sixth year when her acute anorexia, after a number of deteriorations and remissions, seemed now largely to be overcome. Work had been accomplished with regard to the analytic relationship as well as to external conditions. Even though Ivana's relationship with food had improved, it still was not without its problems and sometimes she could relapse into vomiting. She had regained weight to an acceptable level, even if it still was not quite "normal", and the menstrual cycle had returned spontaneously. She had completed her studies successfully and had been involved, to her satisfaction, in some temporary work, and for the first time she had entered into a serious and stable relationship with a peer, despite his work-related move to another city. Ivana was in closer contact with her feelings, and instead of reacting with anger to separation, hardening herself, or breaking off the relationship as she had sometimes done, she tried to keep the relationship alive even during absences. The relationship with me had passed through various phases, some of which had been stormy. Ivana had moved from her formal, detached docility at the beginning of the analysis to a more intense relationship in which she could tolerate differences and separations, even though they remained difficult. I had the impression that even if there had been significant changes, there remained, however, certain unresolved central problems, among which was her intense need for control and her difficulty in fully trusting the relationship. Ivana alternated between moments of great intimacy and emotional contact and sudden withdrawals and blocks, which produced a chronic to-ing and fro-ing in the relationship, as though it were an elastic band, and this demanded a lot of patience and tolerance.

Ivana herself had reached a kind of new equilibrium that provided her with a better life, but, as she remarked to me one day, she had the impression that the nub of the matter had still not really been addressed. This observation presented itself as a message with ambiguous emotional meaning with regard to her relationship with me. If in one sense it seemed to show genuine recognition of a persistent difficulty hiding behind improvements, in another sense it took on a more threatening tone—that of affirming and stressing the stubborn intransigence of her deeper problems. It also sounded like a gentle reminder of my own impotence and the predestined failure of the analysis. I told her that if in a way it seemed to me she was making an effort to express with sincerity how she really felt, I thought at the same time she was telling me, with a certain bitter satisfaction, that inwardly everything was unchanged and perhaps unchangeable, and that in the end I should resign myself to the fact that nothing was to be done and one might as well get used to it. Was it not also a way of "throwing in the towel" and avoiding confrontation with her anxiety about what a real change might bring about? She remained silent for a moment and then said that maybe I was right but she really did not know if she was capable of change at that level and she often thought it would stay like that forever. This time her tone contained more sadness than usual. It seemed to me that we had reached a point which was, so to speak, critical: would it be possible to reach a more genuine transformation? Ivana had managed to sustain her relationship with her far-away fiancé despite a sense of deprivation, anger from a feeling of "having been left by herself", and envy at him having work that was "nice and interesting". The struggle she endured inwardly to keep up the relationship, despite her disappointment and her desire to unleash a vendetta from afar, seemed to be taking the direction of an effort to accommodate and tolerate separation.

Over time, all this seemed to translate itself into an intensified need for closeness and continuity, which each day seemed to become more urgent. The progress she had already made in the analysis led her to consider moving to the city where her fiancé was living, and where she too might find a job, and to try out living with him and in the process leave behind her own family. But this entailed the risk of a premature breaking-off of the analysis. It showed up clearly in dreams that depicted the situation. Ivana was conflicted about the intensification of the analytic relationship, in the sense of an ever-greater acknowledgement of a deep need for dependence, which in the transference made her afraid of becoming imprisoned in a suffocating relationship, that would be a repetition of her relationship with her mother.

Her desire for closeness and continuity were split and displaced almost entirely onto the external world via her relationship with her fiancé, but in the transference she experienced for the most part feelings of impotence and fears of suffocation and imprisonment. In fact, with the removal of her anorexic defences a devastating sense of impotence and incapacity had come to the fore. A further slight increase in body weight once again aroused in her great anxiety and a desperate sense of falling apart: "I feel as if every part of my body could do what it likes." Signs of physical improvement were perceived as dangerous insofar as they were uncontrollable and discordant with her inner feelings: "My body doesn't reflect what's inside me, it does what it likes, it's solid, it gets fat, inside me I feel disgusting. I feel old rather than very little." She returned obsessively to the problem of a paralysing sense of emptiness that constantly intensified in relation to other people whom she envied deeply. Along with the idea of an escape-ending there was an awareness of the fear of being left "without a mother's support", "with a millstone", "the fear of leaving something unresolved that is lurking in me and that could explode from one moment to the next". In the countertransference during this period, I had an image of a small child crying desperately while gripping a table leg. She wanted to walk by herself, and yet she obstinately refused to accept the hand that would help her, while being terribly frightened of the next step, as if this meant leaping into space. I recall the mother's description of how she had been very attached to her dummy and had then suddenly pulled it out of her mouth all on her own.

By the time we had completed the sixth year of analysis, Ivana decided to move away to another town to live with her boyfriend, as this would also give her the possibility of finding some work. It was proposed to continue the analysis but, because of the travel, to reduce the number of sessions to two on two consecutive days. She maintained that she had never considered stopping the analysis altogether but wanted to make "a gradual transition". She said she was "trying to go forward in spite of the fear", but she admitted being unable to give up her anorexic behaviour, which seemed to me at that point like the wooden leg of the table to which she clung so tenaciously. I was concerned at what I saw as a premature separation and that, at least in part, the stopping of two of the sessions was a new anorexic manoeuvre directed at the analysis. I realized that it would have no effect to interpret the move as a way of acting within transference as an anorexic mode that projected onto me feelings of need, of abandonment and loss, as well as of impotence. She seemed in one way to be trying to get closer to her fiancé while distancing herself vigorously from the relationship with me and denying the despair she felt in acknowledging her dependence on the analysis.

At the same time, she projected onto me her distress at the loss and the anxiety about the separation. Seen in this way the disturbance of this period can be read as a response to her attempt to really put an end to the anorexic tactics, an attempt that, even if incomplete, had brought more direct contact with the distress associated with her sense of emptiness. In this situation, the discontinuous presence of analysis, which she felt mostly in terms of dependence, became intolerable. Ivana stated that analysis could not give her real support in the place of the false support offered by the anorexia because "it's not always there", "the analysis is a net with holes in it—if you fall where there's net it's alright, if not you fall". The pain of loss was again projected onto me along with a sense of impotence and failure. The difficulty of feeling herself "inside" and of "belonging" had always made her feel excluded—someone who could only "come in" furtively, "clandestine, something posted"—and this was rooted in feelings of exclusion and envy with respect to the parental couple. "It must be something", she would say, "that developed in me as a child concerning my parents, whom I saw as so beautiful, strong, such a perfect couple. I always felt myself somewhat set apart, in tow."

A few sessions later she added: "It always seems to me that others are better than me. I never take any steps towards anything because I'm always on the side watching. I feel like a goldfish in a glass bowl." I commented that in her "bowl" maybe she felt a bit safer, but also imprisoned and paralysed, with no possibility of being free and of really taking part in life and in relationships.

A dream, a few sessions later, expressed concretely the pain of this inability to "come in" despite her great efforts: "*I was by the sea with friends, and the mask of one of them sank under water and they asked me to go and get it. I put on my mask in order to go and get it, but the surface of the sea was as hard as a floor. It looked like the floor of my old room, where I used to live as a child. I kept banging my head. I saw the mask at the bottom but I couldn't reach it. The wall was giving in in places, it was crumbling, yet I couldn't get to the mask on the bottom. I woke up with a headache.*" On the other hand, closeness too was experienced with distress. She said: "If I stay in my room and read a book, I always think that I could stay there forever without anyone noticing, and without it mattering to anyone." Through her dreams, Ivana expressed, during this period, a concrete fantasy of being installed inside the mother-analyst in a position that is experienced as occupying the mother's rectum ("If I stay here bogged down," she says, "the problem will not resolve itself"), and so, even when I say something reassuring, it comes across as suffocating and as a threat to annihilate her, as if one person were disappearing completely inside another. I was struck by the expression "being bogged down" and the tone of distaste with which she had emphasized it. The "being inside" seemed to have become—I told her—being immersed in something dark, full of amorphous, disgusting, suffocating stuff (Meltzer, 1992). In dreams, but without doubt even more in the countertransference, I could perceive the feeling "inside" the room/analysis, particularly as it was accompanied by a fantasy of projective identification which was very intrusive and "involving". It seemed also to be associated with faecal images of the contents of this inside and of the analysis itself.

During this period, she never failed to emphasize the uselessness and futility of analysis and my helplessness, which she countered with her impelling need to "do" something, a trait that still continued to frighten her. The immobility of this "being inside" which is desired but also feared intensely was expressed, for example, in statements like: "In the morning when I wake I don't want to get up, I'd like to stay for a bit in the warm bed, but then suddenly I have to jump out violently as if I couldn't ever let myself really relax." She feared fusion. She felt it might re-absorb her. It might make it impossible for her to remain "visible". At the same time, it transformed, via a jealous attack, the contents inside the mother-analyst into something alternately false and suffocating. She dreamt, for instance, of a "plastic sea" in which she finds herself immersed, or a faecal "dirty opaque sea" in another dream "on which floats rubbish and bits of excrement which as I swim are hard to shift".

In the countertransference, I had the impression that it was difficult to "hold" her and that, in the actual moment in which she managed to get a little closer emotionally, she tended to slip away and to unload onto me feelings of failure and helplessness so that everything became rubbish, including me. I felt I had my back to the wall: accepting the reduction of sessions seemed like a collusion with a movement towards escape and not accepting the many signals of intense distress that Ivana continued to send me. But had I given her an ultimatum, I would have become immediately the terrible mother who wanted to swallow her up, intolerant of any movement she made. So I decided to say to her that, even though she knew what I thought of this transfer, I would nevertheless agree to see her twice a week.

We went through a period of a few months (from March to December) during which Ivana moved to the other city and came for two sessions of analysis—one in the evening and the other the next morning. During those ten months, Ivana continued to feel great distress and her physical state deteriorated as well. I perceived a progressive stripping of the analysis to a mere survival regime. My concern at her physical state increased: I saw her getting thinner, and she herself said, "I feel as though I am disappearing altogether." I felt that she was allowing herself to fade away and slip through my hands. Yet again there emerged strong anxiety about falling apart and dying. A violent resistance and rage ("a frightful rage") were expressed more clearly and directly, which had previously been hidden behind apparent acquiescence. She told me about her "distancing tactics".

"Sometimes I do things secretly; when someone angers me I cut them off. I keep a space inside myself, and this for me is revenge. I say things but underneath I'm thinking other things, or anyway I don't say everything I'm thinking. I feel a rage and go on steeping myself in my rage. I feel unable to live up to the demands of life, that there are limits, weariness, pain. I'm unable to handle them. When I meet with an obstacle I turn my back and leave. I won't accept effort, sacrifice . . . I just pretend to accept them. I just don't understand a thing. I think: I'll never succeed. I get up and go out or else I stay in but go into the bathroom to be sick. I refuse to make the effort anything will cost me, and I hate the fact of not coming first. Actually, when I'm tired I want at that moment something sweet to put in my mouth—like lots of people. But if I do put a sweet in my mouth I spit it out and am sick. In that moment it's as if someone rapped me on my fingers with a cane; as if a teacher were saying: Pay attention! You're not to stand there eating sweet things, you've got to apply yourself to understanding. I feel it as a punishment for having done something that takes me off the right track. If I eat one sweet I'll want another and another and then I'll spend all day eating sweets. I'll be frightened of not being able to stop. The only way of stopping is by being sick, for in that way it's as if I hadn't started."

As is evident from this account, Ivana shows greater awareness of the destructive force inside her that is directed not only at herself but also at our relationship, as well as at my capacity to continue to carry out genuine analytic work with her.

During those months, it seemed to me that little remained in the analysis beyond an empty ritual, and I often asked myself if I was right to go on with it. Looking back, I think perhaps that Ivana was putting me to the test to see to what extent I could hold out. She was projecting into me that part of her which was terrified and helpless, but also angry, and often I did actually feel this. Anyway, I decided to continue. In the end I decided to say all of the above to her, and to my surprise, perhaps because of the sadness and gravity of the tone I had unwittingly assumed, Ivana said she agreed and that she too had been thinking this for some time but had not had the courage to tell me. Then she began to talk about a part of herself that is isolated and unreachable:

"I've the feeling that there is a little Ivana stuck on a rock at the top of a mountain. She's there and she's got to stay there, and in this way she feels both unreachable and invulnerable. In the meantime anything can happen to the other Ivana. Like that anorexic girl who'd keep saying, they won't get me, they won't get me, and who lived in a state of isolation. It's as if she were frightened of the moment when this part of herself would come down from the mountain and she would lose any defence she had."

Both being inside and being outside are experienced as a great threat. Being inside is tantamount to being imprisoned; being outside, to being shattered. It was in this context that she told me for the first time what her mother had told her about her overdue birth. She was "too large" (4.2 kg) and would not come out, and she was born twenty-one days late, suffering from jaundice. Her coming out "tore" her mother. This account seemed to make sense and led me to reflect on the pain that for her was intimately connected with birth. It seemed like an ill-fated shadow projected onto the analysis, which itself was experienced as a painful "tearing". I, above all, as mother-analyst had to undergo this "tearing" as the only apparent alternative to a suffocating and deadly imprisonment (her delayed birth). I thought, too, that at the birth her mother had had to help the child to come out, pushing together with it: I thought of the difficulty I felt at us not having a reciprocal, synergic force that we could share. She refused to budge, and she clung on or tugged violently. But what was I actually doing to help her to get out? Was I not wanting to hang on to her? Could accepting her leaving be a way of helping her to come out and to be born? Or was it still too early and we would be risking a premature birth or a painful miscarriage?

Often Ivana had communicated her feeling to me—which coincided with mine—that many things had changed in her, or were changing, but nevertheless one problem remained unresolved, one that, according to her, would always remain. It was only in this culminating period of the reduced sessions (it was July, just before the summer break) that I was led to understand what she meant by: "I find that it's as if gradually I were accepting things and was convinced of change but deep down I'm not happy with it. There remains a thread of protest—like those people in mourning who wear a black button, who behave normally but there's always the black button to signal something to others." I was struck by what she said, and in a way I was moved. Then, during the session, I remembered an extract from Frances Tustin concerning the case of one of her young patients, John, who talked about a "black button": John felt that the loss and apparent destruction of the "button", which represented the meeting point of tongue and nipple, had left "a black hole from an evil puncture" (Tustin, 1986). So "the black button"—I thought—was the hole left by the breast. And once again I remembered Bion's words: "The point is the place where the breast was" (Bion, 1965). Ivana had reached a point of not being able to bear the loss of the anorexic part of herself, a part made visible through rebellion.

I thought that it was not only the anorexic part that Ivana could not bear losing. The black button, as I told her, is also the sign of another loss, the loss of the breast, and the black button represents the empty hole. This is the inalienable loss she cannot resign herself to, that she cannot accept, and that the black button is always there to signal. The anorexia is the moment in which this emptiness is held up as an emblem of her life. The session I have discussed came just before the summer break. On her return, Ivana told me that during the holidays, "I felt a kind of inner force", which was an awareness that she should continue with the analysis and that she had not so far talked about a number of important themes—things she had always been ashamed of and about which she felt extreme reticence. "I thought for the first time that the analyst might also miss the patient, and this provoked in me a state of great melancholy. Before, I went through the holidays in anger, but when I thought that maybe she too felt my absence, the anger subsided and I felt more acutely the separation." So along with a decision to stop being sick, Ivana asked me, after a while, to reinstate the usual number of sessions. The course and her work had finished, so she was able to come back to our city and re-enter full-time analysis, while continuing to see her fiancé at weekends. She had planned to pay for the further sessions with the money she had earned.

In this new phase the analysis seemed to proceed at a faster pace, and new material emerged or aspects were clarified that previously had only been sketched in. I had the impression that Ivana had at last decided to bring me into regions of her inner world that until now had been kept obscure. She told me about a feeling of having to undergo an enormous emotional effort to let me in, and often, after the sessions, she complained of tremendous fatigue. She talked about thoughts and fantasies that had occupied her for years and that she had hidden because they made her seem "crazy". The contents of these fantasies, which were concerned for the most part with the inside of her body and its functioning, had a strong psychotic quality. There seemed to exist in Ivana an autistic region into which she withdrew, as the contents of the fantasy were so terrifying. She tried to find a sense, albeit precarious, of security in these autistic refuges of herself through the omnipotent control of her body. She told me that since she was little she'd lived in a world inhabited by imaginary characters with whom she talked.

"... so that I was never alone ... but I did it even when there were people around. ... I was like an iceberg at that time. I had tiny fragments of contact with the external world, but there was an enormous sector of ice, closed off. It was something I had to hide, of which I was very ashamed, for they'd have thought me mad. I've always felt miles away. I grew up with the conviction that nobody knew me. These characters gave me unconditional approval. I've never had the courage to look outside for that reassurance. Then one day this world collapsed. Only emptiness was left."

In this phase of the analysis, it was apparent that there was a particular process at work: on the one hand, as I have said, Ivana had at last decided not to remain alone with these fantasies and to make me "see them" through a transferential process that was clearly intended to be seductive. On the other hand, she went on confirming, through these fantasies, that there existed in her body, as well as in her mind, a whole series of insuperable barriers that only she controlled and that nothing and nobody could contact beyond a certain point. This was something I had always felt through the countertransference but about which she now began to talk more clearly. Paradoxically, while she seemed to be showing greater trust in allowing me in, I felt at another hidden level her intention to make vivid for me just how powerful and absolute her closure was. For example, she would say: "From early childhood I had the sensation that my brain and my mouth were not connected up, as if there were a kind of barrier, a filter. I never really said what I thought. I've always talked very little, even though I thought a lot." Or else, concerning her body: "I have the impression that what's happening in my stomach is also happening in my vagina: as if there were a kind of stopper, an obstruction, a barrier, because of which I never manage to really let anything in, and to let out the blood. It's more than just not being hungry; it's that everything's contracted with a muscular tension so that food can't get in. The stomach's contracted and so is the vagina." The existence of these "barriers", which she felt to be concrete and physical, offered a reason for the impossibility, at the psychic level, of real introjection that would let her establish a nourishing relationship with food but also with analytic food for thought. The inside of her body is, in her fantasy, "completely blocked, rigid, and withered as if it were made of paper and not of living matter. Like fossils, you know, that once were living and then became stone." This deep-frozen, petrified inside also had the function of keeping at bay an extreme fear of breaking up. She said, "If I draw a deep breath and let go, I'm frightened that I'll start losing bits of me, of losing all my blood. I'm frightened of opening myself and disintegrating, and that substances would begin to enter and leave my body without any control." As I have said, I felt, mainly through my counter-transference reactions, that Ivana was putting into practice for my benefit a seductive form of acting out. It was as if she was "letting me further in", illuminating for me the mirage of being shown, personally by her, hidden, secret things that were lodged "inside" her. In the countertransference I realized the risk of being in some way fascinated by this mysterious and terrible world that she disclosed for me: on the other hand, I also had a sense of having ultimately to continue to fight against the obstructions, the wall or "barrier" she presented. It seemed that, despite her unconscious seductive intention, there was a real effort on the patient's part to share with me her fantasies. I chose not to interpret them in terms of their specific content but, rather, to address their general direc-tion; I often stayed silent, simply asking the occasional question or making a comment to clarify something, particularly if it seemed to me that the patient was "hearing" me.

Gradually it became possible to discern a general movement in two directions: an ebbing to and a flowing away, the latter being an attempt to create in the analysis a kind of "dead-end", which happened through the communication of her "crazy" thoughts. Her seductive intention seemed to be aimed at keeping me "blocked" and paralysed while the analysis itself could become for her a kind of "refuge". Later she said that she felt, particularly during this period, that "the analysis, too, had become a bit of a refuge, a kind of limbo in which I could enjoy some protection, a prolonged period of infancy, but which I fear will end suddenly with a rough awakening and a return to reality". Evidently the situation was not as static as it could have been, because progres-sively the image of her frozen, rigid body seemed to change.

Bit by bit, new fantasies emerged, equally distressing certainly, but which now referred to a body made of flesh, perhaps alive and even living, although full of bloody or faecal contents and violently "torn". A process that, seen with hindsight, was engendering increasing animation was also making the body's contents and activities feel bloody and very dangerous. Her menstrual periods, for example, had always been experienced with fear because they were connected to the feeling that a part of herself, or of her internal organs, was falling apart. This feeling was connected to a fantasy of something even more terrifying—that of "something extremely violent happening inside me, something which rips and tears me apart. My image of it is of a hand with claws that tears out something. Every time, I think I could die. I'm astonished that I don't die." So her holding back and her attempts to block and to "petrify" everything were connected with a "tearing" experience inside herself. Through subsequent associations that linked menstruation with giving birth, which in turn was experienced as a bloody laceration of the mother, it was possible to identify and interpret an even more powerful confusion between herself as a child who'd torn her mother when coming out, and the hand of a dreadful and vengeful mother who tore things out from inside her, perhaps babies or bits of herself, just as she, too, had imagined tearing out and destroying the infants inside her mother.

The interpretation of this confusion, in which there arose a reciprocal and awful laceration, led to the emergence of new links between menstruation and birth. This indistinct awareness gave a glimpse of bodily separateness from the mother, which was as yet very limited and was felt as harrowing. This also brought about the experience of an extremely fragile body whose contents now appeared as slimy and disgusting:

"I have a sense of the body as something fragile, which from one moment to the next could rip apart and be dismembered. The idea that there are things there which can come in and go out disturbs me. I have the feeling of things inside us which are slimy and disgusting and that the skin is a smooth covering, polished, white but fragile, which only just manages to contain all this weird slimy red stuff. I always think that suddenly some of it could come out."

During the most acute phase of the anorexia, the doctor's report that her internal organs were reduced in size confirmed her fantasy of the organs becoming smaller and finally disappearing, leaving "only skin and bone", thus ridding herself of this terrifying inside. Ivana seemed to confirm the unchanging nature of these experiences and fantasies but was perhaps entertaining the possibility of their being contained in the analysis—an experience that seemed to her to be missing.

The appearance of dreams, or of fantasies, about pregnancy with uncertain outcome seemed to me to symbolize the process of containment during this period. Dreams of pregnancy paved the way, also for the first time, towards a future of being full that could be perceived as "pleasant", but which in the first instance Ivana associated with what she called her "greed" and which she also related to her current symptoms. Vomiting had actually disappeared, but there was still a feeling of acidity and a persistent regurgitation. The acidity, according to Ivana, came from "an internal struggle and from a repressed desire", and she linked this with the fantasy that the inside of her body was populated by starving and aggressive creatures, "voracious animals which hurl themselves at the food like stray cats. They fight among themselves; I imagine the scene as extremely aggressive and violent. I have the feeling that my body is like a cage full of animals. I open it and give them food but they become enraged and want more."

This dangerous inside clearly points to the need for a barrier, both somatic and psychic, that might keep under control frightening, uncontrollable, and highly concrete feelings and emotions. She says:

"I used to have a problem of not being able to take in big mouthfuls because all my muscles were contracted, as if they formed a barrier between the mouth and the stomach. I compressed my stomach. What I drink doesn't go straight down; it stops and has to go down bit by bit. The mouthful has to be stopped first at a certain point and then the decision made as to whether it goes on down or comes up again. My diaphragm is tense. I have to remove a kind of safety-valve. It's as if I had to take the food to these animals myself and I'm frightened of getting involved in this aggressive scene."

She imagined that this "barrier" placed inside her, somewhere around the middle of her body, performed the functions both of keeping at bay further down what was perceived as insatiable greed, preventing the food from disappearing inside her and being destroyed, and of marking off an intermediate hidden space between the mouth and stomach—a kind of refuge to which in fantasy she retreated, ruminating over food that is continually regurgitated, thereby achieving a feeling of fullness.

Food functions here as a kind of refuge that allows Ivana to keep away feelings that terrify her; food also allows her to feel "away from everything".

> "The thought of food is comforting. Every time I feel uneasy or find it hard to be alone, I think of something sweet I could put in my mouth. It's like closing a door and being wrapped in something, like entering another realm in which if I do something with my hands it will help me. It's as if I needed to wrap myself in a carapace to find myself in this world of mine which I've created . . . a kind of defence, just as my father did with his habits, methodical down to the smallest details. He created for himself a world of small gestures, as if this were a defence against the unforeseen, against unplanned things. I've created this world of eating and of control."

Enclosing herself in a carapace made up of bodily movements and of fantasies became, as I told her, a barrier against a real relationship, a way of preventing anything from coming into her from outside. It led to her distancing herself, making herself feel as if she were outside of it all, and only apparently present. She seemed to be struck by my comment about this and told me that this was exactly what she had felt: of never really feeling as though she were actually present, really there. I told her that she was never anywhere because she was hidden in this region inside herself. By now, however, this process, particularly the one of regurgitation, felt to her to have become "automatic and involuntary" as if inside her "the passage of food were reversed". She said:

> "I have this fantasy. It's as if I had a door inside: when I eat the food goes in and stops at this door; after I've eaten there's a further check to let it enter. It's a way of checking what can go in; some things come back up again. This control is placed at the

height of the stomach. I eat without appearing to think about it, then there's this further check. I imagine it like a round non-human mouth, of an octopus, round, which opens and closes. It stays firmly shut while I eat and then it operates this check. While I'm eating I don't relax. Whatever I eat, there's this second mouth which controls everything."

The fantasy of having a hidden safety-valve ensures that Ivana's eating, at least in part, is only apparent. This is paralleled by a process in the analysis. Many things were only accepted at a certain level, at the rational level. At a deeper emotional level, they were rejected and "nearly no nourishment went to her emotional stomach". Ivana had a strong fear of losing this extreme control, or relaxing this tension, and yet now she is also frightened that the process has become so automatic that, of its own accord, it might take a wrong and opposite direction.

The "second mouth" hidden inside her brought to mind the image of a terrifying internal mother, a voracious octopus with enveloping, suffocating tentacles. Such an octopus, perhaps as a defence against what was perceived as a devouring greed, functioned as a kind of sphincter, which instead of retaining food transformed it in reality to vomit, or to faeces. She vividly described an image of "a round mouth of an octopus".

In the following sessions the meaning of regurgitation became clearer in terms of the transference. Previously when she vomited she had often felt that very little of what I said could be retained. There was an apparent taking in followed by a continuous and all-pervasive "vomiting", which threw out everything that had been given to her and that prevented her from being nourished. The feeling of distance and impenetrability was very strong and sometimes seemed to me to be completely unchangeable. Following more probing questions Ivana explained, with some hesitation, that the process involved regurgitating a certain amount of food, which rose into her throat, and then pushing it back into the oesophagus in a backwards and forwards movement rather like rumination. The movement in two directions—a move to another city and a return—had brought about in her relationship with me a kind of global and macroscopic regurgitation, followed by a kind of mental and physical rumination. Moving to the other city meant that she had probably acted out a fantasy of self-sufficiency and of feeding herself, only then to turn back, and resume the analysis, sending the food back down again and using it mainly for a kind of mental rumination over fantasies that, as she had herself intuited, had a great deal in common with the hypochondriacal anxieties of her father.

Subsequently, reflecting on my feelings and emotions in the countertransference of that period, I was aware that I had often had the quite concrete impression that she wanted to "swallow" me like a mouthful, forcing me down to a certain level inside her, as if in a terrifying and seductive journey to the inside of her body and mind. This was something that, in a paradoxical reversal, took the place of the fantasy of occupying the inside of the mother-analyst: if it could not be her inside me, it was I who now would be swallowed and taken inside her. This could help me to understand the disheartened feeling I had when I felt "vomited up", and with the new sensation of being seductively taken back in only to meet with an obstacle. I still did not really feel that the analysis was being used as a form of nourishment and that there could possibly be a real introjection. The hidden second mouth did not take anything in but, rather, expelled it.

Gradually it became ever clearer that her fear was really of being cured, of growing, and of thus having to give up the "protection" that all the symptoms and the analysis constituted for her. Even though she was actually terrified of it, at a deeper level Ivana had developed a kind of attachment to, or had become addicted to, this rumination. Shutting herself up inside this frightening fantastic world had actually many reassuring features to it, compared with the anxieties that relationships with people "on the outside" provoked in her. On this she had based, as with the anorexia, a deep if idealized aspect of her identity. Nevertheless, despite the repetitive nature of this process, which seemed to result in a situation of immobility, I had the impression that she was liberating herself from these fantasies onto which she had held for so long. The experience of being able to share with me such threatening—because it was aggressive and faecal—material provided a form of silent and barely recognized containment.

Reflecting with hindsight on my countertransference during that period, I would suggest that the patient relied on two elements in me: on the one hand, at a cognitive level, my wish to understand was mobilized regarding the notion of something held secret for a long time and then revealed; on the other hand, she relied on my perception, clear and vivid, of her intense suffering and the dramatic nature of her inner condition of isolation. I believe that, particularly on the basis of this second element, Ivana knew unconsciously that the analysis constituted for me a strong investment, via the countertransference, expressed in terms of my attention and sharing of her suffering. I must also say that, in a certain sense, I admired her courage, and it seemed that her tenacity could be regarded as a source of hope. Over the months, just as one could see changing images in dreams, so the contents of her fantasies were changing, moving gradually away from a "petrified and shrivelled" inside to a body full of contents that were "bleeding and faecal" or, later, on inhabited by "ferocious animals" that turned out to be more like children, often unborn children. Cautiously, for I feared she might take fright and retreat immediately, I tried to help her to notice these changes, and I put forward the idea that, as she was emerging from the dreams, there might be the hope of something inside her, alive and human, that could be born.

After the summer holidays of the eighth year of analysis, a dream seemed to register a significant shift:

"*I was with A____* [a very close friend from childhood] *and her nephew, her sister's son, in the park where we used to live. I'd not seen him for a long time.* He's a child with problems, who, very small at eight months' gestation, was born by caesarean because the placenta was failing to feed him. In his first year he was often ill. He is thin and, at two years, still doesn't talk. In the dream, however, *he was well-fed and chubby.* In real life he has a bony, hollow little face. However, in the dream, *he was also talking. I congratulated A____ on seeing him so well.*"

Associating to this she said that the child, even though he doesn't talk, "has a high-pitched voice. He's extremely strong even though he's so skinny, he's all nerves, he's not a beautiful child but I like him. The fact that he doesn't talk upsets me a great deal more than his poor health. But I think as he grows he'll change." His problems, which "were clearly psychological", according to her, arose from a difficult pregnancy, his mother having been depressed by the illness and death of her own mother. "I think", she said, "that he felt the painful situation in which he spent the first months of his life. His mother's distress, which was perceived by him, must have affected him a great deal." She made the link between herself and the child in the dream and how she saw herself now: "a bit fatter, still skinny, but strong". She had, like the child, "a burden hidden somewhere, like a dark corner", "a fear of facing up to life", which was still present in him.

She said she had always felt, her whole life long, that she was a person who "limped" and who in another era would have died. For this reason, she felt as if she had no right to live.

"All my life long I've had the feeling of someone who limped, was pale and skinny, often ill, delicate, withdrawn, always silent. Like the child in the dream. Now my body's changed, I'm a woman—why should I continue to feel like this? When I was little I was overwhelmed by the fear that I might fall ill from one moment to the next, and by being told about my serious early illness, the possibility that I'd die. My mother always told me that, during that illness, when I had a high temperature she passed her hand in front of my eyes and I didn't follow the hand, and she prayed that I should die rather than be damaged. The fact that I had escaped death has always meant to me that I existed by chance and that I could easily not exist. The Lord had called me but had then thought better of it."

The dream suggested that inside her all this was linked to what she now recognizes as having been her mother's severe depression, present perhaps before her birth, which had clearly left her feeling not only "not properly nourished" and contained, but also weighed down by the inner burden of her mother's unhappiness.

We began to be confronted by an image of a depressed mother burdened by unmetabolized mourning, who was unsupported by a father figure. The mother had been unable to bear the weight of depressive feelings when Ivana was ill, and she was not able to contain her anxiety about Ivana's survival and had projected into her a difficulty in sustaining hope of her survival. The "painful injections" that she had talked about right from the beginning were a symbolic expression—indeed, a concrete expression—of an intrusive projection on the part of her mother of her fears of death. I told Ivana on that occasion that I thought, on the contrary, that she was born to survive. Like the child in the dream, she too had fought off physical illness and had won; this was in itself a sign of her life force. "This was the struggle I had to face in the first years of life," she replied,

> "which has left me feeling weary throughout my life. The burden has been my mother's too, a struggle which she had to face even more than I did. I have an image of her crying next to my cot, it's a struggle we were in together. But in all my mother's stories, there's my illness and her fear that I would die. She never talked about my recovery, or her delight that I was better, or the relief at the danger passed. Unlike you, my mother's dominated by a terrible experience rather than by one in which a battle has been won and life has prevailed. Her fear was so great she never recovered from it. I feel as if I've inherited my mother's sadness."

I think her greatest problem has been the impossibility of separating and differentiating herself from a deeply depressed mother who was unable to provide proper containment of her primitive anxiety about death. The autistic elements that were evident in her and her various strategies of a perverse and auto-erotic nature were no protection against this profound depression, this "black hole" she carried inside her, which was linked to the inner mother from whom she had never differentiated.

After eight years, Ivana decided to finish her work with me in order to move to her fiancé's city where she had found more continuous and more satisfying work. Her relationship with food was now more normal, even though we both knew that this was a particularly fraught area, particularly when Ivana was in a state of anxiety or had to confront some difficult task. Even though I was not entirely convinced by this decision, for I felt that Ivana was still fragile and distressed, I also felt that I could not keep her and that she had a great need to work things out on her own. So, without disguising these thoughts, I accepted the ending of the analysis.

Three years have passed since then, and occasionally Ivana has sent me news of herself. She is reasonably well; after initial uncertainties her work has been a success, and now she likes it a great deal. She has taken on some responsibility and is feeling more sure of herself. The relationship with her fiancé has become more stable, and they are living together. She still suffers sporadic gastro-intestinal problems, which she acknowledges as emotional in origin. Every now and then she considers continuing further with the analysis.

Discussion

In the final phase of the analysis, Ivana had thrown light on the extent to which her difficulties, including the anorexia, were connected with an early disturbance of her relationship with her mother. The last dream she brought and her associations to it show clearly her perception of the link between her own problems and her mother's depression at that early stage.

We could see a wide meaning about the link between the onset of anorexia and her mother's acute depression at her elder sister's marriage. It is likely that this constituted for her a repetition of an infantile situation, already traumatic, confirming her profound intuition that her mother could not tolerate separation from her sister or from her, and that, in a deep sense, she did not accept that they "had a life of their own". At such a fundamental level, her relationship with the depressed mother was experienced as paralysing, immobilizing her vital aspects. After the sister's marriage Ivana had felt imprisoned in a paralysing fusion with a depressed mother who could only be kept alive through her renunciation of some of her aspects on the side of life ("I thought: if I go away too, my mother will die") and the vitality that came and went were derived from reciprocal aggressive investments ("the anorexia had given me something to fight against", but it had also been "an electric shock" that shook her out of her depression). Obviously this paralysing fusion had much earlier roots but had been reawakened by the other daughter's going away, which seemed to have brought about a crisis in the precarious equilibrium maintained by Ivana's docile adaptation to her mother's demands.

The father figure also played an important role in this process; he was not able, because of problems of his own, to come in and unravel the fused relationship between mother and daughter and to set limits. The story of Ivana's infancy bore traces of the failure of an initial oedipal investment of the paternal figure. At this level, the block seemed to be linked both to her perception of her sick father's fragility, as well as to her projection into him of her own infantile aspects ("monstrous and greedy") which turned him into something persecutory. Oedipal investments were not, in fact, maintained by the father figure, but only superficially idealized and felt more deeply as incapacity—because of his fragility—to establish an alternative relationship to the engulfing one with her mother. More than simply a third party, the father was felt to be like "an enormous child", a rival invalid, who was in competition to deprive further an already depressed mother.

Ivana's fluctuation between fusion—experienced both as deadly and intensely idealized—and moments of absolute separation and closure assumed a meaning of being trapped in a suffocating but indispensable relationship with the mother. The mother's depression and deathly aspects were projected into her and were represented concretely as "painful injections" that her mother gave her as a child when she was ill. There followed an attempt, persistently repeated but unsuccessful, to extract herself through an illusion of autonomy which never actually became reality. At this level the anorexia took on, in an aggressively self-sufficient manner, the function of separation from a maternal object experienced as deadly. This process, which is evidence in Ivana's case, supports the hypotheses of authors such as Chasseguet-Smirgel (1940) who have interpreted eating disturbances in adolescent girls as an extreme, but unsuccessful, attempt to achieve separation from the mother and as part of the struggle the child must face in differentiating her own body from that of the mother.

With the onset of puberty, the girl's body becomes dangerously similar to that of her mother. It requires new processes of integration between the bodily self and its impulses and the psychic self. Eating problems at this stage would indicate a girl's difficulty in completing the process of de-identification with the mother, who is thus persecuted violently through the girl's attack on her own sexual body which has been identified with the maternal body. The rebellion against being a woman, against one's own body confused with that of the mother, represents itself in some eating disorders as a wish to escape the control of the omnipotent mother. It is brought about through an illusion of self-sufficiency and accompanying auto-erotic activities and is rooted in an initial failure of maternal care and containment in the initial relationship with the mother.

This helps us to understand the paradox that although struggling for independence and autonomy through eating problems, the girl does not give up the dream of fusion with the primary object, and she goes on trying to bridge the gap prematurely experienced. This is the origin of Ivana's extreme resistance to separation and the fantasy of scooping mother's body of its contents in order to find her place again. For Ivana, getting away from her depressed, lifeless mother seemed the only possibility of salvation, but since this could only be accomplished through angry attacks on the mother through anorexia, this was effected by turning the aggressive elements on herself. The anorexia carried through the attack on the mother via the attack on her own still undifferentiated body. Her symptoms represented a compromise: they were intended as a means of separation from the deadly fusion with the mother, but, at the same time, they merely confirmed the indissolubility of the destructive relationship, as they reduced her to a condition of extreme physical dependence.

The only alternative seemed to be that of raising "barriers" and creating a distance that isolated her and, at the same time, devitalized her. When these barriers were lowered a bit it was clear how the aggression, which had never been integrated, was experienced as an enormous and destructive greed ("an appalling rage") rather than as something with a potential vitality.

This other non-integration of the aggression could, on the one hand, be seen as due to Ivana's perception of its violence, which terrified her and made her believe it could not be kept at bay except by rigid "barriers"; on the other hand, it could be seen as due to a failure of maternal containment. The mother, because of her own depression, had not offered any image of aggression as a vital element or facilitated its integration. On the contrary, she attracted to herself violent and destructive projections that did not get neutralized but, instead, became even more powerful because of her death anxiety. Ivana's idealizing of the mother figure barely hid its intensely persecutory nature; in dreams the image of her mother always appeared too fragile to survive attacks, and thus appeared as both paralysing and deadly. Ivana's intolerance of dependence and envy were intensified by feelings of frustration, and this unleashed a rage that was never expressed openly.

I would like to look briefly at the meaning and function of the fantasies regarding the working of the body which emerged during the final phase of the analysis, and at the symptom of regurgitation. As Ivana told me, these fantasies had for many years since childhood constituted a separate and secret inner world that she saw in quite concrete terms as a "physical location" to which she could escape and in which she could hide.

It became clearer through the analysis that this enclosing herself in a world of fantasy was linked to a series of physical and mental tactics. One of these was the symptom of regurgitation and rumination in which she would sometimes bring the food to the top of the throat, keep it for a while in her mouth, but then push it back down again. After a while, when it was possible to talk more openly about this behaviour, it was possible to ascertain that here was a form of auto-eroticism, linked to perverse aspects, which seemed to me equivalent, at the psychic level, of Ivana's "rumination", during that period of analysis, about her fantasies, terrifying though these were. It is very interesting to observe the similarity and evocation of a fairly rare psychosomatic syndrome consisting of a form of regurgitation (reflux) that can occur in the first year of life, described originally by Gaddini (1959, 1969) and later by Kreisler, Fain, and Soulé (1974). This is a complex defensive reaction of a psycho-physical nature which can arise, according to Gaddini, when the formation of the body image is affected by severe frustration. Without at this point going into the differences of interpretation between Gaddini and the French authors, I would like simply to emphasize the lethal outcome of this syndrome, which, if not treated, can cause the death of the neonate. The "rumination" of the food morsel can become so absorbing that it can prevent the child from sucking, and can lead it to abandon sucking altogether.

The regurgitation and rumination by my patient seemed to reproduce—making allowances, of course, for her age difference—the symptoms of reflux in infancy, which is seen by Fain (Kreisler, Fain, & Soulé, 1974) as one of the most significant deviations from auto-eroticism. It is seen as due to a failure in maternal care. As I have already said, Ivana was in some ways accustomed to this mode of functioning and was addicted to it. It constituted not only a secret region but also a mode of self-sufficiency with respect to food and to other objects. The creation of these mental and physical zones, separated and isolated, had allowed her to reach and maintain a fleeting distance from her mother, and this was experienced by her as self-sufficiency. In the transference and in my analysis of my countertransference experiences, the symptoms carried hidden omnipotent fantasies of being inside the object and occupying it completely, or, vice-versa, of surrounding and enveloping it completely with the aim of obliterating painful feelings of emptiness, separation, and loss. The analysis of fantasies connected with the symptom of regurgitation made it possible to emphasize important and significant differences between Ivana's symptoms, and it showed how the two pathologies are similar in certain respects but clearly not entirely overlapping. These fantasies throw a light on the way regurgitation and rumination, apart from providing a form of sensory self-containment, masking unbearable feelings of loss and loneliness, also carry, through notable confusion between zones, an attack of a perverse kind on the object, in which anal elements play a significant role.

Regurgitation, in one way, tends to reproduce an illusory sense of repletion and to provide the reassurance that the food has not disappeared and thereby, in fantasy, destroyed. On the other hand, it aims to subjugate the object—controlling it and triumphing over it, transforming it into faeces and creating the illusion of being able to do without it. The all-embracing fantasies of fusion that Ivana produced in the transference also took on the character of a kind of return to being a foetus lodged in mother's rectum and presented the claustrophobic and suffocating features described by Meltzer (1966) in his seminal paper on the link between masturbation and projective identification. The inner place where Ivana retreated during the acts of regurgitation–rumination probably in some ways, confused with the throat and mouth and the rectum, had many features in common with the "claustrum" (Meltzer, 1992) but also seemed to perform the functions of a "psychic retreat" (Steiner, 1993). The setting up of this "psychic retreat" and its refuge, with its component "barrier" that did not allow the food to come back, could be linked in my opinion to insufficient maternal containment. This brought about a terror of fragmentation, which demanded the establishment of internal structures that would guarantee rigid containment. The psychic retreat was also linked to invasive projections from deathly feelings by the depressed mother. This demanded a protective barrier to keep at bay the huge, frightening destructiveness felt to be impossible to assimilate.

As she told me in her associations to the dream, Ivana had never felt in her relationship with the depressed mother that her hope to stay alive could be really accepted and contained; on the contrary, she felt invaded by something deathly projected into her by her mother. Especially significant in this respect was the story she told me, in the last phase of the analysis, of how her mother only a few years previously had described a miscarriage that happened some time before her birth. Ivana felt as if she had been born only because this other child had not been, and that for this reason she had no right to live, that she had been born "only by chance". There was a profound retrospective sense of guilt about this miscarriage. She displaced onto the miscarriage undoubtedly her fantasies of attacking and destroying the children inside her mother. This justified her unconscious feeling of living at the expense of the other unborn child.

Apart from these feelings, there was the mother's description of the miscarriage, which the patient had always found terrifying. The mother had told her that "she had not noticed anything"; she had gone to the doctor because she had realized something was wrong, and "the child rolled out like a ball without her feeling any pain, indeed she hardly noticed it". This image of the child "rolling out like a ball" had always horrified her. She used to ask herself how it could have happened, and why the mother hadn't squeezed her legs together to hold onto it. She had always thought if her mother had done that, it would not have "slipped out". I thought that this fantasy, based on her mother's account, expressed clearly the other side of her clinging tenaciously to her mother and of her not being able to come out without lacerating her. It linked with a deep perception of the mother's incapacity to keep her inside her body and her mind long enough to keep her alive. The alternative between remaining clasped in a relationship that easily became suffocating and claustrophobic, or else feeling oneself slipping away too quickly and becoming a miscarriage herself, emerged repeatedly, as I have shown, in the transference.

Many times during the analysis I asked myself if I had been right to accept as a patient someone like Ivana, but I must say that deep down I always believed in her capacity to come through and to live. At the moment, I would argue that she had a great need for the containment of her anxieties about death, destructiveness, and containment, which would reinforce her hope of life, thus replacing the fleeting sense of vitality that she obtained through auto-erotic behaviour. I hope I kept her long enough.

REFERENCES

Abraham, K. (1916–17). The first pregenital stage of the libido. In: *Selected Papers on Psychoanalysis*. London: Karnac, 1988.

Balint, M. (1968). *The Basic Fault: Therapeutic Aspects of Regression*. London: Tavistock.

Bick, E. (1968). The experience of the skin in early object-relations. *International Journal of Psycho-Analysis, 49*: 484–486.

Bion, W. R. (1956). Development of schizophrenic thought. In: *Second Thoughts: Selected Papers on Psycho-Analysis* (pp. 36–42). London: Heinemann, 1967.

Bion, W. R. (1957). On arrogance. In: *Second Thoughts: Selected Papers on Psycho-Analysis* (pp. 86–92). London: Heinemann, 1967.

Bion, W. R. (1958). Attacks on linking. *International Journal of Psycho-Analysis, 40*: 308–315. Also in: *Second Thoughts: Selected Papers on Psycho-Analysis* (pp. 106–107). London: Heinemann, 1967.

Bion, W. R. (1962a). *Learning from Experience*. London: Heinemann. Reprinted London: Karnac, 1984.

Bion, W. R. (1962b). A theory of thinking. In: *Second Thoughts: Selected Papers on Psycho-Analysis* (pp. 110–119). London: Heinemann, 1967.

Bion, W. R. (1965). *Transformations*. London: Heinemann. Also in: *Seven Servants* (pp. 111–136). London: Tavistock, 1977.

Bion, W. R. (1970). *Attention and Interpretation*. London: Tavistock. Reprinted London: Karnac, 1984.

Birksted-Breen, D. (1989). Working with an anorexic patient. *International Journal of Psycho-Analysis, 77*: 29–40.

Bleger, J. (1961). La simbiosi. *Revista de psicoanalisis, 18* (pp. 361–369).

Boris, H. (1984). The problem of anorexia nervosa. *International Journal of Psycho-Analysis, 65*: 315–22.

Bott-Spillius, E. (1993). Varieties of envious experience. *International Journal of Psycho-Analysis, 74*: 1199–1212.

Box, S. (1981). Introduction: Space for thinking in families. In: S. Box, B. Copley, J. Magagna, & E. Moustaki (Eds.), *Psychotherapy with Families: An Analytic Approach* (pp. 1–8). London: Routledge.

Britton, R. (1981). Reenactment as an unwitting professional reponse to family dynamics. In: S. Box, B. Copley, J. Magagna, & E. Moustaki (Eds.), *Psychotherapy with Families: An Analytic Approach* (pp. 48–59). London: Routledge.

Britton, R. (1989). The missing link: Parental sexuality in the Oedipus complex. In: J. Steiner (Ed.), *The Oedipus Complex Today* (pp. 83–101). London: Karnac.

Britton, R. (1992). The Oedipus situation and the depressive position. In: *Clinical Lectures on Klein and Bion* (pp. 34–45). London: Routledge.

Britton, R. (1998). Subjectivity, objectivity and triangular space. In: *Belief and Imagination: Explorations in Psychoanalysis* (pp. 41–58). New Library of Psychoanalysis. London & New York: Routledge.

Chasseguet-Smirgel, J. (1940). "La lotta delle donne per l'autonomia evidenziata dai disturbi alimentari." Unpublished paper presented at the Conference on Feminine Identity, Istituto Italiano per gli Study Filosofici, Naples.

Deutsch, H. (1942). Some forms of emotional disturbance and their relationship to schizophrenia. *Psychoanalytic Quarterly, 11*: 301–321.

Etchegoyen, R. H. (1986). *The Foundations of Psychoanalytic Technique*. London: Karnac [revised edition, 1999].

Fairbairn, W. R. D. (1954). Observations on the nature of hysterical states. *British Journal of Medical Psycholology, 27* (3): 105–125.

Feldman, M. (1995). "Involving the Analyst." Paper presented at the

Conference on Understanding Projective Identification: Clinical Advances, UCL, London.

Freud, S. (1909). Notes upon a case of obsessional neurosis. *S.E., 10*: 153–249.

Freud, S. (1911). Formulations on the two principles of mental functioning. *S.E., 12*: 213–226.

Gaddini, E. (1959). Rumination in infancy. In: *Writings, 1953–85*. Milan: Cortina, 1989.

Gaddini, E. (1969). On imitation. *International Journal of Psycho-Analysis, 50*: 475–484.

Garber, J., & Seligman, M. (Eds.) (1980). *Human Helplessness: Theory and Application*. New York & London: Academic Press.

Graham, P. (1986). *Child Psychiatry: A Developmental Approach*. Oxford: Oxford University Press.

Gray, G. E. (1983). Severe depression: A patient's thoughts. *British Journal of Psychiatry, 143*: 319–322.

Green, A. (1983). La mère morte. In: *Narcissisme de vie, narcissisme de morte*. Paris: Editions de Minuit. [*Life Narcissism, Death Narcissism* (pp. 170–200), trans. A. Weller. London: Free Association Books, 2001.]

Green, J. (1950). *Si j'étais vous. . . .* Paris: Editions Plon. [*If I Were You. . . .*, trans. J. H. G. McEwen. London: Eyre & Spottiswoode, 1950.]

Hinshelwood, R. D. (1989). *A Dictionary of Kleinian Thought*. London: Free Association Books.

Hopper, E. (1991). Encapsulation as a defense against the fear of annihilation. *International Journal of Psycho-Analysis, 72* (4): 607–624.

Jacques, E. (1965). Death and the mid-life crisis. *International Journal of Psycho-Analysis, 46* (4): 502–514.

Joseph, B. (1984). Projective identification: Some clinical aspects. In: *Psychic Equilibrium and Psychic Change* (pp. 168–180), ed. M. Feldman & E. Bott-Spillius. London: Tavistock/Routledge, 1989.

Kernberg, O. (1975). *Borderline Conditions and Pathological Narcissism*. New York: Jason Aronson.

Kernberg, O. (1977). Structural diagnosis of borderline personality organization. In: P. Hartocollis (Ed.), *Borderline Personality Disorders* (pp. 87–121). New York: International Universities Press.

Kestemberg, E., Kestemberg, J., & Decobert, S. (1972). *La faim et le corps*. Paris: PUF.

Klein, G. (1976). *Psychoanalytic Theory: An Exploration of Essential*. New York: International Universities Press.

Klein, M. (1928). Early stages of the Oedipal conflict. *The Writings of Melanie Klein, Vol. 1: Love, Guilt and Reparation and Other Works* (pp. 186–198). London: Hogarth Press, 1975.

Klein, M. (1930). The importance of symbol-formation in the development of the ego. *The Writings of Melanie Klein, Vol. 1: Love, Guilt and Reparation and Other Works* (pp. 219–232). London: Hogarth Press, 1975.

Klein, M. (1935). A contribution to the psychogenesis of the manic-depressive states. *The Writings of Melanie Klein, Vol. 1: Love, Guilt and Reparation and Other Works* (pp. 262–289). London: Hogarth Press, 1975.

Klein, M. (1946). Notes on some schizoid mechanisms. In: *The Writings of Melanie Klein, Vol. 3: Envy and Gratitude and Other Works* (pp. 1–24). London: Hogarth Press, 1975.

Klein, M. (1952). On observing the behaviour of young infants. In: *The Writings of Melanie Klein, Vol. 3: Envy and Gratitude and Other Works* (pp. 94–121). London: Hogarth Press, 1975.

Klein, M. (1955). On identification. In: *The Writings of Melanie Klein, Vol. 3: Envy and Gratitude and Other Works* (pp. 141–175). London: Hogarth Press, 1975.

Klein, M. (1957). Envy and gratitude. In: *The Writings of Melanie Klein, Vol. 3: Envy and Gratitude and Other Works* (pp. 176–235). London: Hogarth Press, 1975.

Kohut, H. (1971). *The Analysis of the Self*. New York: International Universities Press.

Kohut, H. (1977). *The Restoration of the Self*. New York: International Universities Press.

Kreisler, L., Fain, M., & Suolé, M. (1974). *The Infant and Its Body*. Paris: PUF.

Laufer, M., & Laufer, M. E. (1984). *Adolescence and Developmental Breakdown: A Psychoanalytic View*. New Haven, CT: Yale University Press.

Lawrence, M. (2001). Loving them to death: The anorexic and her objects. *International Journal of Psycho-Analysis, 82*: 43–45.

Levi, D., Stierlin, H., & Savard, R. (1971). Fathers and sons: The interlocking crises of integrity and identity. *Psychiatry, 35*: 48–56.

Likierman, M. (1997). On rejection: Adolescent girls and anorexia. *Journal of Child Psychotherapy, 23*: 61–80.

McDougall, J. (1973). L'idéal hermaphrodite et ses avatars. *Nouvelle Revue Psychanalise, 7.*

Meltzer, D. (1966). The relation of anal masturbation to projective identification. *International Journal of Psycho-Analysis, 47*: 335–342. Also in: E. Bott-Spillius (Ed.), *Melanie Klein Today, Vol 1* (pp. 102–116). London: Routledge, 1988.

Meltzer, D. (1967). *The Psychoanalytic Process*. London: Heinemann.

Meltzer, D. (1986). The conceptual distinction between projective identification and container-contained. In: *Studies in Extended Metapsychology* (pp. 50–69). Strathtay: Clunie Press.

Meltzer, D. (1992). *The Claustrum*. Strathtay: Clunie Press.

Nunn, K., & Thompson, L. (1996). The pervasive refusal syndrome: Learned helplessness and hopelessness. *Clinical Child Psychology and Psychiatry, 1*: 121–132.

O'Shaughnessy, E. (1975). Explanatory notes. In: *The Writings of Melanie Klein, Vol. 3* (p. 325). London: Hogarth Press.

O'Shaughnessy, E. (1989). Enclaves and excursions. *International Journal of Psycho-Analysis, 73* (1992): 603–611.

Ravenscroft, K. (1974). Normal family regression at adolescence. *American Journal of Psychiatry, 131*: 1 .

Riesemberg-Malcolm, R. (1995). The three "W's": What, where and when. The rational of interpretation. *International Journal of Psycho-Analysis, 76*: 447–456.

Riviere, J. (1955). The unconscious phantasy of an inner world reflected in examples from literature. In: M. Klein, P. Heimann, & R. E. Money-Kyrle, *New Directions in Psychoanalysis* (pp. 346–369). London: Tavistock Publications.

Rosenfeld, H. (1964). On the psychopathology of narcissism: A clinical approach. In: *Psychotic States* (pp. 170–171). London: Hogarth Press.

Rosenfeld, H. (1971). Contribution to the psychopathology of psychotic states: The importance of projective identification in the ego structure and object relations of the psychotic patient. In: E. Bott-Spillius (Ed.), *Melanie Klein Today, Vol. 1* (pp. 117–137). London: Routledge, 1988.

Rosenfeld, H. (1987a). Destructive narcissism and the death instinct. In: *Impasse and Interpretation*. London: Routledge (pp. 105–132).

234   REFERENCES

Rosenfeld, H. (1987b). Projective identification in clinical practice. In: *Impasse and Interpretation* (pp. 157–190). London: Routledge.

Sandler, J. (1988). *Projection, Identification, Projective Identification.* London: Karnac.

Scharff, D. E., & Scharff, J. S. (Ed.) (1987). *Object Relations Family Therapy.* New York: Jason Aronson.

Segal, H. (1957). Notes on symbol formation. In: *The Works of Hanna Segal* (pp. 49–65). New York: Jason Aronson, 1981.

Segal, H. (1964). *Introduction to the Work of Melanie Klein.* New York: Basic Books; London: Heinemann, 1973.

Segal, H. (1979). *Klein.* London: Fontana.

Sodre, I. (1995). "Who's Who? Notes on Pathological Identification." Paper presented at the Conference on Understanding Projective Identification: Clinical Advances, UCL, London.

Spitz, R. (1965). *The First Year of Life.* New York: International Universities Press.

Steiner, J. (1985). Turning a blind eye: The cover-up for Oedipus. *International Review of Psychoanalysis, 12:* 161–172.

Steiner, J. (1990). Pathological organizations as obstacles to mourning: The unbearable guilt. *International Journal of Psycho-Analysis, 71:* 87–94.

Steiner, J. (1992). The equilibrium between the paranoid–schizoid and the depressive position. In: *Clinical Lectures on Klein and Bion* (pp. 46–58). London: Routledge.

Steiner, J. (1993). *Psychic Retreats: Pathological Organizations in Psychotic, Neurotic and Borderline Patients.* London: Routledge.

Stern, D. N. (1977). *The First Relationship: Infant and Mother.* Cambridge, MA: Harvard University Press.

Stern, D. N. (1985). *The Interpersonal World of the Infant: A View from Psychoanalysis and Developmental Psychology.* New York: Basic Books.

Stierlin, H., & Ravenscroft, K. (1972). Varieties of adolescent separation conflicts. *British Journal of Medical Psychology, 45:* 299–313.

Tirelli, L. C. (1994). Incubi sogni e fantasie: Un bambino ce ne parla. *Richard e Piggle.* Rome: Il pensiero scientifico.

Tustin, F. (1972). *Autism and Childhood Psychosis.* London: Hogarth Press.

Tustin, F. (1981). *Autistic States in Children.* London: Routledge.

Tustin, F. (1986). A significant element in the development of psychogenic autism. In: *Autistic Barriers in Neurotic Patients* (pp. 67–93). London: Karnac.

Waddell, M. (1994). Assessing adolescents: Finding a space to think. In: M. Rustin & E. Quagliata (Eds.), *Assessment in Child Psychotherapy* (pp. 145–161). London: Duckworth, 1999.

Waddell, M. (1999). A mind of one's own: Introjective processes and the capacity to think. In: D. Anastasopoulos et al. (Eds.), *Psychoanalytic Psychotherapy of the Severely Disturbed Adolescent*. London: Karnac.

Williams, G. (1983). Stima di se' e stima dell'oggetto. In: *Quaderni di Psicoterapia Infantile, Vol. 9*. Rome: Borla.

Williams, G. (1997). *Internal Landscapes and Foreign Bodies: Eating Disorders and Other Pathologies*. London: Duckworth.

Williams, G., & Judd, D. (2002). *International Journal of Infant Observation and Its Application, 5* (2).

Winnicott, D. W. (1956). Primary maternal preoccupation. In: *The Maturational Processes and the Facilitating Environment* (pp. 45–59). London: Hogarth Press, 1965.

Winnicott, D. W. (1971). The location of cultural experience. In: *Playing and Reality* (pp. 95–103). London: Routledge.

INDEX

Abraham, K., 155
acceptance, generosity of, xviii, xx
accepting, risk of, defences against, xiii
acting out, 93, 102, 147, 158, 173, 212
    self-destructive, 165, 173
adhesive identification, 47
alopecia, 143
alpha function, 146
ambivalence, 3, 183–184
    incapacity for, 65
amenorrhoea, 32, 45, 195
    menstruation, 36, 42, 44, 202, 213
annihilation anxiety, 46, 79
anorexia/anorexic(s), xv, xix, xxi, 51,
    72, 108
    difficulty in associating, 47
    fantasies concerning body
        functioning [case study:
        "Ivana"], 195–227
    function of receiving [case study:
        "Aurora"], 29–49
    lack of identity [case study:
        "Lydia"], 83–105
    of mind, 27
    oedipal illusions in, protection of,
        xv

search for identity and fear of
    contamination [case study:
    "Rebecca"], 1–28
terror of separateness and
    differentiation, xv
"transitional" space in, poverty of,
    xv
very damaged persecutory internal
    object [case study: "Julie"],
    175–194
anorexic syndrome, fundamental
    characteristics of, 45
"Anthony", catastrophic birth
    experience [case study], xvii,
    xxii
anxiety(ies):
    annihilation, 79
    castration, 46
    primitive, 32, 88, 140, 220
    separation, 46, 47, 119, 123, 134, 149
    signal, 79
attachment, 27, 28
    vicissitudes of, 27
"Aurora", function of receiving [case
    study], 29–49
separateness, achievement of, xx

237

over needy self, xx
omnipotent, *see* omnipotent control
projective identification used for, 21
cornucopia fantasy, infantile, 74
countertransference:
transference–, relationship, 83
use of:
with anorexic patient [case
studies]:
"Ivana", 195, 199–200, 204,
206, 211–212, 217–218, 225
"Lydia", 87
"Rebecca", 2
with bulimic patient [case study:
"Paula"], 53, 57
with patients with eating
disorders [case study:
"Deborah", 145, 155, 157, 162,
169, 173
with pervasive refusal syndrome
[case study: "Yufang"], 108,
114, 116, 119, 133
couple, attacks on, xx–xxiii
Creak, M., 108
Crohn's disease, 137

death:
claustrum as space of, 48
destructive superego on side of, xvi,
107–138, 170
dreams and fantasies about, 37–38,
48
father's, 36
fear of, 34, 88, 224, 227
mother's projection of, 220, 226
primitive, 220
of starving to death, 11, 12, 19, 24
mother's, 219
nanny's, 38
"Deborah", processes of projection
and introjection, loss of
identity in projective
identification [case study],
xviii, 139–173
Decobert, S., 45
defence(s), 150–151, 198, 203, 208
claustrophobia as, 15
denial as, 149
against dependency, xiii, 95, 193
against depressive feelings, xx
against envy, xx

fear of persecution as, 119
fragile, 74, 77, 78
fusion between object and self as,
141
against gratitude, xx
healthy, 72
hyperactivity as, 15
of incorporation and projection, 72
massive denial of conflictual
feelings as, 119
narcissistic, *see* narcissistic defences
"no-entry" system of, xiv, xvii, 83
pathological, 72
projection of aggression as, 119
projective identification as, 88, 149
against psychic pain, xx
psychosomatic, xv, 79
splitting as, 149
transformation of in analysis, 151
defensive organization, primitive, 149
de-identification, 223
denial, 149
of destructiveness, 119
engendered by projective
identification, 19
dependence:
fear of, xv, xviii
feelings of, defences against, xiii,
xvi, xviii
healthy, achievement of, xx
intolerance of, xix, xx
depersonalization, xviii, 79, 117, 118,
140
depression, 48, 131, 222
in anorexia [case studies]: "Julie",
175, 176, 178, 180, 181, 189, 191,
192, 194; "Lydia", 86
and eating disorders [case study:
"Deborah"], 172
father's [case study: "Paula"], 68
manic–, 192
mother's, 30, 32, 66, 142
case studies:
"Aurora", 33, 39, 48
"Deborah", 142
"Ivana", 196–197, 219–224, 226
"Paula", 66
"Rebecca", xxii, 6, 15, 23, 27, 28
"Yufang", 109, 112
pervasive refusal syndrome, 119,
122, 134

depression (*continued*):
  psychotic, and pervasive refusal
    syndrome [case study:
    "Yufang"], 108, 109, 124
depressive feelings, defences against,
    xx
depressive position, 164, 167, 172
  achieving, 30–31, 161–163, 165
    difficulties with, xvi
    and Oedipus complex, 172
    and weaning, 30–31
    pain of, defences against, xv
    working through, 164, 166
depressive stupor, in pervasive refusal
    syndrome [case study:
    "Yufang"], 107–108
deprivation, silence as, 120–121
derealization, 79
Desmarais, J., xiii
destructiveness, denial of, 119
Deutsch, H., 69, 80
differentiation, xx, 41, 201
  fear of, in anorexia, xv
distance, emotional, 3
Dubinsky, H., xx, xxiii, 175–194
dyadic couple, space within, denial of,
    xv
dyadic relationship:
  early, "fit" or "lack of fit", xv
  space within, obliteration of, xvi
  third element in, space as, xvi, xx
dyadic transference, 51

early mechanisms, primitive, 83
early relationships, failure of, xv, xvii
ego-destructive superego, xv, xvi,
    xxiii–xxiv, 107–138, 170
electroshock treatments (ECT), 108,
    110, 111, 113
emotional distance, 3
emptiness, feeling of, 9, 40, 42, 52, 81,
    143, 147, 163, 179, 191, 197,
    204–205, 210, 225
envy, defences against, xx
epilepsy, 199
epistemophilic drives, 30
Etchegoyen, R. H., 46

Fain, M., 224, 225
Fairbairn, W. R. D., 63

false self, 62, 69, 73, 74, 77, 79, 80
father:
  anger towards, 13
  denial of existence of, xxii
  denigration of, xvi, 15
  hate campaign against, 4
  obliteration of, xxi, 91–92
  obsession with snoring of, xxii
  violent attack on, suicide as, 199
Feldman, M., 160, 165
food (*passim*):
  as displacement of chaos within, xv
  as refuge, 215
Freud, S., xx, 170
  primary narcissism, theory of, 30
  "Rat Man" case, xix–xx
fusion, xv, xviii–xx, 222, 225
  with depressed mother, 221, 223
    fear of, xv
  fear of, 206
  idealized but deadly, experience of,
    xviii, 201
  with mother, fear of, xv
  obliteration of otherness through,
    xv, xvi, xviii, xx–xxiii
  with primary object, 223
  of subject and object, fear of, xv, 141

Gaddini, E., 224
Garber, J., 118
genitality, attainment of, 41
"George", catastrophic weaning [case
    study], xvii, xxii
Graham, P., 110
gratitude:
  defences against, xx
  fear of, xix
Gray, G. E., 131
Great Ormond Street Hospital for
    Children (London), 133
  Mildred Creak Eating Disorders
    Team, 108
Green, A., 48
Green, J., *Si j'etais vous*, 98–99
guilt, persecutory, xxiii, 183–184
  and eradication of paternal
    function, xxi

hallucination, of monstrous "male
    figure", 136

and triadic relationships, 65
    phallic, 66
oedipal situation, 5, 15, 30, 172, 187
    working through, failure of, xiv
oedipal structure, 30, 44
oedipal wish, 8, 14
Oedipus complex, 172
omnipotence, 18, 119, 141, 155, 164,
        171–173, 184, 197, 225
    fantasy of, 201
    loss of, 201
omnipotent control, 192
    over body, 180, 210
    over self and objects, 191
omnipotent functioning, 139, 173
omnipotent mother, 223
omnipotent phantasy(ies), 28, 150, 154,
        160
    grandiose, 150
oral incorporation, 77, 81
oral stage, 31
O'Shaughnessy, E., 141, 158
otherness, need to obliterate, xv, xviii

paranoia, 14, 26, 28, 65, 177, 182–183
paranoid anxiety(ies), 115
paranoid–schizoid position, 73, 80,
        149, 150, 164, 165, 167
parasitism, 156, 157, 161
parents:
    need to keep separated, xxi, xxii,
        xxiii
    oral attack on, xxiii
paternal function:
    attacks on, xv, xx–xxiii
        case study ["Lydia"], 83–105
    obliteration of, xvi
"Paula", bulimia and absence of
        paternal function [case study],
        xxii, 51–82
penetration, fear of, xiv
Perocevic, S., xvii, xviii, xxi, xxii
persecution, feelings of, xvi
persecutory anxiety(ies), 31, 159
persecutory guilt, xxiii, 134, 183–184,
        187
    and eradication of paternal
        function, xxi
personality structure, defective, 77
pervasive refusal syndrome, xviii
    case study ["Yufang"], 107–138

summary of treatment for, 137–138
Petrelli, D., xvi, xviii, xxii, xxiii, 195–
        227
Pinheiro, M. Mendes de Almeida, xvii
pleasure principle, 170
post-traumatic stress disorder (PTSD),
        118
primal scene:
    noises, denigration of, xxii
    primitive, 200
primary narcissism, 30
primary object, 30, 31, 45, 223
    internalization of, 65
primitive anxiety(ies), 32, 88, 140, 220
projection(s), xiv, 72, 78, 79, 89, 113,
        134, 187, 222
    of aggression, as defence, 119, 135
    into analyst, 88, 92, 98, 204, 205, 208
    of body image, 86
    child's, 116, 146
    of disembodied drives, 73
    envious, controlling, intrusive
        phantasies, 14
    of good parts, 69, 74–76
    immobilizing, 74
    infant's, 140
        hostile, 146
    of intrusive fantasies, 26
    of intrusiveness, xix
    Klein's concept of, 151
    maternal, 226
        depressed, 30, 89, 220
        infant as receptacle for, 190
        invasive, 226
        negative, 191
        unbearable, 89
    mechanism of, primitive, 83, 108
    micro, 57, 69
    of oedipal wishes, 14
    parental, xiv, xv, 57, 58, 62, 67, 116
        child as receptacle of, xvii
    patients', acceptance of, xiv
    processes of, 28
        in eating disorders [case study:
            "Deborah"], 139–173
    of split-off parts of self, 88
    violent, 20, 224
projective identification, xvi, 6, 21, 26,
        27, 28, 47, 63, 74, 75, 80, 89, 206
    Bion, 19, 46, 88, 139–141
    with body of mother, xix